Nikolay Milkov
Hermann Lotze's Influence on Twentieth Century Philosophy

New Studies in the History and Historiography of Philosophy

Edited by
Sebastian Luft

Editorial Board
Karl P. Ameriks (Notre Dame University, West Bend, IN, USA), Margaret Atherton (University of Wisconsin, Milwaukee, WI, USA), Frederick Beiser (Syracuse University, Syracuse, NY, USA), Fabien Capeillères (University of Caen Normandy, Caen, France), Faustino Fabbianelli (University of Parma, Parma, Italy), Daniel Garber (Princeton University, Princeton, NJ, USA), Rudolf A. Makkreel (Emory University, Atlanta, GA, USA), Steven Nadler (University of Wisconsin, Madison, WI, USA), Alan Nelson (University of North Carolina, Chapel Hill, NC, USA), Christof Rapp (LMU Munich, Munich, Germany), Ursula Renz (University of Klagenfurt, Klagenfurt, Austria), Wilhelm Schmidt-Biggemann (FU Berlin, Berlin, Germany), Denis Thouard (HU Berlin, Berlin, Germany), Paul Ziche (University of Utrecht, Utrecht, Netherlands), Günter Zöller (LMU Munich, Munich, Germany)

Volume 12

Nikolay Milkov

Hermann Lotze's Influence on Twentieth Century Philosophy

—

DE GRUYTER

ISBN 978-3-11-162034-3
e-ISBN (PDF) 978-3-11-072628-2
e-ISBN (EPUB) 978-3-11-072638-1
ISSN 2364-3161

Library of Congress Control Number: 2023930678

Bibliographic information published by the Deutsche Nationalbibliothek
The Deutsche Nationalbibliothek lists this publication in the Deutsche Nationalbibliografie;
detailed bibliographic data are available on the internet at http://dnb.dnb.de.

© 2024 Walter de Gruyter GmbH, Berlin/Boston
This volume is text- and page-identical with the hardback published in 2023.

www.degruyter.com

Contents

Preface —— IX

Acknowledgements —— XIII

Introduction: Why Lotze? —— 1
1   Opening —— 1
2   Lotze and the Phenomenology Movement —— 2
3   Hegel, Lotze and Early Cambridge Analytic Philosophy —— 3
4   The Idiosyncrasy of Lotze's Philosophy —— 6
4.1 Lotze's Second Logical Turn in Modern Philosophy —— 6
4.2 Implications —— 8
4.3 Lotze's Influence and Its Decline —— 9
5   Final Remarks —— 10

Part I: Lotze's Philosophy

Chapter 1
Lotze's Philosophy: An Outline —— 15
1   Opening —— 15
2   Life and Works —— 16
2.1 Biography —— 16
2.2 Works —— 17
3   Philosophical Principles and Methods —— 18
3.1 Regressive Analysis —— 18
3.2 Anthropology as *prima philosophia* —— 20
3.3 Lotze's Dialectics —— 21
4   Theoretical Philosophy —— 22
4.1 Ethics —— 22
4.2 Metaphysics (Ontology) —— 24
4.3 The Importance of Relations —— 26
4.4 Epistemology —— 27
4.5 Logic —— 29
4.6 Philosophy of Nature (Cosmology) —— 30
4.7 Philosophy of Language —— 32

Chapter 2
Lotze's Philosophy of Psychology — 33
1   Introductory Remarks — 33
2   Lotze's Project — 34
3   Materialism, Identity Theory, or Spiritualism? — 36
4   The Principle of Teleomechanism — 39
5   Lotze's Physical-Psychological Mechanism — 41
6   Lotze's Occasionalism — 43
7   The Emergence of the New — 44
8   The Local-Signs Theory — 46
9   Lotze's Theory of Space — 48
10   The Location and the Essence of the Soul — 50
11   Lotze's Concept of Philosophy — 52
12   Logic and Psychology — 54

Chapter 3
Lotze's Philosophical Anthropology — 56
1   Opening — 56
2   Setup — 56
2.1   First Description — 56
2.2   Three Traditions of Microcosmic Studies — 59
2.3   History of Lotze's *Mikrokosmus*-Project — 60
3   Methods — 61
3.1   Ontological Approach — 62
3.2   Ecological Stance — 63
3.3   Theoretical Liberalism — 64
4   Life and Society — 65
4.1   Forms of Life — 65
4.2   Social Progress — 66
4.3   Philosophy of History — 68
4.4   Political Philosophy — 70
4.5   Philosophy of Religion — 71
4.6   Religious Practices — 72

Part II: Lotze and the Descriptive Psychology

Chapter 4
Lotze and Franz Brentano — 77
1   Brentano and the Neo-Brentanists — 77

2	An Overview of the Relationship between Lotze and Brentano —— **78**	
3	Relatedness —— **80**	
3.1	Judgment and Its Content —— **81**	
3.2	The Content of Perception —— **82**	
3.3	Intentionality —— **84**	
3.4	Descriptive Psychology —— **85**	
3.5	Perception, Knowledge, and Emotions —— **87**	
4	Agreements —— **87**	
4.1	Philosophy as a Rigorous Science —— **88**	
4.2	Similarity of Philosophical Approach —— **89**	
5	Differences between Lotze and Brentano —— **90**	

Chapter 5
Lotze and Carl Stumpf —— **92**

1	Introduction —— **92**	
2	Biographical Notes —— **92**	
3	Zeitgeist —— **95**	
4	Stumpf's Descriptive Psychology —— **96**	
5	Stumpf's Analytic Method —— **98**	
6	Further Points of Relatedness Between Lotze and Stumpf —— **100**	
7	Stumpf's Ontology —— **102**	
8	Carl Stumpf's Philosophical Acolytes —— **103**	

Part III: **Lotze and Bertrand Russell**

Chapter 6
Lotze and Bertrand Russell —— **109**

1	Russell: Hegelian or Lotzean? —— **109**	
2	Lotze and Russell: An Overview —— **110**	
3	Lotze's First Impact on Russell (1896) —— **111**	
4	Lotze's Second Impact on Russell (1897) —— **114**	
5	Lotze's Third Impact on Russell (1898) —— **115**	
6	Lotze and Russell's Philosophical Logic —— **117**	
7	Russell Misinterprets his own Philosophical Development —— **119**	
8	Russell's Supposed Disagreement with Lotze —— **121**	

Chapter 7
Bertrand Russell's Notes on McTaggart's Lectures on Lotze —— **123**

1	Introduction —— **123**	

2   Lectures on Lotze —— 125
3   Commentary —— 141

Chapter 8
Lotze, William James, and Bertrand Russell —— 144
1   Opening —— 144
2   William James as a Philosopher —— 144
3   James' Direct Influence on Russell —— 145
4   James' and Russell's Debt to Lotze —— 145
4.1   Lotze and William James —— 145
4.2   Hermann Lotze and Bertrand Russell: Propositions are Believed —— 146
5   Russell's Propositional Attitudes —— 149
6   Analytic Revolt Against Russell's Propositional Attitudes —— 151
7   James' Late Influence on Russell: Truth-Making —— 152
8   Russell's Troubles with Truth-Making —— 154
9   Epilogue —— 155

Part IV: Lotze and the Philosophy of Logical Empiricism

Chapter 9
Lotze, Heinrich Rickert, and Logical Empiricism —— 159
1   Opening —— 159
2   The Philosophy of Logical Empiricism and the Southwest Neo-Kantians —— 159
3   Rickert's Impact on the Logical Empiricists: A First Approximation —— 161
4   History of the Notion of Concept Formation in Science —— 162
4.1   Kant and Fries —— 163
4.2   Hermann Lotze —— 164
5   Heinrich Rickert on Concept Formations in Science —— 165
6   Comparing Heinrich Rickert and Ernst Cassirer —— 167
7   Comparing Marburg and Southwest Neo-Kantians —— 168
8   Rickert and the Logical Empiricists before the Vienna Circle —— 170
9   Rickert and the Logical Empiricists of the Vienna Circle —— 172
10   Heinrich Rickert as a Philosopher of Science —— 173
11   Epilogue —— 175

References —— 177

Index —— 195

Preface

The present book is revisionist in style. It presents Lotze as the hidden central figure of German philosophy in the 19th century who decisively influenced Western philosophy in the *fin de siècle*. It opposes the conventional approach, according to which Kant introduced his "Copernican revolution" in philosophy that was later followed by the appearance of German Idealism, the two "late German idealists", Trendelenburg and Lotze, and ultimately the Neo-Kantians (Beiser 2008, 2013, and 2014). The approach I follow in this book is different, and this deviation is easy to explain. While conventional interpreters start their histories with Kant and Hegel, my understanding was based on the background of years of intensive studies in the history of analytic philosophy. In fact, Rudolph Hermann Lotze (1817–1881) was never the main subject of my academic interest. In the 1990's, I worked mainly on the history of early analytic philosophy in England, producing two books on it (1997 and 2003). However, in the process of these explorations, I discovered, to my surprise, that the "philosophical revolution" of G. E. Moore and Bertrand Russell was properly prepared by some German philosophers, not merely by Gottlob Frege. Until that point, I followed A. J. Ayers' mantra from his *Language, Truth, and Logic* (1936) that analytic philosophy was a further development of the philosophy of the British Empiricists.

Significantly, I was not the first scholar who realized that early Cambridge analytic philosophy developed under massive Teutonic influence. While preparing his *Hundred Years of Philosophy* (1966; first ed. 1957), John Passmore devoted considerable space to the philosophy of Christoph Sigwart, Hermann Lotze, J. F. Herbart, and Friedrich Ueberweg. Without any doubt, the most prominent figure among this circle of philosophers was Hermann Lotze. Lamentably, the final book's coverage of these thinkers was only "a residue of a much more expanded account which Arthur Prior had persuaded [him] to castrate" (Passmore 1995, p. 194).

I was personally awakened to embrace this position after I read the excellent new edition of Parts I and III of Lotze's "greater" *Logic*,[1] prepared by Gottfried Gabriel (1989a, 1989b). I first wrote on Hermann Lotze and early analytic philosophy in my first book on the history of analytic philosophy (1997, pp. 91–94). At the beginning of the 2000s, I delved into this topic more intensively, producing two papers on it (2000, 2002a). Unfortunately, when I was working on my second book on the history of analytic philosophy in England (2003), the editors convinced me to abandon the pre-history of this movement for reasons of parsimony: the book was to be no more than 300 pages in length.

---

1 On Lotze's "greater" *Logic* and "greater" *Metaphysics*, see Chapter 1, § 2.2.

A few years later, in 2006, I published a comprehensive paper on Lotze's *Mikrokosmus* (Chapter 3), following the invitation of Anna-Teresa Tymieniecka. I composed the paper "Russell's Debt to Lotze" (2008a) (part of it is published here as Chapter 6) while I was Visiting Fellow at the Center for Philosophy of Science at the University of Pittsburgh (2005–2006). In 2010, I authored the entry on Lotze in the *Internet Encyclopedia of Philosophy* (some parts of it are incorporated into Chapter 1).

Between 2007 and 2013, however, I worked less on this topic. Instead, I intensively explored the history of the Berlin Group of logical empiricists around Hans Reichenbach, a theme suggested to me by Nicholas Rescher while I was in Pittsburgh. The products of this exploration include seven my works (2008b, 2011a, 2013a, 2015a, 2015b, 2021a, and 2021b).

I renewed my investigations of Lotze's philosophy only after I had finished this work. My first new essay on this subject from this period was "Carl Stumpf's Debt to Hermann Lotze" (2015a; Chapter 5). Shortly afterwards, I wrote a review article on William Woodward's seminal *Hermann Lotze: An Intellectual Biography* (Milkov 2016a). On May 21, 2017, Lotze's 200th birthday, I presented (in German) a paper on "Hermann Lotze and Franz Brentano" (2017a) at a conference held on this occasion in Bautzen, the town where Lotze was born. The German version of this paper was printed in (2017a), and a revised and adapted form of it is reproduced here as Chapter 4.

Also, to celebrate Lotze's second centenary in 2017, I edited and published with Felix Meiner a new, 7th edition of Lotze's *Mikrokosmus*. It included an "Introduction" of more than 16,000 words, 3 addenda, Lotze's short abstracts of Volumes I and II, and an index of names and concepts. Finally, in 2021, I published a new edition of Lotze's *Medicinische Psychologie* with Springer Spektrum. This edition was accompanied by an introduction of some 12,000 words (part of it is reproduced in English translation as Chapter 2 of the present book), with Lotze's extensive abstract for the book and a newly prepared index of names and concepts.

Two years ago, I also wrote an introduction to Russell's "Notes on McTaggart's Lectures on Lotze" which were published in the journal *Russell* (40. No 1, 2020e). Unfortunately, I had very limited space for this "Introduction"—slightly more than 1,000 words. In the present book, Russell's "Notes" are republished as Chapter 7, where they are accompanied by a more extensive introduction and some exegetical remarks. The "Notes" demonstrate how significant the study of Lotze's philosophy was for Russell's philosophical development, which was, at that moment in time, at a turning point.

In 2020, I also issued my most recent book, *Early Analytic Philosophy and the German Philosophical Tradition*. In it, I tried to demonstrate that analytic philosophy, as it emerged in Cambridge, England, was well prepared by some specific developments in German philosophy after Leibniz. Part III of that work is expressly dedicated to the role that Lotze played in this development. In fact, one of the tasks of the present book is to substantiate and supplement this thesis. In general, this approach is not new. In (1973), Michael Dummett convincingly demonstrated that the roots of analytic philosophy went back to Frege. The task of the present book is even more challenging. Namely, it intends to show that the roots not only of analytic philosophy but also of phenomenology go a step back to the imposing figure of Hermann Lotze. Lotze was the source from which these two leading streams of philosophical thought of the *fin de siècle* emerged in order to "flood out" the whole of Western philosophy for more than a century. In other words—let me here use Michael Dummett's metaphor (1993, p. 24)—Lotze was that philosophical Black Forest (*Schwarzwald*) from which the Danube and the Rhine of analytic philosophy and phenomenology started on their long journeys, albeit in different directions. To be more specific, he achieved this by introducing a new method that made philosophy more formal and also logically more precise (Introduction, § 4.1).

As a final remark, it should be noted that the present book is not a systematic study. In line with the objective to demonstrate Lotze's position as the leading figure in German philosophy after Hegel and before the emergence of analytic philosophy and phenomenology, that is, before Frege and Husserl, Part I of the book first sketches a general outline of Lotze's philosophy (in Chapter 1) and then discusses (in Chapter 2) his philosophy of psychology and (in Chapter 3) his philosophical anthropology. At the same time, there is no detailed discussion of his logic and metaphysics; they are described briefly in Chapter 1. Clearly, my exploration of Lotze's philosophy in this book is highly selective.

I follow this approach further in Part II, where I do not explore the relation between Lotze and Edmund Husserl, the founding father of phenomenology, but rather those between Lotze and Franz Brentano and Carl Stumpf, Husserl's teachers. Similarly, Part III does not discuss Lotze's influence on Frege but rather Russell's debt to Lotze.

Finally, Chapters 8 and 9 give an example of the deep but cryptic influence that Lotze exercised on the philosophy of the *fin de siècle* and the first half of the 20th century. To be more explicit, the objective of Chapter 8 is not to demonstrate that William James and Bertrand Russell directly adopted the theory of truth-making or propositional attitudes from Lotze or that the logical empiricists in Vienna and Berlin, in their explorations of the subject of conceptual construction in science, followed the pace of Lotze's devotee Heinrich Rickert. Rather, it explores what can be called the "echo" of Lotze's thought, which played a considerable role in shaping the ideas not only of the early analytic philosophers and logical empiricists but also of the Neo-Kantians and the pragmatists.

Acknowledgements

Versions of each chapter have previously appeared in print or online in the following order: Chapter 1, "Lotze's Philosophy: An Outline" is based on my entry in the *Internet Encyclopedia of Philosophy*, "Hermann Lotze", which was first published in 2010 (https://www.iep.utm.edu/lotze; last accessed on December 3, 2022); Chapter 2, "Lotze's Philosophy of Psychology" is based on my Introduction "Hermann Lotzes Philosophie der Psychologie" in Lotze, Hermann (2021): *Medizinische Psychologie oder Physiologie der Seele*, Heidelberg and Berlin: Springer Spektrum, pp. v–viii, 1–25; Chapter 3, "Lotze's Philosophical Anthropology", is based on my paper "Hermann Lotze's *Microcosm*", in Tymieniecka, Anna-Teresa (Ed.) (2006): *Islamic Philosophy and Occidental Phenomenology on the Perennial Issue of Microcosm and Macrocosm, Islamic Philosophy and Occidental Phenomenology in Dialogue*, Vol. II, Dordrecht: Springer, pp. 41–65, and on my Introduction "Hermann Lotzes philosophische Synthese" in Lotze, Hermann (2017): *Mikrokosmos*, 3 Volumes, Nikolay Milkov (Ed.) ("Philosophische Bibliothek", Volumes 705a–c), Hamburg: Felix Meiner, pp. xii–xxv; Chapter 4, "Lotze and Franz Brentano", is based on my 2018 paper "Hermann Lotze and Franz Brentano", *Philosophical Readings* 10, No. 2, pp. 115–122; Chapter 5, "Carl Stumpf's Debt to Hermann Lotze", is based on my paper in Fisette, Denis and Martinelli, Riccardo (Eds.) (2015): *Philosophy from an Empirical Standpoint: Essays on Carl Stumpf*, Leiden: Brill, pp. 101–122; Chapter 6, "Lotze and Bertrand Russell", is based on my June 2008 paper "Russell's Debt to Lotze", *Studies in History and Philosophy of Science, Part A*, 39, No. 2, pp. 186–193; Chapter 7, "Russell's Notes on McTaggart's Lectures on Lotze", was first published with another Introduction and without Commentary in "Russell" 40, No. 2 (Summer 2020), pp. 57–74; Chapter 8, "Lotze, Bertrand Russell, and William James", was published in 2020, in an abbreviated version, as "Russell's Conception of Propositional Attitudes in Relation to Pragmatism" in *An Anthology of Philosophical Studies* 14, pp. 117–128; Chapter 9, "Lotze, Heinrich Rickert, and Logical Empiricism", is based on a paper I read in Paderborn, Bad Neuenahr-Ahrweiler, Konstanz, and at the Central Division Meeting of the APA in Chicago in 2018. I am grateful for the permission I received to use material from these articles. It deserves notice, however, that the material adapted from the works listed above has been corrected, revised, and recast to suit the unified aims of this book. Additionally, content from several of the book's chapters was presented at a number of professional meetings and workshops, to whose participants I owe a debt of thanks for their valuable input and helpful suggestions.

My thanks go also to the Bertrand Russell Archives, McMaster University, Canada, for permission to republish Bertrand Russell's notes on McTaggart's lectures on Lotze, which were delivered in the Lent Term of 1898 at Trinity College, Cambridge; in particular, thanks are due to Mr. Rick Stapleton, B.Ed., M.A.S., Head of the Archives & Research Collections at McMaster University Library. I am grateful to Prof. Sebastian Luft, who encouraged me to publish the book with de Gruyter. Christoph Schirmer at de Gruyter helped me to come to grips with the technical tasks associated with this project. On the theoretical side, my work was supported by Dr. Michele Vagnetti, while an anonymous reviewer with the publishing house made helpful comments. Dr. Phillip Stambovsky (Fairfield University) helped me improve the language of Chapters 4, 5 and 9. Mrs. Lilli Isabel Förster translated Chapters 2 and 4 into English and also helped me prepare the index. Most of all, I thank my wife Michaela for her constant encouragement and inspiration.

Introduction: Why Lotze?

1 Opening

In 2013, the well-known and widely respected American expert on the 19th century German philosophy, Frederick Beiser, published the book *Late German Idealism: Trendelenburg and Lotze*. In 2015, Cambridge University Press issued William Woodward's long awaited *Intellectual Biography* of Lotze (Milkov 2016a). In 2017, the three volumes of Rudolph Hermann Lotze's *Mikrokosmos* were reissued by the Felix Meiner publishing house, Hamburg, in their 7th edition.[2] In the same year, the anthology *Lotze et son heritage* appeared, edited by Federico Boccaccini. In 2018, the Italian journal *Philosophical Readings* presented online the issue *Lotze's Back!* edited by Daniele de Santis. Finally, in 2021, Springer–Spektrum Verlag in Germany published a new edition of Lotze's *Medicinische Psychologie*.

How can this renewed interest in Lotze be explained? First of all, it was prompted by the intensive work carried out on the history of philosophy of the 19th and 20th centuries in the last few decades. It revealed the division of Western philosophy into analytic and continental, naturalistic and idealistic, etc., as simplified and highly problematic. Gradually, one became aware of the fact that the history of philosophy after Hegel needs a more fine-grained consideration. To be more specific, detailed investigations made it clear that around 1880, Hermann Lotze was the leading philosopher not only in Germany but in the whole Western world (Milkov 2008a, 2010, 2015a). Lotze decisively influenced the early analytic philosophy (Gottlob Frege and partly also Bertrand Russell), phenomenology (Carl Stumpf and Edmund Husserl), the Neo-Kantians (especially the Southwestern school of Wilhelm Windelband and Heinrich Rickert but also the Marburg Neo-Kantians Paul Natorp and Ernst Cassirer), the philosophy of life (Wilhelm Dilthey), the British Idealists (Bernard Bosanquet und F. H. Bradley) and the American pragmatists William James and Josiah Royce. In the next two sections, we shall demonstrate this in brief in respect of the two leading philosophical movements of the 20th century philosophy, analytic philosophy and phenomenology.

---

[2] The 6th edition of Raymund Schmidt (Lotze 1912) set Lotze's three volumes for the first time in Antiqua instead of in blackletter style and also latinized their title to *Mikrokosmos*. Since the 7th edition of Lotze's *Mikrokosmus* is a photomechanical reprint of the 6th edition with a new Introduction and Indexes, it also adopted the latinized title of the book.

2 Lotze and the Phenomenology Movement

As already noted in the Preface, in the present book, we shall not deal with Lotze's influence on Husserl in particular. Instead, in Part Two we are going to discuss the indebtedness of Husserl's philosophy teachers Franz Brentano and Carl Stumpf to Lotze. To partially make up for this decision, in this section, we shall say a few words about the direct indebtedness of Husserl to Lotze's works.

Husserl often spoke about Lotze's "decisive influence" on himself (1900, p. 229) which was especially prominent in his *Logical Investigations*. It can be no surprise, therefore, that in the first volume of the book, the *Prolegomena* (1900, p. 222), Husserl declared his intention to discuss, in the later parts of a new edition of the *Logical Investigations*, Chapter 4 of the 3rd book of Lotze's "greater" *Logic*, which was dedicated to the "real and formal significance of the logical". Unfortunately, this promise remained unfulfilled. Be this as it may, Husserl was also deeply involved in studying Lotze's thought during the 1910s. In the summer terms of 1912 and 1919, he gave classes on Lotze's epistemology (Varga 2013, p. 181).

To start, in *Logical Investigations* Husserl suggested a form of anti-psychologism[3] and a theory of ideas that are substantially Lotzean (1939b, pp. 323 f.). Especially important for Husserl's philosophical development were Lotze's theory of value alongside his theory of "idealities" (§ 4.1). As Husserl saw it, among the denizens of Lotze's realm of "idealities" were the "truths in themselves" (*Wahrheiten an sich*) (1939a, p. 129). It is true that this term was already used by Bernard Bolzano (Bolzano 1984, pp. 28, 80). In fact, however, there is no evidence that Lotze knew Bolzano's theory of "truths and propositions in themselves". He simply rediscovered it. This cannot be said about Frege—he clearly adopted this term from Lotze, later (in 1918/1919) calling it "thought".

Husserl also praised Lotze's "scholastic realism",[4] his "Platonism", and "his brilliant [*genius*] interpretation of Plato's theory of ideas" (1939a, p. 129). But let us be more specific regarding Lotze's contributions here. He transformed the Hegelian dichotomy between *being* and *becoming* into the trichotomy *being, becoming,* and *value*. The given (the being) is; it is opposed to both what happens (e.g., to changes, to becoming) and to the validities. Transitions among these three are impossible. Furthermore, from the perspective of his conception of values, Lotze suggested a new interpretation of Plato's theory of ideas. Ideas have two characteristics: (i) they have their own autonomous being; (ii) at the same time, however, ideas

---

[3] On the conception of anti-psychologism see Kusch (1995).
[4] To remind the reader, today not Lotze but Brentano is considered as the man who rediscovered the scholastic tradition in philosophy (Chapter 4).

have properties similar to those of the objects of reality. Lotze's claim was that these two conditions are only met by values. In fact, Plato's ideas are nothing but validities of truths. Plato misrepresented them as "ideas" only because in Ancient Greek language there was no expression for things which have no being—and values are just such things (1874, § 317). The fact that Plato's ideas are validities, Lotze argues further, explains why they are beyond space and time, beyond things and minds.[5]

Husserl also maintained that "Lotze discovered the realm of sense-data [*Empfindungsdaten*], the data of colour and tone as a field of ideal, i.e. 'ontological' cognitions" (1939b, p. 321). The only problem in Lotze's system, as the later Husserl saw it, was that he was a *realist* (§ 4.2). Lotze namely failed to realize that these data are only and exclusively part of the consciousness, that the human mind itself is an endless field of a priori cognitions. In contrast, Husserl's phenomenology explored only the latter.[6]

These considerations urge us to preliminary revise the history of the "logical turn" in the 19th century philosophy we are going to discuss in § 4. The received view underlines on this count the relatedness between Bolzano and Husserl as well as between Bolzano and Frege (Føllesdal 2001). What it misses to see is that one can clearly discern, at the center of the philosophical–logical triangle Bolzano–Husserl–Frege, the imposing figure of Hermann Lotze.

3 Hegel, Lotze and Early Cambridge Analytic Philosophy

Frege, arguably the founding father of analytic philosophy, attended at least one course of Lotze's lectures in Göttingen, on philosophy of religion, and, as it is clear from Frege's "17 Key Sentences on Logic" (1882), he industriously explored Lotze's "greater" *Logic* (Sluga 1980, p. 45) (Chapter 1, § 2.2). The special concerns of the present book, however, preclude an investigation of Lotze's influences on Frege,[7] a complex topic that calls for monograph study of its own. The focus in this section is on how Lotze's extensive logicalization of philosophy (§ 4.1 below)

---

5 Lotze's interpretation of Plato's ideas was further elaborated by Paul Natorp (1902).
6 As a matter of fact, in the first four "logical investigations" (1900/1901) Husserl was a logical realist as well. Later, the realist phenomenologists Adolf Reinach and Johannes Daubert highly praised Husserl's *Logical Investigations* (especially the first four investigations), but not his later works.
7 On this topic, one can consult Gabriel (1984, 1989a, 1989b, and 2002). Frege himself underlined that Lotze's ideas were "of decisive importance" (*von entscheidender Bedeutung*) for his work (Gabriel and Schlotter 2017, p. 209).

influenced the leading figures of the early Cambridge analytic philosophy, Bertrand Russell and G. E. Moore.

The conventional wisdom has it that the early philosophy of Moore and Russell was under the strong sway of the British "neo-Hegelians". Yet those historians who investigate the British "neo-Hegelians" of 1880–1920 in detail call attention to the fact that the latter were anything but epigones of Hegel. Geoffrey Thomas made this point in regard to Thomas Green (1987), William Sweet in regard to Bosanquet (1995), and Peter Nicholson in regard to F. H. Bradley (1990). Finally, Nicholas Griffin has shown that Russell from 1895–1898, then an alleged neo-Hegelian, "was very strongly influenced by Kant and hardly at all by Hegel" (1996, p. 215).

This can be hardly surprising if we keep in mind that the members of the school of T. H. Green—arguably the founding father of the British "Neo-Hegelianism"—F. H. Bradley, B. Bosanquet, W. Wallace, R. L. Nettleship, were only called "Neo-Hegelians" by their opponents. As it turns out, that term had little explanatory value from the outset. To be sure, the students of Green "had some knowledge of Hegel, and a good deal more of Kant. The fact of their having this knowledge was used by their opponents ... to discredit them in the eyes of a public always contemptuous of foreigners" (Collingwood 1944, p. 16). The "Neo-Hegelians" themselves categorically repudiated the application. The only Neo-Hegelian in England of the time was Moore's and Russell's elder friend and fellow Cambridge Apostle J. E. McTaggart. In fact, however, McTaggart's study of Hegel was far from being truly Hegelian. Arguably, "no one has ever been convinced that the Hegel he described exists outside McTaggart's fertile imagination" (Passmore 1966, p. 76).

This claim is supported by the fact that scholars well-versed in German philosophy of the 19th century find the statement that the mainstream British philosophy of 1870–1910 was "Hegelian" rather puzzling. Historically speaking, after 1840, there was scarcely any German philosopher of importance who would have openly declared that he was Hegelian.[8] The principal reason for this was that after Hegel's death, a host of new, paradigm-changing scientific discoveries revealed that many of Hegel's speculations were mistaken. In consequence, Hegelianism in the strict sense started to be judged unsupportable. The question thus arises as to whether the leading philosophers in Britain were so ill-informed about this development in Germany that between 1870 and 1910 they embraced Hegelianism as their philosophical credo? In fact, there is clear evidence that suggests that this was not the case. In 1877, Wilhelm Wundt had informed his British colleagues in the

---

[8] A prominent exception was the historian of philosophy Kuno Fischer. This cannot be a surprise since, arguably, Hegel was the founder of the academic history of philosophy. He was the first to see past philosophers as struggling with problems, with internal logical relations between them, not simply as holding views (Milkov 2020b, p. 22).

newly founded journal *Mind* (old series) that the Hegelian school had "at the present day the fewest thoroughgoing adherents [in Germany]" (p. 511). In what follows in this section, we shall show that the leading British philosophers of that time were not really Hegelian, not even Kantian, but were more under the influence of Hermann Lotze.

To be sure, the philosophers who influenced the young Moore and Russell through reading most, the putative neo-Hegelians Bradley and Bosanquet, were strongly under Lotze's sway. This should be no surprise since their philosophy professor we already mentioned, Thomas Green, was so enthusiastic about Lotze that in 1880, he started a major project of translating Lotze's *System of Philosophy* which included Lotze's "greater" *Logic* (1874) and "greater" *Metaphysic* (1879) (Chapter 1, § 2.2) into English.[9] After Green's untimely death two years later, this project was continued by a team under the guidance of Bosanquet. Besides Green and Bosanquet, A. C. Bradley (brother of F. H. Bradley), R. L. Nettleship and J. Cook Wilson contributed to the translation and editing of Lotze's work. The two volumes appeared in English in 1884 and 1885. At the same time, at Cambridge, James Ward and Henry Sidgwick were instrumental in preparing the translation of Lotze's three volumes of *Mikrokosmus* by Elisabeth Hamilton and E. E. Constance Jones. This translation appeared in two volumes in 1885.

Furthermore, while G. F. Stout and James Ward, Russell's and Moore's tutors at Cambridge, were widely believed to be Hegelian, in truth, they were under the direct influence of Lotze.[10] This is clearly shown by the fact that Lotze was one of the philosophers set for examinations at Cambridge between 1890 and 1910. Moore later remembered that Ward encouraged him "to read pieces of Lotze's *Metaphysic* and to write essays on these pieces [which] then [... Ward] discussed privately with [him]" (1942, p. 17). Towards the end of this period, C. D. Broad won the Burney Prize with an essay on Lotze's Philosophy of Religion (Kuntz 1971, p. 57).

Even more, while the Cambridge man James Ward was Lotze's student in 1869/1870, the Oxonian John Cook Wilson was the same in 1873/1874. Josiah Royce of Harvard, for his part, visited Lotze's lectures in 1875/1876. Later, he remembered: "In Germany I heard Lotze at Göttingen, and was for a while strongly under his influence" (Roth 1982, p. 406). On September 8, 1879, William James, for his part, wrote in a letter: "[Lotze] is the most delectable, certainly, of all German writers—a pure genius" (Perry 1935, p. 16). Another upcoming Harvard philosophy professor, George

---

9 Green said once to Bosanquet: "The time which one spent on such a book as that (the ['greater'] *Metaphysic* [of Lotze]) could not be wasted as regards one's own work" (Lotze 1888).
10 This is especially true of Ward, who studied with Lotze in Göttingen in 1869/1870. Note that in comparison to his two other tutors in Cambridge, Sidgwick and Stout, Ward exercised the strongest influence on Russell (Griffin 1991, p. 35). Stout was more of a follower of Franz Brentano.

Santayana, studied at the University of Berlin only in 1887–1888, when Lotze was already dead. As if in compensation, he wrote his PhD Dissertation on Lotze, which he defended in 1889 at Harvard.

These are undeniable facts. Those who want to argue against our thesis of the leading role of Lotze in both German and Western philosophy in general after Hegel's death face the challenge of suggesting examples in which other German philosophers of this period exercised such an influence in Oxford, Cambridge (England), and Harvard. There is simply no basis for comparison of Lotze with Herbart, Trendelenburg,[11] Dilthey or any of the Neo-Kantians on this score. None of them was thus esteemed in the most respected universities of the West.

4 The Idiosyncrasy of Lotze's Philosophy

But how did Lotze achieve this standing? How he became the most influential German philosopher in the second half of the 19th century?

4.1 Lotze's Second Logical Turn in Modern Philosophy

Lotze won this prominent position in the German philosophy of the 19th century mainly because he took a new *logical turn* in modern philosophy. It should be observed that the first logical turn in this context was made by Kant (Milkov 2013c; Lapointe 2019).[12] To be more explicit, Kant's project of transcendental idealism was no less than an advancement of a new formal discipline in philosophy: of a new, *transcendental* logic that outlines the capacities of pure reason. It set the scope and validation of the a priori functioning of thinking (understanding) and of the way in which it is connected with material content. Its final objective was to suggest "a complete table of the moments of thinking in general" (KrV, A 71/B 96).

Lotze continued the logical turn in modern philosophy started by Kant but developed it in a new form. In contrast to Kant, he did not view logic as purely formal. Following a wink made by Schleiermacher, Lotze tried to set up logic of con-

---

[11] Köhnke (1986, pp. 23 ff.), for example, sees Trendelenburg, not Lotze, as the key figure of the German philosophy after Hegel's death.

[12] In Milkov (2013c), we defined Kant's transcendental turn as the second step of logicalization of philosophy, the first step being Plato's logicalization of the Socratic method of philosophy in his theory of Forms, which Aristotle later transformed into his theory of syllogism (Milkov 1997, i, pp. 53 ff.). In this sense, Lotze logicalization of philosophy was a third step in this direction. It was the *second* step of logicalization in *modern* philosophy.

tent. To be more explicit, his lucky find was to merge together logic with metaphysics (also with philosophy of mind,[13] understood, at that point in time, as part of metaphysics), epistemology, and ethics.

A typical example in this respect was Lotze's new approach to studying thinking. He connected thinking to two "logically different" domains, validating and becoming, and considered each of them to be explored by a specific science: logic investigates the validity of thinking, while psychology investigates the development of thinking. The implication of this move was that Lotze's new method formalized metaphysics and ethics, on the one hand, and enriched logic, on the other. It made metaphysics and ethics exact disciplines while turning logic philosophical.

In other words, according to Lotze, "metaphysics is to be developed as *a formal science*" (Misch 1912, p. xxii; italics added). Significantly, Lotze's primary motive for embracing this approach was his desire to eliminate the bitter disagreements that had characterized philosophical theorizing for centuries—a main source of philosophy's reputation of being unscientific. This can be achieved since the *formal—logical*—presentation of philosophical theories eliminates their subjective side which is the principal source of philosophical animus. Thus purified, seemingly contradictory systems could be shown consistent with one another. In other words, adopting the formal approach to metaphysics implies that philosophical systems are not exceptional; they have alternative value.[14] And as we know today, the belief of the German idealists that they advance the "only true" philosophical system (Hegel 1830, § 14), which gives the correct account of the systematic self-explication of the reality from the one and only Absolute, was their major flaw.

In more technical terms, Lotze achieved this, reshaping the already mentioned concept of "idealities" that was widely used by the German idealists (§§ 95 f.) into a new form. Lotze's idealities are formal terms that serve as *orientation* both in science and in philosophy (Chapter 1, §§ 3.1–2; Chapter 2, § 9). They have the form of *values* that are products of the human mind—to be more precise, of human culture. However, idealities require "matter" in order to come into being—i.e., they do not exist autonomously.

---

[13] In Chapter 2, § 13, we shall say more about how Lotze connected his explorations of philosophy of mind with logic.
[14] For this position and its implications, which we are going to discuss in § 4.2, Lotze's interpreters often maintain that his writings "lack the masculine power" (Vorländer 1927, i, p. 150).

4.2 Implications

Lotze's commitment to this approach led to radical changes in his philosophical practice. He started to investigate philosophical problems bit by bit, piecemeal, so that a later discovery of a mistake in his investigation did not make his overall philosophy mistaken.[15] Correspondingly, Lotze recommended other philosophers to view his writings as "an open market, where the reader may simply pass by the goods he does not want" (Lotze 1874, Preface) (n. 14). This side of Lotze's philosophy made him the most "pillaged" philosopher of the 19th century (Passmore 1966, p. 51). Many of his theses were embraced and further developed without mentioning their origin, e.g., the anti-psychologism adopted by Frege and Husserl or the context principle in logic according to which one is to "ask for the meaning of a word, not in isolation but only in the context of a proposition" (Frege 1884, Introduction).

Lotze's logical turn in philosophy also went hand-in-hand with his belief that "after centuries of philosophical work, it is impossible to suggest new ideas" in it (Becher 1929, p. 51). In this sense, one can consider him a "philosophical conservative". As already seen, Lotze saw his task as an examination of the old ideas in philosophy from a new, logical perspective. He aimed to give a new meaning to some specific philosophical ideas introduced in philosophy, in particular, after 1781—the year Kant's first *Critique* was published. In an original move, Lotze endeavored to recast these notions as problems of logic.

Following this understanding, Lotze subscribed to the method of eclecticism. Today, the term "eclecticism" is only used and understood in a pejorative sense. However, it is remarkable how successfully Lotze used a method with this label.[16] From the very beginning, his slogan was: "When we cannot necessarily join one of the dominating parties, we [shall …] stay in the middle via free eclecticism" (1843, p. 1). Lotze adapted to his purpose the ideas of different philosophers, above all, of Kant, of the German idealists Fichte and Schelling, and also of Hegel, distilling what he took to be the most valuable of them and expressing them in a new, exact form. Among other things, this explains the manifest presence of Hegel's ideas in Lotze's writings, which made it easy—but mistaken—to interpret him as a Hegelian.

Lotze's innovative logical turn in philosophy introduced—or simply revived—a number of seminal philosophical concepts some of which we already mentioned.

---

15 This practice was later also followed by Russell (1918b, p. 85) (Chapter 6) and became central to analytic philosophy (Milkov 2020b, p. 116).
16 Lotze showed admiration towards eclecticism already in his pre-theoretical period: in 1840, he wrote the poem "Eclecticism" (Kronenberg 1899, p. 218).

Among them are: (i) the concept of value in logic—its most notorious successor being the concept of truth-value; (ii) the notion of anti-psychologism in logic; (iii) the context principle; (iv) the objective content of judgment—a conception that Brentano later developed into the idea of radical distinction between subject and object of knowledge (Chapter 4); (v) the idea that perception features objective content—its most notorious successor was a concept that Russell would later transform into that of sense-data (Milkov 2001);[17] (vi) the idea of concept/judgment as a function; (vii) the metaphors of coloring expressions and of saturated–unsaturated expressions; (viii) the concept of a state of affairs (Sachverhalt) (Milkov 2002a) that played an important role in the philosophy of both Husserl and Wittgenstein. These concepts are still widely discussed in philosophy today.

The last three ideas signal what can be characterized as Lotze's "logical realism". According to it, "propositions and their parts, generally understood as concepts, ... have some form of being independently of the mind that thinks them" (van der Schaar 2013, p. 8). It shows Lotze's treatment as a forthright "idealist" (Beiser 2013, p. 222) to be problematic. This is also confirmed by the fact that Lotze's student, James Ward, paved the way for G. E. Moore's and Russell's philosophical realism, while another British student of Lotze, John Cook Wilson, groomed the Oxonian realism of H. A. Prichard, the tutor of J. L. Austin.

4.3 Lotze's Influence and Its Decline

The significance of Lotze's new logic, which we justly can call "philosophical",[18] was widely acknowledged in Europe after Hegel's death. The point is that through the new way in which Lotze blended philosophy with logic, moreover, through introducing a logic that is not deductive but piecemeal, he became "most acceptable to the post-[and anti-]Hegelians", in particular because he freed logic "of many of the abstractions and rigid dogmas which Hegel had fixed upon" (Kraushaar 1940, pp. 440 f.).

The innovations in this rapidly developing kind of logic that has no specific formulas or axioms, spread quickly and were adopted in a short period of time. A typical example in this respect is the context principle, (re)discovered by

---

[17] As already have seen in § 2, Husserl maintained that already Lotze discovered the "realm of sense-data". In fact, Lotze only set up the condition for exploring this realm.
[18] Husserl openly spoke about Lotze's "pure", or "philosophical logic" (1939a, p. 123). The concept of philosophical logic also played important role in Russell's philosophy (Milkov 2020b, pp. 200 ff., and 2022a).

Lotze as early as in the 1840s.[19] Vehemently criticized by J. S. Mill, "the slogan 'Only in the context of a proposition [or judgment] do words have meaning' [... became] an Anglo-Hegelian commonplace" after 1875, assumed also by Green and Bosanquet (Manser 1983, p. 62).

In fact, the philosophers "of the Lotzean period were well aware of the roots of the *Logic* of Bradley and the *Logic* of Bosanquet in Lotze's *Logic*" (Kunz 1971, p. 61). As Agnes Cuming noted long ago, what Bradley and Bosanquet adopted from German philosophy were, above all, some ideas of Lotze's logic: "Their treatment of the problems of logic is almost a continuation from the point at which the German writer [Lotze] left off" (1917, p. 165).

The situation did not change in the early years of the 20th century. In 1912, Heidegger called Lotze's "greater" *Logic* "the basic book in modern logic" (1978, p. 22). A few years later, the neo-Kantian Bruno Bauch wrote: "Of everything that has followed in the area of logic from Hegel to the present day, there is nothing that has surpassed Lotze's achievements in value" (1918, p. 45). One is here reminded of the fact that in the 1910s, Bruno Bauch was a colleague of Frege in Jena and one of his few devoted admirers in Germany.[20] This, however, did not hinder him to appreciate Lotze as the most prominent among the logicians of his age.

Unfortunately, with the rapidly growing predominance of mathematical logic, awareness of the importance of Lotze's achievements in philosophical logic declined perceptibly after 1920. This decline progressed to such an extent that in the early 1960s, the name of Lotze warranted not so much as a footnote in *The Development of Logic* of William and Martha Kneale (1962), still one of the standard historical texts in this realm of study.

5 Final Remarks

In summary, it should be noted that the study of Lotze's thought today is not only significant because of the formative influence he exercised on Western philosophy at the *fin de siècle*. It is interesting in its own right. We refer here to the old wisdom that good philosophy does not age. Copernican cosmology has refuted the Ptolemaic worldview, but modern philosophy has not made Plato and Aristotle obsolete. Just like the good old books of fiction, the old masters of philosophy are always up to date. This also applies to Lotze's philosophy.

---

19 On the history of the context principle, see Milkov (2003, pp. 126 f.).
20 Bruno Bauch was also the supervisor of Rudolf Carnap's 1923 PhD Dissertation.

5 Final Remarks — 11

The implication is that his work is not only of archival importance. It contains positions that can still be worked out today. Following this stance, our interpretation challenges the tendency to treat Lotze like a "dead dog".[21] Unfortunately, such a tendency is also perceptible in the latest publications on Lotze. To be fair to the facts, Lotze himself is partly to blame for this. He followed a cunning dialectical method that openly admitted contradicting claims (Chapter 1, § 3.3). At the same time, however, Lotze emphasized that the statements of philosophy must be rigorously and clearly formulated. That makes him a philosopher who is difficult to interpret.

Among other things, exploring Lotze's ideas can help to better understand the cleavage of the Western philosophy into analytic and continental as well as into academic and popular philosophy. Apparently, Lotze already sensed the danger of splitting philosophy into continental and analytic. As we understand it (Milkov 2020b, pp. 217 ff.), this is a split: (i) between philosophy that explores *conditio humana* and philosophy that investigates the *being qua being*; (ii) between philosophy that finds expression in essays or popular (mundane) philosophy and philosophy that produces argumentative analyses.

Regarding (i), Lotze made anthropology prima philosophia (Chapter 1, § 3.3). In this way he tried to explore problems of being *qua* being and of *conditio humana* together. Regarding (ii), in his *Mikrokosmus*, Lotze tried to unify popular philosophy and the "philosopher's philosophy" (Elisabeth Anscombe's fitting description of Wittgenstein's philosophy (1990, p. 2) (Chapter 3, § 2.1).

---

[21] It is allowed to use here this phrase coined by Karl Marx in relation to Hegel (Marx 1867, p. 26).

Part I: **Lotze's Philosophy**

Chapter 1
Lotze's Philosophy: An Outline

1 Opening

Rudolph Hermann Lotze began his career in philosophy as a contributor to an anti-Hegelian, objectivist movement in German-speaking Europe (Gabriel 1989b). Closely following Adolf Trendelenburg, he advanced a philosophy that did not start from the opposition between matter and spirit (mind) (Lotze 1841, p. 281). Trendelenburg abolished it, referring to the concept of movement, which is common to them both. Lotze went further, however. He insisted that the relation between matter and spirit is based on metaphysical nexus that is more fundamental (Schnädelbach 1983, p. 219). Lotze suggested as uniting the *order* between all objects and terms—it is the "universal inner connection of all reality" (1879, § iii). Especially important in Lotze's theory of order is the concept of *relation*. A favorite saying of his illustrates this point: "The proposition, 'things exist'", he repeatedly said, "has no intelligible meaning except that they stand in relations to each other" (1887a, p. 186).

The priority of orderly relations in Lotze's ontology was an implication of the fact that nature is a cosmos, not chaos. Furthermore, since the activity that is typical of humans—thinking—is nothing but an activity of relating, man is a *microcosm*. The latter point convinced Lotze to study microcosm and macrocosm jointly, a conviction which found expression in his three-volume book *Mikrokosmus* (1856/1864) (Chapter 3).

The distinction between the universe as macrocosm and humanity as microcosm gave rise to another important side of Lotze's philosophy—its anthropological stance. Following Kant, Lotze assumed that the fundamental metaphysical and logical problems of philosophy are to be discussed and answered through the lens of the microcosm, that is, in terms of the specific perceptual and rational characteristics of human beings. There is no alternative access to them.

Lotze's philosophical work was guided by his double qualification in medicine and philosophy (§ 2.1 below). While he chose academic philosophy as his profession, his medical training was an ever-present influence on his philosophy in at least three respects. First of all, his overall philosophy was characterized by a concern for scientific exactness. Secondly, Lotze's philosophical conceptions were scientifically well-informed: Lotze criticized any philosophical doctrine that discards the results of science. Thirdly, he devoted many academic years to more or less philosophic studies in medicine and physiology. Lotze's efforts in this direction resulted in foundational works in psychology, in virtue of which he counts as one of psychology's founding fathers (Hall 1912).

2 Life and Works

2.1 Biography

Hermann Lotze was born in Bautzen (Saxony) on May 21, 1817, as the third child of a military medical doctor. Two years later, the family moved to nearby Zittau. Lotze's father, Carl Friedrich, died in 1829, when Hermann was 12. Soon thereafter, the family encountered serious financial troubles. This series of events shaped Lotze's character in significant ways. He grew up independent, ambitious, serious and thrifty but also melancholic, reserved, even shy.

Between 1828 and 1834, Hermann attended the local high school (*Gymnasium*) in Zittau. In 1834, he matriculated at the University of Leipzig. Lotze wanted to study philosophy—a wish also nourished by his love of art and poetry—and he did so. However, his experience with financial hardship urged him simultaneously to pursue a degree in the more practical and lucrative field of medicine. Four years later, in 1838, he received doctorates in both disciplines.

After practicing medicine for a year in Zittau, Lotze joined the University of Leipzig as an adjunct lecturer in the Department of Medicine in 1839 and in the Department of Philosophy in 1840. In the same year, Lotze achieved dual degrees based on post-doctoral dissertations (*Habilitationen*) in medicine and philosophy. As a result, he received a license to teach (*venia legendi*) at German universities in these two fields.

In 1839, Lotze became engaged to Ferdinande Hoffmann of Zittau (b. 1819). They married in 1844. The marriage produced four sons. Lotze was deeply attached to his wife, and her death in 1875 was a loss from which he never recovered. One of his numerous British students, Richard Haldane (who later became Lord Chancellor and Secretary of State of the United Kingdom), described him after his wife's death as one who "seldom sees people, as he lives a sort of solitary life in the country where his home is, about half a mile from Göttingen, and is looked upon as unsociable" (Kuntz 1971, p. 50).

In the year of his marriage, 1844, Lotze was named J. F. Herbart's successor as Professor of Philosophy at the University of Göttingen. He remained at Göttingen until 1880, when he was named Professor of Philosophy at the University of Berlin. A few months later (on July 1, 1881), Lotze died of a cardiac defect from which he had suffered for years. He was succeeded in the Berlin chair by Wilhelm Dilthey.

Among Lotze's professors in Leipzig were G. T. Fechner, from whom he learned the importance of quantitative experiment in psychology, and Christian Weiße, who helped the young Hermann to see the philosophy of German Idealism from an aesthetic perspective. Lotze was also influenced by Kant, Hegel, Herbart, Schelling, and J. F. Fries. He was personally introduced to Fries, who at the time was a Professor in Jena, by his fellow countryman, friend, and Fries' student Ernst Friedrich Apelt.

Some interpreters maintain that Lotze was also influenced by his countryman Leibniz (Leibniz was born and raised in Leipzig, Saxony). Indeed, there are some common points between these two philosophers: the occasionalism, the atomism, the active–passive dichotomy in epistemology and ontology. A hidden influence (seldom discussed in the literature) came from Schleiermacher—via Trendelenburg—who held, against the project of formal logic pursued by Kant and M.W. Drobisch, that logic must be developed alongside metaphysics.

2.2 Works

Lotze charted his philosophical program early on in his "lesser" *Metaphysic* (1841) and "lesser" *Logic* (1843a). His *Habilitation* in medicine was published in between these two texts under the title *Allgemeine Pathologie und Therapie als mechanische Naturwissenschaften* (1842).

Over the next ten years, Lotze worked on problems at the intersection of medicine and philosophy, in particular on the relation between mind and body. The results of these studies were published in two books: *Allgemeine Physiologie des körperlichen Lebens* (1851) and *Medicinische Psychologie oder Physiologie der Seele* (1852a) (Chapter 2). During this period, Lotze also published extensive essays on the philosophy of biology and the philosophy of mind: "Leben. Lebenskraft" (1843b), "Instinct" (1844), and "Seele und Seelenleben" (1846). In the late 1840s, he produced important works on aesthetics: "Über den Begriff der Schönheit" (1845), "Über Bedingungen der Kunstschönheit" (1847), and *"Quaestiones Lucretianae"* (1852b).

Mikrokosmus, published in 3 volumes between 1856 and 1864 (Chapter 3), marked a new period in Lotze's philosophical development. In this monumental work, he synthesized his earlier ideas: the logico-metaphysical thoughts of 1841–1843, his studies in philosophy of biology and in philosophy of physiology and psychology of 1842–1852, and his ideas in aesthetics of 1845–1852. Despite some interpretations to the contrary, the book was not only a popular treatise. It developed important logical and metaphysical ideas and discussions of the mind–body problem in a form that cannot be found in his earlier work.

Shortly after Lotze finished *Mikrokosmus*, he started his *System of Philosophy*, which consisted of his "greater" *Logic* (1874), and "greater" *Metaphysic* (1879). A third part of the system on ethics, aesthetics and religious philosophy remained unfinished at the time of his death. Briefly, the difference between *Mikrokosmus* and *System of Philosophy* can be expressed as follows. While *Mikrokosmus* was something of an encyclopedia of philosophical deliberations on human life, private and public, supported by some technically advanced philosophical discussions, the *System* was an encyclopedia of the philosophical disciplines. In other words, *Mikrokosmus* was mainly directed to the general educated public, while the *System* was addressed, above all, to professional philosophers.

Lotze possessed an extraordinary ability for studying languages. Many of his papers were written in French, some of them in Latin (e.g., "*Quaestiones lucretianae*"). Lotze also published a volume of poetry (Lotze 1840).

3 Philosophical Principles and Methods

In the Introduction (§ 4.1 below), we already said something about Lotze's second step of logicalization of modern philosophy. In Chapter 2, we are going to present Lotze's principle of teleomechanism, his form of occasionalism and his conception of physical-psychological mechanism. In the present section, we shall shortly pass in review some other elements of Lotze's principles and methods in philosophy.

3.1 Regressive Analysis

The declared objective of Lotze's philosophy was a "reflection on the meaning of our human being [*Dasein*]" (1856b, p. 304). The urgency of this task was a consequence of the scientific and industrial revolution of the beginning and the middle of the 19th century. That revolution dramatically changed the way in which humans view the cosmos and universe. It eroded the unity of God and humanity; traditional mythology proved to be inconsistent. As a consequence, the world started to seem alien and cold. A substantial weakening in religious belief followed. Lotze saw danger in the numerous attempts, in particular, on the side of the mechanic philosopher-scientists like Ludwig Friedrich Büchner, Heinrich Czolbe, Franz Fick, Jacob Moleschott and Karl Vogt (Chapter 2, § 3), to prove that the microcosm of human beings is merely mechanical and materialistic. His objective was to disprove such attempts and to make people feel at home in the world again.

Contrary to the trends in then-current anthropology (for example, that of Karl Marx), Lotze did not seek to explain humanity in terms of the technologies and goods it produced. Rather, he thought that the keys for understanding the human race are to be found in the results of human education and schooling (*Bildung*), as they have been developed throughout history. This meant that the philosophical investigations are to begin not simply with the elements of human culture but with developed human cultures taken as wholes and, even more so, with the history of such cultures taken as a whole. From these wholes, one should work "backwards", ultimately in order to analyze logic, metaphysics, science, and mathematics. This is the approach of *regressive analysis* (1874, § 208; 1879, § 93).[22]

Lotze further believed that the main educational goods (*Bildungsgüter*) of human culture are usually conveyed by poetry and religion. They provide a "higher perspective on things", the "point of view of the heart". This means that the mechanistic processes upon which science focuses are not the only key to understanding the world; they are not even the most important key. On the contrary, science becomes intelligible and useful for humans only in connection with the historically developed values and forms of schooling and education characteristic of an advanced human culture.

But how exactly can the history of culture command the shape of logic, metaphysics, and science? Lotze's answer in brief is: through the already mentioned (in Introduction, § 4.1) *idealities* they produce. As magnitudes that are identifiable in experience, the idealities serve as orientating concepts for all academic disciplines, giving them direction and purpose within the framework of a unified human life in a developed human culture.

Following Kant, Lotze further claimed that idealities pertain to the mental rather than to the material reality.[23] However, they require matter in order to be exemplified or articulated by human beings. That is why we can only understand idealities *in experience*. We find them at work already in our sensual life and in our feelings of pleasure and displeasure. So, they are presented in aesthetics and ethics. But they are also of cardinal importance in science, mathematics, metaphysics and logic. The spatial order, for example, is such an ideality (Chapter 2, §§ 8 f.). However, the idealities are not given as another thing among things, as substances. Rather, they are simply "noticed" as a necessary "backdrop" to or a "condition of the possibility of" the matrix of material things.

Given his views on the relation of the material to the ideal, Lotze was convinced that the quarrel between materialism and idealism is misguided. It is a

---

22 The method of regressive analysis was not first introduced by Lotze. It was practiced and also discussed by Pappus of Alexandria and also by Kant (1800) before Lotze and by Russell (1907b) after him.
23 Lotze's position was markedly different from that of Kant, however. We shall say more about this in Chapter 2, § 3.

quarrel about meaning: idealists see too much meaning (borne by ideal entities) in reality, while materialists see no meaning in it at all. Fearing that the characteristically vague aesthetic elements of human experience would undermine exact science, the materialists had tried to purge all humanistic meaning from reality by sanctioning only mathematical descriptions of mechanically-construed natural processes. Lotze thought such fears were in vain. Just as mechanism was compatible with teleology (Chapter 2, § 4), so Lotze thought that aesthetics (poetry) and religion (revealed truth) were compatible with the mathematics and calculation preferred by the materialists. By the same token, the acceptance of mechanism as a purely methodological principle in science did not invalidate the belief in free will. On the contrary, since mechanism made the spiritual effort to achieve the trans-sensual more strenuous, it only "increased the poetical appeal of the world" (Lotze 1856b, p. 306).

3.2 Anthropology as *prima philosophia*

It can be no surprise therefore that Lotze's main objective was the investigation of the concrete human being alongside her imaginings, dreams, and feelings. He considered these elements—as expressed in poetry and art—to be constitutive of a human person and her life. This explains the central role that the concept of home (*Heimat*) plays in his metaphysics. The related concept in his philosophy of mind is feeling and heart (*Gemüt*), as distinguished from mind (*Geist*) and soul (*Seele*). In fact, Lotze introduced the concept of *heart* in the wake of German mysticism (of Meister Eckhart and Jakob Böhme). However, he used it in a quite realistic sense. Heart is what makes us long for home. The longing itself is a result of our desires, which we strive to satisfy. Life consists, above all, in consuming (*genießen*) goods, both material and ideal. Clearly, Lotze's conception of human life is close to hedonism (§ 4.1 below). For this purpose, he also introduced and widely used the concept of *coloring*: "An immense color intensity of our lively, concrete world examination grants an endless occupation"[24] (1858, p. 383).

It is no surprise, therefore, that Lotze's *Mikrokosmus* greatly influenced young philosophers of the time such as Wilhelm Dilthey. On Christmas 1858, the latter (then 25) noted in his *Notebook*: "The second volume of Lotze's *Mikrokosmus* had really grasped me. This is a marvelous book" (Dilthey 1933, p. 55). Clearly, Lotze was attractive to Dilthey due to his realism, which emphasizes the individual

---

[24] Today, we connect the concept of coloring mainly with Frege's logic who, apparently, borrowed it from Lotze.

and her concrete life.[25] From this starting point, Dilthey developed his philosophy of life.

In fact, Lotze did not introduce anthropological investigation into philosophy. Rather, it was started in the 16th century in an effort to renovate theology. During the next three centuries, anthropology became a favorite subject among German university philosophers, including Kant. In his anthropology, however, Lotze did not follow Kant. Kant distinguished between theoretical philosophy and mundane philosophy, with anthropology falling in the latter category (Introduction, § 5; Chapter 3, § 3.1). Lotze openly criticized Kant on this count (1841, p. 17) and developed his "theoretical anthropology" specifically in order to merge the two philosophical disciplines into one.

The conclusion to which Lotze came was that Kant's question "what can I know?" cannot be answered in the abstract; it can be only addressed in terms of embodied persons in concrete socio-historical situations. Only when we embrace this perspective, Lotze thought, can we also grasp the depth and the importance of metaphysical problems. This point brings us to the most important characteristic of Lotze's philosophy. Lotze did not simply shift from metaphysics to anthropology. Rather, his anthropology became philosophy proper (Orth 1986, p. 43).

3.3 Lotze's Dialectics

In the "Introduction" (§ 4.2), we already spoke about Lotze's method of eclecticism. Consistent with his eclecticism, he also used something approaching Hegel's dialectical method (Lotze 1841, p. 320). This found expression in the fact that "there are some passages [in Lotze's writings] in which he does seem conscious of the contradictions and [nevertheless] attempts to mediate between the two" rather than eliminating one of them (Kuntz 1971, p. 34).

Some authors judge these tendencies in Lotze negatively. For example, Eduard von Hartmann complained that "there is scarcely a 'yes' by Lotze, which is not undermined at another place by a 'no'" (1888, p. 147). Yet other philosophers, like George Santayana, have recognized that, despite the apparent contradictions, Lotze's philosophy remained astonishingly consistent overall. Careful attention reveals that most of the supposed contradictions are apparent only as a result from

---

[25] On the joint program for a new, concrete philosophy of Lotze and Dilthey, see Orth (1984a, 1984b).

the failure to notice the varying perspectives from which Lotze conducted his philosophical research.

For instance, Lotze insisted that mechanistic descriptions were appropriate and, indeed, *required* in science but inappropriate in philosophy, where teleological explanations are simply indispensable. It is easy to see this double-demand for mechanism and teleology as contradictory if one fails to recognize that each demand is only a "methodological" demand made by the requirements of two disciplines with differing norms and purposes. The idealistic tendencies of Lotze's system, for example, were part of an aesthetic description of reality, "a personal manner of reading things, a poetic intuition of the cosmic life" (Santayana 1889, p. 155). Other aspects of his system—like his atomism—were radically objectivistic, suited only to the demands of scientific description and scientific work.

Lotze's perspectivism—the tendency to treat some views as "merely methodological", i.e., as rooted in a given disciplinary perspective (Chapter 2, § 11)—can make him difficult to follow. The problem is compounded by his tendency to, on occasion, switch perspectives throughout the course of a single work. For instance, he begins his ontological investigations with pluralistic realism only to end it with monistic idealism. This explains why Lotze's views are often difficult to understand, difficult to state, and also difficult to criticize correctly and effectively.[26]

Lotze also followed a specific approach by discussing different views (*Ansichten*) on the subject under scrutiny. He was against the hasty satisfaction of our "theoretical needs" and expectations through one-sided theories. Moreover, Lotze claimed that his final solutions were merely views that satisfy "needs of the heart". Incidentally, this point can be comfortably interpreted in the sense of Freud and Wittgenstein in the sense that philosophical puzzles are similar to mental neuroses, which can be treated by changing one's perspective.[27]

4 Theoretical Philosophy

4.1 Ethics

The starting point of Lotze's predecessor in the philosophy chair in Göttingen, J. F. Herbart, was the *given:* i.e., he began his philosophical explorations with analysis of the objects immediately given in inner and outer experience (Pester 1997, p. 119).

---

[26] As we are going to see in Chapters 6 and 7, one who became trapped in the "labyrinth" of Lotze's philosophy was Bertrand Russell.
[27] On the relatedness of Lotze's philosophy to psychoanalysis, see Chapter 4, § 3.5.

Being was, for Herbart, real—beyond and independent of the world of ideas. From this point followed a strict division between theoretical and practical philosophy—reality and values, being and obligation, are independent one from another.

Lotze agreed with Herbart that we cannot draw conclusions about value from facts about reality. However, he insisted that we can do the reverse; that is, we can draw conclusions about reality from value-relevant facts. He expressed this belief in the claim that both logic and metaphysics are ultimately based on ethics. Lotze already proposed this idea in his first philosophical work, his "lesser" *Metaphysic*, where he maintained that "the beginning of metaphysics lies not in itself but in ethics" (1841, p. 329). Two years later, he postulated that "the logical forms cannot be independent from metaphysical presupposition, and they also cannot be totally detached from the realm of morality" (1843a, p. 7).[28]

Of course, ethics is not presented in metaphysics in propositional form. It enters metaphysics in judgments in which possibilities for ordering facts correspond to an ideally presupposed order or to Lotze's idealities (§ 3.2 above). In this sense, there is no knowledge without ethical presuppositions. In "Introduction", § 4.1, we have already seen that Lotze's idealities found expression above all in the concept of value. Furthermore, Lotze claimed that "values are the key for the world of forms" (1857, p. 22).[29]

Lotze was adamant that the only measure of values is the "satisfaction of the sentimental needs [*Gemütsbedürfnisse*]" (Misch 1912, p. xx) and nothing beyond that. The most natural result of these satisfactions is pleasure. This means that moral principles are to be founded on the principle of delight (*Lustprincip*). In fact, this is a typically empirical solution to the problems of ethics that is clearly related to Epicurean hedonism. Lotze thus avoided Kant's formalism of the categorical imperative. Instead, following Fries, he proposed a psychological basis for the maxims of ethics, claiming that we draw our moral principles from the immediate certainty with which we consider something as true or good (1858, p. 287).

The point that unites the subjectivism of this position with Lotze's idiosyncratic objectivism (§ 1 above) is that, despite assuming values to be recognized via delight, he did not limit them to aesthetics and ethics. Rather, Lotze understood values—by way of being idealities—also as crucial for the apprehension of physical facts: they constitute the "meaning of the world in general—as a universal method for speculative expansion of all appearances" (Misch 1912, p. lxv) (§ 3.1 above). This is the case since also our perceptions of the external world, with which we make

---

28 This is a typical case of the fusion of metaphysics with logic practiced by Lotze (Introduction, § 4.1).
29 Lotze's debt to Plato here is easy to recognize.

scientific observations and experiments, are formed through idealities (Chapter 2, n. 96).

4.2 Metaphysics (Ontology)

In conformity with the tradition of his time, Lotze's metaphysics consists of three parts: ontology, philosophy of nature (or cosmology), and philosophy of mind. Ontology explores "the connection of things"[30] or problems of compositionality. It does not investigate the origins (the genesis) of things. Its results are valid for all possible worlds, i.e., for everything that can be thinkable or intelligible at all.[31] In contrast, cosmology investigates the available, real world. Lotze's position here is apparently connected with his insistence on a radical distinction between genesis and being, between "happened" and "is" (Chapter 2, § 12).

Lotze's ontology has two kinds of objects—substances and relations. Let's examine them more closely, beginning with substances. In the Aristotelian tradition, only wholes exhibiting an organic unity, such as a particular human being or a particular horse, count as substances—arbitrary collections of things, like a heap of sand or the random assortment of items in a person's pocket, do not count. Lotze did not embrace either of these two conceptions. Instead, he defended a constructivist position which assumes that a substance is a whole composed of parts that hang together in a particular relation of dependence. More particularly, the elements of the substance (the whole) stand to one another in a relation in which the elements affect each other reciprocally, binding each other together in this way into the whole that they constitute.

In other words, the elements of a substance (of a whole) stand to one another in a reciprocal relation C and in a certain order (*Folge*) F that excludes all other orders. The same is also the structure of the minimal composite unity. If we call the whole (the substance) M, and its elements A, B, and R (A and B are particular elements which are in the focus of our attention, and R designates the sum of all unspecified elements which *can* occur in the whole), we can designate the substance with the formula M=φ[A B R], where φ stands for the connection between the elements, A and B are determinate elements, and R is the sum of all implicit

---

[30] This is the title of Book I of Lotze's *Metaphysic* and also of Book IX of *Mikrokosmus*, which was also published as a separate book (1913).
[31] The discipline and also the very term "ontology" were introduced at the beginning of the 17th century in this sense (Lorhard 1606): ontology does not explore reality, what exists here and now, but all that is intelligible, i.e., what human reason can comprehend, in principle, in all possible worlds. This understanding of ontology was preserved in German philosophy for centuries to come.

elements (1879, § 70).³² The type of connection is a resultant of the specific relations and positions of the elements of the substance, as well as of their order in it. In fact, this is the structure of the *minimal composite unity.*³³

Lotze further specified that the elements of the substance (the whole) stay in a *reciproca tantum* relation to one another.³⁴ Moreover, they mutually exert on one another *effectus transeunt*, which is the opposite of the *effectus immanens.* In other words, all the elements of the whole exert on one another a kind of minimal effect.³⁵

Here are some further elucidations on this point. Lotze's terms in German here are *transeuntes Wirken* and *immanentes Wirken.* Now, *transeuntes Wirken* is usually translated (for example, in Lotze 1885) as "transeuter action". In his critique of Lotze in *The Principles of Mathematics*, Russell calls *effectus immanens* and *effectus transeunt* "immediate" and "mediate action" (1903, p. 452). Yet "action" in German is *Handlung*. However, what Lotze had in mind here is neither *Handlung* nor *Verursachung* (causation) but rather functional connecting that does not lead to changes in the objects of the substance but instead to some kind of minimal internal alteration in the substance seen as a network of elements. Most importantly, these alterations produce that "ontological glue",³⁶ which keeps the elements of the states of the whole or the substance in it. In short, *effectus transeunt* (or "action in passing", "cursory action") is the minimal effect that A exercises on B in the substance M and B on A, thanks to which they stay connected in M. Through it, the isolated, autonomous elements of the substance became interdependent.

---

32 Following Lotze, Ernst Cassirer (1910) embraced a theory of concepts keyed to the model of the mathematical notion of function, specifically on the seriality of members ("particulars") as a function of a serial principle ("universal"). Cassirer explicitly credited Hermann Lotze as the father of this new theory of concepts (Chapter 9, § 6).
33 Between 1912 and 1919, Russell and Wittgenstein also tried to explicate the minimal composite unity (Milkov 1997, i, p. 268). These efforts were epitomized in Wittgenstein's Tractarian "general propositional form" (1922, 4.5).
34 This concept of being in *reciproca tantum* relation is often referred to in constructivist ontologies (Smith 1998, pp. 524, 533, and 539; Milkov 2020b, pp. 106 and 234) but is still not explored in its full form. This is a realm of ontology that still awaits appropriate elaboration.
35 Cf. the discussion of the most economic type of connection between the entities of mereological unities in Chapter 4, § 8.
36 The term "ontological glue" was intensively discussed in the contemporary analytic ontology (Armstrong 1978, i, pp. 113–116; Vallicella 2000; Priest 2014, pp. 16 ff.).

4.3 The Importance of Relations

Lotze's ontology also assumed that there are different systems of relations in the world every one of which giving rise to what may be called different "states of something". This position cannot be a surprise since Lotze was convinced that to *exist* means to stand in relation (Chapter 6, § 8). The systems of relations in the world are of miscellaneous kinds, every one of which has its specific co-ordinates, for example:
- the system of geometrical relations;
- the system of colors.

These two networks of relations are necessary in the world of the real but not in the world of art, in the spiritual world of men, or in other forms of life (e. g., in the "lion's form of life", as Wittgenstein would later say (1953, p. 223)). There are also other kinds of relation-nets (1879, § 108). From the perspective of the cognizing subject, Lotze singles out two in particular:
- that of perception; this net is the universe of what he calls "local-signs" (*Localzeichen*) (Chapter 2, § 8);
- that of judgments and concepts; this net is the universe of interrelations of objective things (*sachliche Verhalten*) or of states of affairs (*Sachverhalte*) (Milkov 2002a).[37]

Moreover, the *sachliche Verhalten* themselves can take different forms. There are:
i.   relations of extension (*Raumverhältnisse*; 1879: §§ 114, 132);
ii. relations of places (*Lagenverhältnisse*) (§ 77);
iii. relations of weight;
iv. we can add to them "*Wunschverhalt*" (Mulligan 1985: 145). Etc.

In summary, we shall say that Lotze's philosophy suggested a form of relationism, or "connectionism"—connectionism not in the sense of the contemporary philosophy of mind (Smolensky 1988) but in the sense of the "general inner connection of all reality[, ... of] the connection passing throughout all reality" (1879, §§ iii and iv). The ultimate "points" of the universe—the substances (the things)—are nothing but the traction points (*Kraftpunkte*) of different systems of such connections. Lotze related them "to optical instruments that reflect ... not convertible beams in a direction which they themselves cannot follow" (1841, p. 232).

---

37 We are going to say more about them in § 4.5 below.

In the literature Lotze's connectionism was described in a variety of ways. P. G. Kuntz, for example, presented it as a *theory of order*. To be more specific, Kuntz took Lotze to be interested not in formal order but rather in concrete, "actual series, networks of series, causal regularities, analogies, and processes that are encountered, not merely thought" (1971, p. 29). Other authors insisted that Lotze's "philosophy is essentially an analysis of the concept of mechanism of the nature" (Høffding 1896, ii, p. 571), i.e., of the concept of all-embracing causal connection, whereby the particulars of our experience are related to all other elements by way of lawful connection.

4.4 Epistemology

In epistemology, Lotze claimed that thoughts are just tools (*organa*) for *deciphering* messages of *reality*. This deciphering takes place in the form of realizing values. The implication is that the aim of human thought is not to serve as a lens for immediate grasping reality. We understand reality through its validities for human beings. This means that the *structure* of thoughts is not identical with the *structure* of facts (Chapter 9, § 6). Be this as it may, their effects coincide (1874, § 342, p. 562).[38] This conception is supported by the fact that although there are no general ideas in reality, we understand *it* via general ideas.

Lotze did not believe that this conception had anything to do with epistemological pessimism. On the contrary, he adopted the principle of self-confidence of human reason (§ 303) (Chapter 7, en. iii). It is true that "reality may be more extensive than our capacities for representing it (whether by knowledge, feeling, etc.) [can ever comprehend]" (Cuming 1917, p. 163). Lotze insisted, however, that these features of reality, these supposed "things in themselves", are beyond the interests of philosophers, since they are beyond their (human) reach—in essence, along the lines of the saying: "What the eye does not see, the heart does not grieve over".

In more concrete terms, the task of Lotze's epistemology was to secure knowledge that is to be separated from perception. The main characteristic of knowledge is that it is true. To Lotze, this means that it and only it presents the things as they really are *for us*, as value-guided recipients—in fact, that is what is expected from thinking as a result.

---

[38] This claim is related to Lotze's occasionalist treatment of the mind–body problem that we are going to discuss in Chapter 2, § 6.

The difference between perception and knowledge (or thinking)[39] can be set out in the following way. *Perception* (including imagining, daydreaming, etc.) notes accidental relations of ideas, while *knowledge* asserts a natural fit (a "necessary connection") among these ideas: they belong together (*zusammengehören*). In other words, the perceiving mind conceives "kaleidoscopically" a multiplicity of contingent pictures (*Bilder*) (1843a, p. 72). Only *then* (in non-temporal sense, though) comes thinking, which consists in going through the ideas a second time, producing in this way "secondary thoughts" (*Nebengedanken*). The latter connect solely those ideas that intrinsically belong together. Lotze describes the "secondary thoughts" as taking "a critical stand towards an idea". These are satellite thoughts that accompany the "kaleidoscope" of the stream of consciousness, making part of it *knowledge*.

Some authors maintain that this conception is a further transformation of Hegel's method of dialectical self-development of the truth (Misch 1912, p. xxvii). In a sense, this is true. According to the German idealists, to think means to be aware (*bewusst zu sein*) that it is *correct* to judge in this particular way (Rödl 2018). It would be more accurate to say, however, that Lotze's secondary thoughts are incorporation into logic of the old method of dialectic of Plato's Socrates—tentative, experimental inquiry that tests different opinions and decides which connection of ideas they realize is true and which are false.[40] To be sure, the kernel of Lotze's method of examining lies in the conviction that we somehow can grasp, in a vague form, what we intend to find in our analysis.[41] In other words, this conception assumes that we have a kind of intuition that helps us to judge is the connection of ideas that lie before us—in our perception—as true or false. Indeed, Lotze was adamant that

> this inner regularity of the content sought-after, being unknown yet, is not open to us in specific realistic definitions of thought. However, being present in the form of opinion, it really has [...] the defensive [intuitive] force to negotiate what is not suitable to her. (1841, p. 33)

Thanks to this ability, we can assert, in our secondary thoughts, that the connection of ideas that lie before us in our perception is either true or false.

---

[39] In identifying thinking with knowledge, Lotze was followed by Frege (1918/1919).
[40] This interpretation was also suggested by Lotze's former doctoral student Wilhelm Windelband (1884, p. 170). See also Milkov (2020b, pp. 37–38 and 170–171).
[41] Cf. Jakob Friedrich Fries' concept "sense of truth" (Milkov 2020b, p. 171).

4.5 Logic

But how it can be that the judgment, at least in one of its understandings, connects the ideas in the same way in which objects are connected in reality? In order to answer this question, we must bear in mind that Lotze's content of judgment (*Urteilsinhalt*) is not an interrelation of ideas (*Vorstellungen*), as Hume, Herbart and Mill maintained, but an interrelation of objective contents, or things (Chapters 4 and 5): it is a *Sachverhalt* (state of affairs).[42] In turn, the minimal objective interrelation ("connection") of things is nothing but a possible content of judgments. Since there is no difference between the content of judgments and reality as conceived by us,[43] the state of affairs has the structure of the substance or of the minimal composite unity (§ 4.2 above). This position was another expression of Lotze's objectivism (§ 1 above).

But the content of judgment also has two other dimensions that have little to do with its structural characteristics. First of all, it is *asserted* by the judging person. Thus, the judgment has an assertoric quality, or what Lotze called its "affirmation" (*Bejahung*), or "positing" (*Setzung*).[44] For Lotze, this is the ultimate quality of a judgment—it is what makes a judgment a *judgment*, as opposed to complex of terms. Later, this conception was also adopted by Brentano, Stumpf (Chapters 4 and 5, again) and Frege. The latter, in particular, maintained that the judgment acknowledges the truth of its content so that only this acknowledgement makes the combination of ideas a judgment. In other words, the judgment is an acceptance, or assumption of content as true, or rejecting it as false (Gabriel und Schlotter 2017, p. 159; Mulligan 2013, p. 99).

Above all, this characteristic of judgment was connected with a variant of the context principle (Introduction, §§ 4.2, 4.3), according to which a word has a meaning not in isolation but in the context of a proposition in which it occurs: "The affirmation of a single notion has no meaning which we can specify; we can affirm nothing but a judgment in which the content of one notion is brought into relation with that of another" (1864, p. 465; 1885, ii, p. 582). Frege followed Lotze also on this point.

Second, the content of judgment has a value—in fact, this is the point that connects Lotze's logic with his ethics (§ 4.1 above). In contrast, concepts have meaning

---

[42] This concept was introduced by Lotze and later also used by Carl Stumpf, Husserl and Wittgenstein (Milkov 2002a).
[43] Lotze distinguishes between "reality" (*Realität*) and "*Wirklichkeit*" (1864, p. 515). Roughly, reality is explored by ontology, *Wirklichkeit* by cosmology.
[44] Similar concept was already used by Descartes (Steinvorth 2007, p. 136) and Spinoza (*Ethica* II, prop. 48).

(*Bedeutung*) but not value. They can have a value only through the propositions in which they occur—in their contexts (Lotze 1874, § 321). Eight years later, Lotze's closest pupil, Wilhelm Windelband, introduced the concept of truth-value in the wake of this conception (1882). Other nine years later, this concept was also embraced by Frege in his paper "Function and Concept" (1891). Frege's distinction between the sense and meaning of propositions also has its roots in Lotze's "greater" *Logic* (§ 353)—to be more explicit, in the distinction he made between the value of a sentence and the "different ways" in which it can be realized (Gabriel and Schlotter 2017, pp. 142 ff.).

Following Herbart, and developing further the idea of content of judgment, Lotze also explored the idea of the "given" (*Gegebene*) in philosophy (§ 4.1 above). To be more explicit, Lotze understood the given as an "experienced content of perception" which is different from the content of judgment, or the state of affairs. Later, this conception of the given was instrumental by coining the concept of sense-data,[45] which was epitomized by Bertrand Russell (Milkov 2001).

4.6 Philosophy of Nature (Cosmology)

As already noted in § 2.1 above, as a young man, Lotze was friends with E. F. Apelt, a pupil of J. F. Fries. Through Apelt, Lotze became familiar with Friesian philosophy of nature, which he often used as a convenient foil in the development of some of his own views. Fries' philosophy formally followed Kant but was in fact more mechanical and calculative, and it was notably more mechanical and calculative than the philosophy of Herbart, who himself was often interpreted as a "mechanistic Kantian".

Lotze criticized Fries for being too formal and forgetting the "deep problems" of philosophy. Beyond this general remark, Lotze attacked Fries' (and arguably also Kant's) "dynamic understanding of matter", which presents it as the interplay of powers. Thus construed, the standard, empirically verifiable properties of matter, such as extension, solidity, place, etc., remain outside the system of science. Against this conception, Lotze embraced a form of atomism, which he saw as necessary for the individuation in the material world. Indeed, humans understand something only when the content of their judgment is articulated, and there cannot be an articulation without individuation;[46] furthermore, individuation is best carried out

---

[45] See n. 17.
[46] This statement is a good example of the way in which Lotze associated philosophy of nature and logic. Russell, among others, followed Lotze closely on this count (Chapter 6, § 3).

when we accept that there are atoms. Besides, Lotze was convinced that the order in the world cannot come into being from a purposeless and planless beginning, from a chaos. It is ordered, and the order too presupposes an articulation and individuation: it is order among individuals—for example, among the variables A, B, and R (§ 4.2).

Significantly, Lotze did not understand atoms as they were understood in antiquity—as ultimate elements of reality that have different forms but the same substance (stuff). He did not conceive of them as the ultimate building blocks of the material world but rather as idiosyncratic and as remaining unmodified in all compositions and divisions. In other words, whereas the ancient atomism saw atoms as made out of the same kind of stuff, Lotze saw each atom as being made of a unique, specific kind of matter.

A further difference with the atomism of the antiquity was that Lotze's atoms were punctual (i.e., point-like) and without extension (*unräumlich*) (Chapter 2, § 9). This is supported by the fact that extension is only possible where there are many points that can be easily identified and differentiated. To be more specific, we conceive the extensionless atoms as impermeable unities, filling up the space, only because of their demonstrated reciprocal resistance (1856a, p. 402).

An important characteristic of matter is its passivity, i.e., its ability to be affected from the outside. True to his anthropological stance, Lotze further maintained that only if two essences mutually produce their respective "sufferings" (*Leiden*) can they be their respective interacting causes.[47] At the same time, however, he was adamant that the concepts of suffering, effecting, and interaction are only—although inescapable—scientific metaphors. These are not to be conceived of literally. They simply help us better grasp the nature of the problem.

Clearly, one can interpret this conception of Lotze in the sense of the doctrine of Panpsychism.[48] Be this as it may, Lotze was not a true Panpsychist. He simply maintained that "the law that makes the substantial unity of a thing is an individual law; it is conceived on the analogy of human character, or of aesthetic unity like melodies" (Santayana 1971, p. 183). This position makes it understandable why Lotze claimed that the elements of the states of affairs in his ontology "take care [*kümmern sich*]" of one another (1879, § 69); they have "fate [*Schicksale*]" and "sensitivity [*Reizbarkeit*]" (§ 70).

In questions of space, Lotze used his teacher Weiße, rather than Fries, as a foil. Weiße had distinguished between space and interaction (*Wechselwirkung*) of sub-

---

[47] The concept of "suffering" shows the influence on Lotze of his countryman—both were born in Upper Lusatia, Saxony—Jacob Böhme.
[48] On Lotze's alleged Panpsychism, see Kuntz (1971, p. 34).

stances. Moreover, for Weiße, interaction is the condition of space (Lotze 2003, pp. 85f.). In contrast, Lotze did not differentiate between interaction and space (he was convinced that the two coincide) but between extension and place (Chapter 2, § 9).

4.7 Philosophy of Language

Starting with his "lesser" *Logic*, Lotze made great efforts to elaborate a coherent philosophy of language. Like Frege later, his first step in this direction was to connect language with logic by claiming that logic begins with exploring language forms (1843a, p. 40). The reason for this assumption of Lotze's was that the living, unconscious "spirit of [ordinary] language" connects what one experiences concretely in sense-perception with the abstract forms that one extracts from sense perception (p. 82).[49] Indeed, our language functions on the level of perceptions. This, however, is not a hindrance to our using it to convey truths of a higher order: truths of science, mathematics, and logic (1856a, p. 304).

Lotze criticized the idea that language achieves meanings by picturing reality.[50] As he saw it, not even the pictures formed by perceiving are pictures proper (§ 4.4 above),[51] and even less are the pictures supposedly embedded in the structures of language. Rather than performing a picturing function, language provides something of a method. To be more specific, it provides rules for transforming (for translating) signals from the sensual world into the phenomena of our mental world and vice-versa: from our perception into the meanings we formulate and communicate with the help of the language (Chapter 2, § 12). In fact, the very relation between microcosm and macrocosm was understood by Lotze in this way. The microcosm can be characterized as a "language of the macrocosm" and at the same time as a place for understanding the possibilities of speaking about the macrocosm (Orth 1986, p. 48). Lotze developed this idea further in his theory of local-signs, which we are going to consider in more detail in the next chapter.

---

[49] This idea was also adopted—via Frege—in Wittgenstein's *Tractatus*, 3.1: "In a proposition a thought finds expression that can be perceived by the senses".
[50] In his *Tractatus*, Wittgenstein *prima facie* defended this conception. In fact, however, Wittgenstein's "pictures" are logical and so do not really resemble the facts and states of affairs they model.
[51] On this point, Lotze clearly opposed Hume's Copy Principle of knowledge.

Chapter 2
Lotze's Philosophy of Psychology

1 Introductory Remarks

In the second quarter of the 19th century, psychology developed slowly into an autonomous discipline. In contrast to the other figures involved in this development —J. F. Herbart, E. H. Weber and G. T. Fechner—Lotze brought the new discipline, psychology, into close connection with philosophy from the beginning.[52] In so doing, he shuttered the hope of leaving psychology entirely to experimental investigation, an approach that many of his colleagues were following at the time.[53] Lotze, however, refused to call this discipline "philosophical psychology". For him it was only "physiological psychology", which was worked out with the help of philosophy. It examines the ways in which body and mind relate to one another not only empirically but also philosophically.[54] In the case that one day one would build up a "philosophical psychology",[55] it would describe the various developments "that the *content of self-consciousness* undergoes partly in the course of everyday experience of life, partly in the explicit processing through scientific reflection" (1852a, p. 495). It would be a real "analytic psychology" (Seron 2015, p. 29).

As a matter of fact, Lotze's prospective project for a philosophical psychology was only developed by the eminent figures in philosophy of the late 19th and early 20th centuries Franz Brentano, Carl Stumpf and Edmund Husserl, whose descriptive psychology (discussed in Part II below) and phenomenology were advanced as an analysis of psychological phenomena. In the 20th century, philosophical psychology was magisterially explored by Wittgenstein, e.g., in his *Philosophical Investigations* (1953).[56] Just like Lotze, Wittgenstein claimed that mind and body are "incompara-

---

[52] Incidentally, Fechner too maintained that psychology and philosophy are to be developed in conjunction with one another. In contrast to Lotze, however, Fechner had full confidence in "mathematical psychology" for which he was sharply criticized by Lotze (§ 3 below).
[53] Théodule Ribot wrote with this in mind: "[Lotze] n'a jamais séparé les recherches psychologiques des hypothèses métaphysiques, et l'on peut affirmer sans hésitation que cette 'psychologie sans aime' qui a gagné bon nombre d'adhérents en Allemagne, dans ces dernier temps, ne sera jamais celle qu'il préfère" (1879, p. 60).
[54] Apparently, Erich Becher spoke about Lotze's "metaphysical psychology" (1917, § 2) in this sense.
[55] This, however, was not the task of Lotze's *Medicinische Psychologie* (1852a, pp. 455, 464, 474, and 495). Lotze was not sure that this task is feasible.
[56] See also Wittgenstein (1984).

ble". Even more: the main problems of philosophy, its paradoxes, arise when we think about psychological processes in terms of physics.[57]

Lotze's view of psychology is magisterially presented in his book *Medicinische Psychologie, oder Physiologie der Seele* (1852a).[58] This explains why the present chapter shall discuss primarily this work. Significantly, it was a philosopher's product—it is to be seen as a work in the field of the philosophy of psychology. Understanding the book as a philosophical work helps us apprehend it better (Introduction, § 4.4).

2 Lotze's Project

Lotze's book *Medicinische Psychologie* was written shortly after he finished his *Allgemeine Physiologie des körperlichen Lebens* (*General Physiology of the Bodily Life*) (1851). The two books actually share "the same purposes, the same method of presentation" (Lotze 2021b, p. 669). They discuss Lotze's philosophy of physiology, which consists of two parts: (i) physiology of body and (ii) physiology of mind. In short, in these years, Lotze dealt with the philosophy of the physical nature of man—for a medical professional, habilitated in philosophy, this was a matter of course. From a more general perspective, Lotze's physiological psychology was a part of his philosophical medicine and, still more generally, of his philosophical science in general.

Importantly enough, Lotze's *Medicinische Psychologie* is not a purely philosophical work. Rather, its task is to clarify the relationship between body and mind, between spiritual life and the functioning of the body. The main problem is that in this area—as everywhere in science—observations alone are not enough. The scientific enterprise in general shows that the data of the observation can be interpreted *ad libitum*. In the words of the physiologist A. W. Volkmann,[59] to whom Lotze dedicated his book, "Even the most proven observation [is] an ambiguous thing. ... With such observations everyone does what he *wants*" (1852a, p. vi).

It is clear only that experience and observation alone must be the *start* of science. The crucial point, however, is that "every experience, in order to become a science, presupposes *principles of its assessment,* which cannot again be presented

---

[57] A similar position was defended in Ryle (1949).
[58] In 1886, the Dannenberg Verlag, Berlin, published a second edition of the book. In 1876, an abridged translation of the book into French appeared: *Psychologie médicale: principes généraux de psychologie physiologique*, Auguste Penjon (Trans.), Paris: Germer Baillière.
[59] Lotze studied under Alfred Volkmann in Göttingen. Among other things, Volkmann published an important work in optical physiology (1836).

by experience and by the microscope, but only by the metaphysical knowledge of things" (Lotze 2021b, p. 669; italics added). That is why medical students and practicing physicians are to be well trained in philosophy. In general, Lotze saw the relation between experience and theory (speculation) as a conundrum. In this area, no definite conclusions are possible. Be this as it may, one can clearly differentiate between three levels of investigation: (i) The "microscopic observation" (Kölliker 1850) or the collection of facts; (ii) with the help of "reflective observation",[60] one draws up "concrete laws"; (iii) the purely speculative (theoretical) formulation of the basic laws of science.

At this point it might be appropriate to make a short comment about the title of the book. To today's reader, the phrase "medical psychology" might be misleading.[61] In fact, the book was named that way partly because it was written for medical students. The subtitle of the book, "Physiology of the Mind", gives more information about its content. The main focus is on physiological psychology, which is opposed to speculative psychology, developed from purely philosophical point of view (Hegel 1830, iii, 1st Part). Typically for Lotze, in so doing, he refused to join a particular philosophical school.

The task of Lotze's book is to develop a robust "*applicable comprehension [anwendbare Anschauung]* of the relationship between mental life and physiological functions" (1852a, p. v; emphasis added). In particular, such a comprehension is required in order to make an appropriate interpretation of the facts provided by empirical psychology. Ultimately, the task is to put this knowledge into practice successfully. The point is that, in contrast to other areas, mental life is interpreted and understood not only scientifically but also speculatively. Indeed, with regard to the soul, each of us has his "practical wisdom" (p. 4) and attitudes that are supported by our "moral and religious reflections" (p. 8) as well as by poetry and imaginative literature. Such knowledge clearly helps to grasp "the necessary objectives" by acting—in fact, one could not act successfully without it. Importantly enough, the two types of knowledge of the mind, scientific and speculative, are complementary (§ 6 below).

It is also problematic that mental phenomena are often "accompanied by the incessant activity of semi-unconscious reflections mixed up with unfinished metaphysics" (p. 7). At the same time, the eminently important task to better understand the soul and to come to a psychological understanding urges scientists to "seek an ensuing view of [them] with often inadequate cognitive means" (p. 6). That is why

---

[60] We shall say more about this term in § 11 below.
[61] Théodule Ribot already found the title "un peu bizarre" (1879, p. 60).

so many scientists are inclined to commit bad fallacies in this area. Philosophers have to fight this tendency.

This explains why physiological psychology, in contrast to science, cannot replace the practical view—and vice versa. Generally, the interior of the soul "remains unknown in its true essence, and in the original laws of its work" (1852a, p. 5). It is a riddle. That is why it is problematic to claim that psychology is allowed to adopt the method of science.[62] Psychology is nothing like physics. That is also why we can perhaps speak about philosophical psychology but not about philosophical physics.[63] Furthermore, psychology has the important task of mediating between natural science and philosophy (§ 8 below). On the one hand, it is an empirical science; on the other hand, however, it is a philosophical discipline. Apparently, psychology is a quite specific academic field. Perhaps this explains why "psychology had become Lotze's most enduring teaching concern. He lectured on it every winter semester from 1842/1843 through 1880/1881, while altering his other courses" (Woodward 2015, p. 206).

3 Materialism, Identity Theory, or Spiritualism?

An important development in the context in which Lotze worked on the *Medicinische Psychologie* was that in the mid-19th century, as a reaction against German Idealism and as an expression of the new achievements of natural science, some scientists, including L. F. Büchner, Jacob Moleschott and A. C. C. Vogt, worked out a materialistic conception of the relationship between body and mind. They reduced the mind to the physiology of the brain, claiming that everything in humans, including the activity of the mind, can be explained materialistically. This is the only way, they said, that scientists can free themselves from the concept of vitalism. Although Lotze too was an opponent of vitalism (§ 4 below), he did not want to approve reductionism in any of its forms.

Lotze held that the position of the materialists, which became quite popular at the time, is actually nothing but a modern metaphysical claim that tried to bring everything to the level of natural science. For the materialists, psychology is a natural science—the two follow the same explanatory principles.[64] Against this posi-

---

[62] This is what Lotze's professors in Leipzig E. H. Weber and G. T. Fechner claimed (§ 3 below).
[63] Later, Wittgenstein will make the same claim, adding mathematics to psychology. For him, both psychology and mathematics are also to be examined philosophically.
[64] Karl Popper and Carl Hempel revived this thesis in the middle of the 20th century. See in particular Hempel (1942).

tion, Lotze advocated a "philosophical natural science" (1852a, p. 32) that does not see science as a sum of fragments but rather from a uniform perspective:

> Against materialism we maintain that in terms of those properties and effects of the things that we designate with the name of materiality, the mental can never be explained. Therefore, psychology can never be transformed into natural science (p. 65)

Another group of scientists, among them G. R. Treviranus and J. F. von Autenrieth, tried to substantiate the identity of mind and body. According to them, humans lead a "double life": they are "ideal-real substances" (p. 49). The solution of the mind–body problem is not a matter of reducing the mind to the body, but of merging the two into an indissoluble unit in order to achieve an identity of the real and the ideal. Some identity theorists refer to the term "life force" (*Lebenskraft*) as what constitutes the inner side of this unit, while the outer side is just an aggregate of physiological atoms. Against them, Lotze insists that the term "life force" explains nothing.[65] An organism cannot have just one drive for its existence, even if this drive is called "life force". It is also not clear how the connection between the supposedly all-encompassing life force and the individual physiological forces is supposed to emerge.

While a student in Leipzig, Lotze attended the lectures of G. T. Fechner, the founder of the identity theory of the mind and body. Fechner called his teaching "psychophysics" and developed it in a perspectival sense: for him, body and mind are two aspects of a unity.[66] The scientists examine the relationship between body and mind from different perspectives. To be more explicit,

> Natural science consistently takes the external standpoint of comprehending the things, the science of the mind from the internal one. The conceptions of life are based on the change of point of view: the philosophy of nature on the identity of what appears double from a two-fold point of view. A doctrine of the relationships between mind and body will have to trace the relationships of both modes of appearing of the One. (Fechner 1860, i, p. 6)

In this sense, Fechner spoke about the "identity comprehension" of mind and body, which he considered to be first advanced by Spinoza. He hoped that this view would explain, among other things, why physiologists are usually materialists while psychologists are generally idealists. Metaphysically, body and mind are only two parts of a unit. And since the body can be examined in an exact, scientific way, Fechner further held that it is possible to achieve exactness in psychology as

---

[65] We shall come back to Lotze's criticism of the concept "life force" in § 7 below.
[66] This view was later adopted and further developed by Ernst Mach, William James and, after 1919, by Bertrand Russell in his theory of "neutral monism" (1921).

well. In other words, he tried to make psychology "an exact doctrine of the functional or dependent relationships between body and mind" (Fechner 1860, i, p. 8; emphasis added). Moreover, following E. H. Weber, Fechner introduced the famous measurement formula for assessing sensations. According to it, the connection between stimulus and sensation is not causal but functional. In short, the Weber–Fechner law states that a linear increase in the subjectively (psychologically) perceived strength of sensory impressions corresponds to the logarithm of the increase in the objectively (physically) measurable intensity of the stimulus.

Lotze, who also studied under E. H. Weber in Leipzig, did not maintain that this view is wrong. It is merely inadequate (Lotze 1846, p. 183f.). In this sense, Lotze developed a position opposed to that of his old professors. Lotze called it "spiritualism". With this position, following his method of regressive analysis (Chapter 1, § 3.2), Lotze tried to connect natural science (in this case, physiology) with the aesthetic and moral needs of human mind. In other words, he "put the emphasis on the spiritual [*das Geistige*]" in science (Lotze 1852a, p. 55). Spiritualism is motivated by the idea that only the human mind can ensure the unity—but not the identity—of body and soul. This principle is of utmost importance since the unifying comprehension of reality has an absolute priority in philosophy. It should be noted that according to spiritualism, there is only one real dimension of reality—the supersensible. In contrast, the world of matter is only a world of appearances. In fact, matter is "to be seen as an appearance of something supersensible in itself" (p. 64). What scientists are investigating is not the world itself, but its properties that can be observed and verified in experiments.

In order to better understand Lotze's approach here, we must return to his main objective: to bring the latest results of the science of his time into harmony with the needs of the inner life of humans. Some scholars label the position "romantic" (Beiser 2013, p. 196). In reality, it was an expression of Lotze's transcendental conviction that humans can only understand what their abilities allow them to gain knowledge of. In contrast to Kant, however, he stated that this ability is not fixed a priori. It is determined by human culture.[67] The latter builds up idealities that serve as ultimate points of orientation both in perceiving and thinking, and also in science. Without them, we cannot understand reality.

At this point, we shall make three further remarks on Lotze's conception of spiritualism:

i. It was an expression of Lotze's anthropologically oriented metaphysics. As already noted (Chapter 1, § 3.3), Lotze did not simply reduce metaphysics to an-

---

[67] This position is consistent with Lotze's concept of space, which is based on the active role of the subject (§ 9 below).

thropology. Rather, his transcendental anthropology became for him the leading philosophical discipline, *prima philosophia*.
ii. Lotze's philosophical inquiry followed a regressive order: he practiced "regressive analysis" (Chapter 1, § 3.2). For him, philosophical exploration begins with the history of culture and then moves on to logic and metaphysics. In other words, Lotze tried to understand how science, but also how human practical life works on the basis of cultural history.
iii. The relation between mind and body is not a question of two perspectives—material and ideal—from which one can observe the relationship between mind and body, as Fechner maintained. Rather, there are two dimensions of reality, the nature and the world of the spirit, of which only the second is real. However, the second dimension cannot determine the first. It follows that reductionism or identification between the two is mistaken.[68] Here, Lotze puts into use his specific dialectical method, which, however, is markedly different from that of Hegel.[69]

4 The Principle of Teleomechanism

Although Lotze did not follow the "exact psychology" of his professor in Leipzig, E. H. Weber, he adopted Webber's principle of mechanism, according to which science must regard its objects as mechanisms. Lotze firmly believed that this principle is omnipresent both in physics, in physiology, and also in cultural theory. The extension of the mechanism is "universal without exception". In fact,

> the whole process of formation always depends on a circle of purely mechanically determined forces whose start-up, once initiated, without reflection or consideration of its goal, goes on exactly as far as the law of inertia goes on, as long as it is not opposed or its serving means are withdrawn. (1851, p. 114)

For example, if a fetus is conceived without a brain, it will continue to grow also without a definite goal.

The principle of mechanism can be easily formalized. In psychology, it is extensive in form—it follows the laws of inertia. Its main advantage is that it elim-

---

[68] This also explains why idealism, which reduces the material to the ideal, and spiritualism are not the same thing for Lotze as well as why it is mistaken to call Lotze an idealist.
[69] On Lotze's dialectics, see Chapter 1, § 3.3. See also the last paragraph of § 11 below.

inates all metaphysical entities, e.g., what the vitalists later called *elan vital*.[70] Particularly important is that the processes of culture are mechanical as well. Lotze also believed that since sciences follow the same principle, that of mechanism, his philosophical considerations on physiology and psychology he presented in *Medicinischen Psychologie* are valid in all sciences.

However, the principle of the mechanism is only a methodological, not a metaphysical device. It cannot *explain* the origin of life, of human culture, or free will; it *describes* them (§ 5 below). Moreover, it also delimits the realm in which it, the principle of the mechanism, does not apply. For Lotze, this *realm* is that of the spirit. As already mentioned in § 3 above, there are two dimensions of reality that complement each other—a mechanical and a spiritualistic, or a teleological one. Furthermore, Lotze underlined that the teleological reality has relative priority over the mechanical.

In order to limit the validity of the principle of the mechanism in psychology as well as to show that the two dimensions of reality are complimentary, Lotze developed the so-called principle of the teleomechanism. The latter settles the direction of further development of a system as its *value* which also determines the *meaning* of the system. As we already know, when a system has taken its course, its further development unfolds quasi mechanically. The biological nature in particular orients itself towards finality: its driving force is the Aristotelian *causa finalis* (*Met.*, 1013a33).

Something new arises (§ 7 below), when the two dimensions of reality, i.e., the mechanical dimension examined by natural science and the teleological dimension examined by metaphysics, cross one another. This shows that science alone cannot unlock the meaning of the world. It can only *describe* the phenomena. One of the tasks of Lotze's philosophy is to relate these meanings to human values and so to *explain* them. In this context, Lotze distinguished between two forms of knowledge: *cognitio rei* and *cognitio circa rem* (1852a, pp. 57f., 148). *Cognitio rei* is the knowledge of indefinable entities which were already tracked down by Plato (*Theaitetos*, 201d–202b) and Aristotle (*Met.*, 1039b27).[71] One cannot put *cognitio rei* into words. It is ineffable. *Cognitio circa rem*, on the other hand, is the knowledge of the relationships among objects. The difference between these two kinds of knowledge also signals the difference between intuitive and discursive knowledge

---

70 In § 5 below, we shall see that Lotze did not advocate a dogmatic but rather what can be called an indicative (*hinweisende*) metaphysics. He fought against all superfluous metaphysical entities in this sense.
71 Otto Kraushaar maintains (1936, p. 255) that this distinction corresponds to that made by William James (in 1890) between knowledge by acquaintance and knowledge by description (Milkov 2001).

and, furthermore, between value and evolvement. This is exactly what Lotze's principle of the teleomechanism claims. One can describe the world scientifically but interpret it only teleologically, explain it critically, or analyze it logically.

These two principles, that of mechanism and that of teleology, have different norms and goals. That is why they do not contradict one another. Even more:

> In this mediation [of the two principles lies] the true vital point of science; admittedly not in that we now make fragmented concessions to one viewpoint and now to the other, but rather in showing how *invariably universal the extension*, and at the same time *how completely subordinate the meaning of the mission is which the mechanism in the construction of the world has to meet.*[72] (Lotze 2017, p. XIII*)

This interpretation is supported by Lotze's claim that spiritualism is only to be understood as "the target point of [his] conception, and not as a formula useful for practical use in explaining particular cases. ... It would therefore be necessary to mention it only for the sake of completeness" (2021b, p. 672). In other words, spiritualism is only a regulative principle of investigation, nothing more than that. In general, one is to distinguish between the *ideal of science*, to which the spiritualism pertains, and the *practice of science*. That is also why it is wrong to call Lotze a spiritualist *sui generis* without further qualifications. This mistake is committed by Abbagnano (2006, pp. 8–16) and Beiser (2013, pp. 232ff.), whereas most of Lotze's interpreters (Kunz 1971, Misch 1912, Orth 1986, Pester 1997, Sullivan 2018, and Woodward 2015) avoid doing this.

5 Lotze's Physical-Psychological Mechanism

As we have seen, Lotze was firmly convinced that science must follow the mechanical conception of nature (§ 6 below). However, this is only one part of the story. One must also critically inspect the results of science in a philosophical manner. In other words, we have to reach reality in two ways, on two levels: the scientific and the philosophical.

The basic idea of Lotze's philosophy of psychology is that body and mind have no causal connection. Because of this, they are incomparable. Be this as is may, the "ponderable" (or calculable) part, i.e., physiology, and the "imponderable" (or incalculable) part, i.e., psychology, interact (Lotze 1852a, p. 33). Body and mind "do not exist separately; they are different but coordinated kinds of the concept of *sub-*

---

[72] Lotze first formulated the idea of mediating between mechanism and teleology in his medical dissertation (1838).

stance" (p. 74).⁷³ They work together. However, the interaction between the two cannot be explained and therefore cannot be fully understood.⁷⁴ It follows that one cannot understand human mind as constructed by physical (physiological) elements.

Lotze called this conception the *physical-psychological mechanism*. However, he emphasized that this is not a theory—in fact, philosophy cannot, in principle, build a positive theory. It is merely a methodological teaching that could help us develop the basic concepts in the field. Most importantly, it could enable us to study the "composition of the elements" or things (Chapter 1, § 4.2). But it permits "no further use" (p. 78); or, as we have already noted in § 3 above, it is of no technical value.

It should be observed that the term "the connection of things" is the title of the 9th book of Lotze's *Mikrokosmus*, which presents his metaphysics or, to be more precise, his ontology (Chapter 1, § 4.2). As just noted, however, Lotze's metaphysics was not a positive theory or a doctrine—it had only an indicative (*hinweisende*) function.⁷⁵ This goes hand-in-hand with Lotze's belief that metaphysics is, in principle, incomplete; in addition, its development is contradictory (2021b, p. 670). This speaks against the hope that it could serve as a well-worked out foundation of the psychological investigations.⁷⁶ Rather, Lotze suggested a kind of a minimalist metaphysics⁷⁷ that, incidentally, was related to the minimalist metaphysics of the early analytical philosophers Frege, G. E. Moore and Russell.⁷⁸ Be this as it may, Lotze's minimalist metaphysics could help by developing a theoretical perspective in order to better orientate ourselves in the problems of psychology and also in other disciplines. Such a perspective can be very fruitful in science—it can determine specific philosophical attitude (or "applicable comprehension" (§ 2 above)) towards the facts that the scientists have gathered through observations.

---

73 For more on Lotze's conception of the soul as substance, see § 10 below.
74 Today, a similar view is maintained in the philosophy of "the new mysterians"—Colin McGinn, Thomas Nagel, Jerry Fodor, and Noam Chomsky (Flanagan 1991, p. 313). They claim that humans cannot, in principle, answer the question of how mind and body relate to one another. It lies outside of the capacities of human knowledge.
75 The ontology of Wittgenstein's *Tractatus* also has indicative functions in the sense that it can only *teach* us to think and speak better; but it is not a theory (Milkov 2017c and 2022b). Like Lotze's ontology, it explicates the minimal composite unity (see n. 33), showing how the things relate to one another (*wie die Sachen sich zu einander verhalten*) (1922, 4.5).
76 Frederick Beiser, in contrast, claims that, according to Lotze, psychology "must have metaphysical foundation" (2013, p. 211).
77 In § 4 above, we have already seen that Lotze fought against the superfluous entities of metaphysics. See also n. 70.
78 See more on this topic in Milkov (2000) and Gabriel (2002).

Due to the special character of the relationship between body and mind, Lotze maintained that one could present physiological psychology as the doctrine of the principles of the being *par excellence*. This is the case since it suggests a unified view of the world. Psychology thus becomes a "philosophical natural science" proper. Physics, in contrast, is simply a doctrine of the multiplicity of phenomena. In short:

> Psychology [is] the doctrine of the essential principles of all existence and activity, while physics, on the other hand, is only to be cited as evidence of the particular forms which the liveliness of the mental life develops within the area of spatial-temporal perceptions. (Lotze 1852a, p. 64)

6 Lotze's Occasionalism

As an implication of adopting the incomparability of mind and body and in order to derive a unity from the combination of the two, Lotze subscribed to the occasionalist philosophy of mind. Recall that according to Leibniz' occasionalism, body and mind are like two clocks that show the same time. However, they are not directly connected. God mediates between the two, so that their relationship has the form of a pre-established harmony. Lotze's occasionalism followed a different track, however.[79] Mind and body are two autonomous spheres of the world that are nonetheless connected, although, as we already know, this connection is not causal. The changes in one of the spheres are rather remodeled in the other.[80] Furthermore, Lotze spoke about the induction (*Veranlassungen*) of mental phenomena by physiological processes. Those are realized in certain "occasions" (1852a, p. 78).

In other words, the fact that there is no causal connection between the two sides of the being, body and mind, does not mean that there is no connection between them. It merely makes it impossible to develop psychology, in contrast to natural sciences, as a "constructive science". It also shows that Weber's, Fechner's, and Herbart's "mathematical psychology", which examined the "mechanics of the mind" (§ 3 above), are not the last word in this realm.

As can be expected, Lotze understood his form of occasionalism simply as a methodological principle that can help us to conduct scientific research in this area. It is not a positive theory. It is simply impossible to reveal all intermediary

---

[79] For this reason, F. Beiser maintains that Lotze's use of the term "occasionalism" here is misleading (2013, p. 221).
[80] This remodeling can also be understood as a kind of "translation". We shall return to this concept in § 12 below.

links of inducing of the mental through the physiological. Nevertheless, one can examine the human mind scientifically. In fact, this is the primary task of physiological psychology. It describes the interrelation between mind and body or what Lotze called the physical-psychological mechanism empirically. To be more explicit, it allows for "no construction of mental states from [psychological] movements, but only factual and proportional chaining of both" (p. 78):

> Therefore, we *cannot* state how a material stimulus of movement that hits our body may begin to produce a mental state; but we can hope for an answer to the question *which* simple stimuli are generally and lawfully interlinked with *which* simple internal states, and how from the further combination of these pairs of internal and external events the whole of the interaction between body and mind, i.e. the physiological mind-life arises. By borrowing from experience the fact that a body state *a*, produced by external stimuli, is always and generally connected to a mind state *α*, or that a body state *β* always follows consecutively from a mind state *b*, we see *a* and *b* as inductions [*Veranlassungen*] in which the natural course permanently and generally bounds the reality of *α* and *β*. (pp. 77–78)

In other words, Lotze's occasionalism does not defend any content or qualitative connection between body and mind. It simply allows us to clear up the quantitative or proportional (structural) linkages (chaining) between them. With this assumption, Lotze left the door open to empirical studies in psychology.

7 The Emergence of the New

The principle of the mechanism cannot explain why exactly this specific event or phenomenon takes place. Many alternative developments can be realized that can be elucidated through this principle. In Leibniz's language (which Lotze, however, does not use), the principle of the mechanism cannot determine which specific world among all possible worlds will be realized. In a mechanical course of events, everything happens with necessity; there is no room for contingency. In other words, a mechanical process does not happen spontaneously. The spontaneity that triggers what really happens has to be explained with the help of another principle. In such cases, the course of nature takes on *new forms*. It is not a simple movement that can be mathematically recorded but rather a complex development that is determined by a "transcendent image" or a "transcendental plastic" (Lotze 1838, pp. 14f.).[81] More precisely, this transcendent image determines the spe-

---

81 Lotze also spoke of "plan" (1879, §§ x, 67).

cific order in certain complexes of individuals.[82] The *quid*—the individual—is created in exactly this way.

In order to explain this phenomenon more clearly, as early as in his first dissertation in medicine (1838), Lotze suggested a new interpretation of Aristotle's term "δύναμις" ("*dynamis*", "ability") (*Met.*, 1019a15ff.).[83] This is a metaphysical term that refers specifically to the emergence of individuals (Lotze 1879, § 41). It sets out what will actually be realized among innumerable possible options. At the same time, Lotze fought against the interpretation of Aristotle's term *dynamis* as "life force".[84]

In psychology, the cross-point at which mechanism and *dynamis* meet in psychology lies in sensations. The mechanical processes are the substructure of reality, while the mind is its higher level. As Lotze put it,

> We assume that the nerves act dynamically and thus we reject the contention that mathematical laws exclude dynamic effects. If we invoke this term [*dynamis*], the meaning of which is not far away from that of Aristotle, we shall then see how the *dynamis* and the mechanical system come into equilibrium. (1838, p. 11)

The conceiving of a mental *quid* occurs through what Lotze calls "striving".[85] Striving is a product of the interaction of impulses driven by the matter and the irritability of the body. Thus, the stimulus is the primary property of the mental *dynamis*, just as *actio* and *reaction*—the principles of interaction—are the primary properties of the mechanism. The teleology of reality is secured in this way. The impulse is transferred from the material system to the mental and appears as a reaction to it.

One can explain the connection between *causa efficiens* and *dynamis* of the material life in the same way. That is, reality acquires its forms through the *dynamis*. But it develops progressively and with "mathematical necessity" only thanks to the mechanism. Leibniz describes this connection as follows:

> The souls act according to the laws of the final causes [*causa finalis*] by means of desire, ends and means. The bodies act according to the laws of active causes [*causa efficiens*], or movement. And these two realms, that of the final causes and that of the effective causes, are harmonious with one another. [The pre-established harmony between the two ...] causes the bod-

---

[82] Similarly, in his *Tractatus* Wittgenstein presents the generation of the different levels of reality —the world, language, thought—as new *arrangements* of elements of the lower level in new complexes (Milkov 2020d).
[83] See also Plato (*Hippias major*, 295c3ff.).
[84] In § 3 above, we already discussed Lotze's criticism of the term "life force".
[85] Cf. Aristotle's ἐπιθυμία (*De anima* 414b33) and Spinoza's *conatus* (*Ethica* III, prop. 6ff.).

ies to act as if, which is impossible, they had no souls at all, and the souls act as if they had no bodies, and yet both act as though they were acting one on the other.[86]

Although Lotze never used the term "pre-established harmony", he explicitly claimed that both systems ("realms"), the mechanical and the dynamic, act in tandem—the quantitative side of reality goes hand-in-hand with its qualitative side. The impulses from the outside world induce the bodies to react spontaneously, thereby breaking the causal chain. This is also how one could understand the freedom of the will—it does not contradict the laws of causality. But it can be understood this way only metaphysically, not physiologically.

8 The Local-Signs Theory

Lotze's doctrine of the physical-psychological mechanism found clear expression in his local-signs theory.[87] Local-signs are the qualia that humans perceive. The mind's sense of place assigns them a specific location which further determines the space itself. In other words, in this process, specific intense marks are transformed into extensive local-signs which the mind eventually transforms back into intense spatial sensations. One can describe this remodeling of signs or the establishment of common-sense spatiality with the help of three terms, while the remodeling itself proceeds in three stages: (i) signs, which are determined by the external world and physiology; (ii) the sense of movement of the psychic sensors of the mind, which makes them local-signs; and (iii) space-perception (*Raumanschauung*):[88]

> If, therefore, we are to gain a perception of the real position of external objects, it cannot be via *apprehension*, but via *regeneration* [*Wiedererzeugung*] *of the spatiality.* Everywhere the extensive is transformed into an intensive, and from the latter the soul has to reconstruct a new inner world of space in which the images of the external objects find their corresponding places. Just as a variable quantity can decrease to a value of zero and can grow again beyond it, so the regularity of the geometrically ordered evolution infallibly fades away to a point of perfect standstill and is regenerated after that. (Lotze 1852a, pp. 328–329)

---

86 Leibniz, *Monadology* (1714), §§ 79 and 81, Jonathan Bennett (Trans., 2017), https://www.earlymoderntexts.com/assets/pdfs/leibniz1714b.pdf (last accessed on December 3, 2022).
87 In Lotze's decision to introduce this term, we can see the connection between his psychology and his logic. We are going to say more about this in § 12 below.
88 Hermann von Helmholtz, who followed Lotze on this point, maintained that the soul "reads" the "signs" that the nerves generate and thus forms the space-perception (1867, pp. 433–434).

8 The Local-Signs Theory — 47

To summarize, when the nerves are stimulated by the physical world, they create a system of marks that are transformed into local-signs. More precisely, this happens with the help of the muscles of the sensory organs which thereby get a direct impression—which is nothing more than a muscular feeling—of the size of the movement.[89] For example, in visual space-perception, the spatial arrangement is realized through the optical muscle. The implication is that mental phenomena are also determined by events in the body. The body thereby functions as the substructure of the mind.[90]

In other words, the physical object or event produces a qualitative sensation or sign in us. But we do not know where exactly this object or event is located. In order to find this out, we need secondary sensations, a feeling of movement that is formed by the muscles of the sensory organs (Chapter 1, § 4.4).[91] Only they enable us to localize the object or the stimulated nerve. Precisely this operation creates a "sense of place" (*Ortssinn*) (p. 409). The system of local-signs itself has no spatial order. The latter is determined only by the mind:

> Once all the geometrical relations between the parts of the external stimuli and also between the corresponding impressions in the nerves have disappeared in the merely intense existence that belongs to the ideas in the mind alone, and if they are to be reconstructed from them, then to the individual sensations there must be attached intensive marks that represent the position of their objects in space and from which the mind can restore the spatial order. (p. 335)

Lotze occupied a middle position in the dispute between the nativists and the empiricists. The nativists—J. P. Müller, and later also Konstantin Hering and Franz Brentano—claim that the intuitions of space and time are innate. On the one hand, Lotze criticized this view. As we already know, he assumed that the mind arranges the local-signs in a space with three dimensions. The space is therefore something subjective. However, this subjective view of space does not come to us in a finished form. It is recurrently constructed by the mind (§ 9 below).[92]

---

89 Lotze adopted this conception from G. A. Spieß (Vagnetti 2020b, n. 72).
90 We shall say more about the psychological functions of the body in § 10 below.
91 That both Lotze's physiological psychology and his epistemology adopted the principle of secondary sensations or thoughts should not come as a surprise. Both followed the general Principle of Reflection to which Lotze also adheres in the form of "critical reflection". (Lotze's term "critical reflection" will be discussed in further detail in § 11 below.)
92 For this position, Lotze's local-signs theory was criticized by the nativists and also Lotze's followers Franz Brentano and Carl Stumpf (Milkov 2020a; on Lotze's relationship with Brentano and Stumpf, see Chapters 4 and 5). William James, who followed Lotze in many ways, also claimed against Lotze that the sensory organs have a direct connection with space.

At the same time, however, Lotze emphasized that mental *phenomena* are definite, they are not composed. In that sense, Lotze was a nativist. He was convinced that we have "a positive and immediate view" of the content of mental life—of "what it means to feel and strive, love, hate, yearn and be satisfied" (1852a, p. 58). These phenomena could be explored in Lotze's prospective discipline of "philosophical psychology" (§ 1 above).

Lotze's middle position, his hybrid approach on this subject, opened the door to empirical studies in psychology also for nativists.[93] The first who went through it was Lotze's doctoral, and post-poctoral student Carl Stumpf. On the one hand, Stumpf followed Franz Brentano's nativism. On the other hand and in contrast to his first teacher Brentano, he was an avid experimental psychologist who founded the famous Psychological Institute at the Kaiser-Wilhelm-University in Berlin in 1894 (Chapter 5).

9 Lotze's Theory of Space

Lotze's atoms (Chapter 1, § 4.6) are "metaphysical points"[94] that have no extension. They are non-spatial and form substances (things) through relationships. Lotze's statement "The being of things [is] standing in relation [to one another]" (1864, p. 453) is well known. The relations themselves are based on the reciprocal *resistance* of their elements.[95] All three, i.e., atoms, relations, and substances, evolve in time. This creates the possibility of extensions in an unlimited number of dimensions and directions.

Space itself is not a concept of metaphysics (of ontology). It is a concept of science (of cosmology). It is merely a form of intuition *generated* by human mind—space is not available a priori. It is an *ideality*.[96] In other words, space is not a product of intuition, as Kant postulated. It is not a priori. Lotze thus also distanced himself from Newton's conception of space as an infinite container and came close to Leibniz's view that it is not absolute but consists of relations. In addition, Lotze's

---

[93] In § 6, we have already seen that Lotze did not intend to slow down the development of empirical psychology.
[94] The term "metaphysical points" was introduced by Leibniz. For Leibniz, however, the metaphysical points are the numbers, not the atoms (Milkov 2020b, p. 34).
[95] Lotze considered the atoms to be alive, albeit metaphorically speaking (§ 4 above). They are open to stimulus and can have "fates" (Lotze 1879, § 70). This conception was an expression of Lotze's alleged Panpsychism (Chapter 1, § 4.6). See more on it in Beiser (2013, pp. 232–238).
[96] Time (Lotze 1864, p. 576), extent, shape and size are *idealities* as well, and not "material" factors that cause our perception.

position shows relatedness to J. G. Fichte, who has expressly underlined the active role of the subject of knowledge.[97] To be more specific, Lotze took over the view that the space-perception is a product of mind's activity from his professor in Leipzig, E. H. Weber.

An implication of Lotze's distinction between metaphysical atoms (points) and space-perception was that he also distinguished between *place* (location) and *extension*. Place is simply a geometric term that is not precise enough in order to be included in the philosophical (metaphysical) investigation. In this context, it is better to speak of extension (Pester 1997, p. 110). The geometrical directions are three, while the metaphysical (ontological) directions are innumerable. In geometry, a location is determined by three coordinates, thus making the possible dimensions concrete and suitable for mathematical calculations. Individuation plays an important role in this context.[98]

Be this as is may, humans are convinced that space has three dimensions. Lotze highlighted the fact (1852a, pp. 335–336) that only a careful reflection[99] can enable us to track down the infinite number of dimensions. He, however, was a *realist* insofar as he maintained that science explores and learns something about the structure of *the world*[100]—despite the fact that science does not *represent* it. The world is not made by us. It really exists and so is not an illusion. However, consciousness is not a mirror of nature. It is a product of the critical activity of the mind. The reality that the mind creates is not analogous to the outside world (Chapter 1, § 4.7; Chapter 9, § 9). For example, "our idea of the bigger is no bigger than that of the smaller" (Lotze 1864, p. 487). Lotze concludes that

> just as little as the sound of the struck string is fed through the wood of the key [of the piano] in the nature in which there is rather no hint at the world of tones, just as little could the soul pick up its well-formed sensations from the nerves that feed it. (1852a, p. 177)

However, there are general laws of formation that govern all levels of reality.

Despite Lotze's clear avowals to the contrary, his theory of space was often brushed aside as "idealistic". Curiously enough, the development of science in recent decades has strengthened Lotze's view that while human mind creates space

---

97 In contrast, the Russian philosopher M. I. Karinski, who visited Lotze's lectures in Göttingen in 1871–1872, maintained that Lotze's philosophy of space is close to that of Hegel and Trendelenburg. Karinski's argument for paying credit on this count to Hegel and Trendelenburg instead to Fichte was that according to the former, space is the result of a process (1873, p. 193).
98 One can see here the merging of psychology with logic in Lotze's argument (n. 87).
99 On Lotze's Principle of Reflection, see n. 91 and § 11 below.
100 Husserl (1939b, p. 323) strongly criticized Lotze for this position (Introduction, § 2). On Lotze's realism, see Introduction, § 4.2.

with three dimensions, reality has more dimensions. Today, many leading cosmologists claim that while we perceive the world in only three dimensions, it can be explained more convincingly if we assume that it has ten or eleven inherent dimensions (Hawking 2004, pp. 186 f.).[101]

Lotze's philosophy of space also bears a resemblance to Husserl's somewhat obscure—and therefore little investigated—but rather sophisticated theory of manifolds, which he developed by reference to Bernard Riemann's and Hermann Großmann's n-dimensional manifolds.[102] Husserl namely maintained that instead of space and time, one could speak of axiomatic forms in which the individuals find their specific coordinates (Milkov 2005a). The conventional concept of space can be understood as a Euclidean manifold of three dimensions.

Last but not least, Lotze's emphasis on the creative power of the human mind helps to understand how humans can produce, through the sparse and formal means of ordinary language, new, plastic worlds that are just as convincing as reality. Successful pieces of literature can put us in "misery and shudder" (Aristotle, *De Poetica*, 1449b27–28) to the same extent as scenes in reality sometimes do.

10 The Location and the Essence of the Soul

The problem of the location of the soul was of central importance for Lotze. He criticized phrenology, which enjoyed widespread attention in the mid-19th century (1852a, pp. 106–115; 1856a, pp. 372–379). The theorists of phrenology tried to assign mental properties and states to clearly defined parts of the brain. In opposition, Lotze emphasized that it is problematic to link specific mental phenomena exclusively to particular parts of the brain. The mind is not simply an aggregate of mental states which, like physical forces, come together at one point (1852a, p. 16 f.). This argument was based on Lotze's maxim not to confuse the mental world with the physical. The nature of the mental is different in principle. The soul is an organic unity that is realized in interactions among the different parts of the brain. One implication of this position is that the mind is numerically identical and so cannot be broken down into parts (1846, p. 144). The numerous nerves do not work autonomously but rather work together until a resonance is achieved among them—similarly to the way the music produced by a piano does not come from pressing

---

[101] New scientific studies also indicate that the brains of animals, e.g., that of a mouse, *composes* topographic maps to orient itself in space and time-schemes to improve its ability to orient itself in time. It also *composes* social maps that can help by orienting in the mouse kinship (Schafer and Schiller 2020).

[102] As we already know (Introduction, § 2), Husserl was demonstrably influenced by Lotze.

the piano keys alone but also from the piano's soundboard (§ 9 above). In contrast, nature is divisible.

As already seen in § 8 above, according to Lotze, a stimulus from the outside world is transformed into an impression (sign) in the sensory organs of the body, then into a local-sign, and further into a spatial-perception that is generated by the mind. Lotze understood this transformation as a dynamic process. The mind is

> kept *mobile* in the brain. ... She should not sit quietly and wait until the impression reaches her but should rather hurry up towards it and collect the impressions that are presented to her everywhere on the spot, namely, at the central ends of the stimulated fibers. (Lotze 1852a, p. 121)

Lotze's conclusion was that the mental appearances (phenomena) do not come from a "specific principle" of the mind which makes it problematic to think of the mind as a substance. "The name soul is inasmuch a *phenomenological expression*" (pp. 137 f.). Lotze thus rejects a main thesis of the rational psychology of the Leibnizians. The soul is not a substance.

But souls can also be understood as "substantial minds" (p. 75).[103] The point is that the ideas that the soul generates can in fact cause actions and thus also has impact on the physical world. The soul thus drives the body:

> The soul is *ideal* in relation to the nature of its content and in contrast to the *material* whose properties it does not have; but like this, it is an actually existing substance and enjoys in no less degree that *reality* of independent existence on which rests the ability to set something in motion in the world. (p. 75)

However, actions are also carried out automatically, or with graduated participation. Such actions are caused not by the soul but by the muscles alone. The leading role in this kind of acting is the attempt—the striving—to achieve something:[104]

> Thus, when we are writing, or playing the piano, we see a large number of movements, some of which are very complex, taking place in quick succession, the exemplary images of which hardly passed through the consciousness for a moment and certainly did not remain in it long enough to awaken a will other than the general one to surrender without resistance to the transition of ideas into movements. All the ordinary movements of our everyday life happen in this way; our getting up, walking, speaking; none of this requires any special will impulses but is adequately justified by the course of images. (pp. 293–294)

---

[103] By this turn of thought from rejecting the view that soul is a substance to accepting that it is such, Lotze made use of his dialectical method again (§ 3 above).
[104] A similar conception was presented some time ago by Brian O'Shaughnessy (2000, pp. 98–100).

These observations provide further evidence that the human body is also of psychological importance. "We believe [writes Lotze in conclusion] that we have to look for the first and most important footing of the mental functions not in the *central* but rather in the *peripheral organs* and their *functions*" (p. 554). Feelings, in particular, are determined by the movements of the body.[105] There is no central organ of feelings.

A few decades later, following Lotze's ideas on this topic, William James developed his famous somatic theory of feelings. According to it,

> our emotions must always be *inwardly* what they are, whatever be the physiological ground of their apparition. If they are deep, pure, worthy, spiritual facts on any conceivable theory of their physiological source, they remain no less deep, pure, spiritual, and worthy of regard on this present sensational theory. [...] If such a theory is true, then each emotion is the result of a sum of elements, and each element is caused by a physiological process of a sort already well known. The elements are all organic changes, and each of them is the reflex effect of the exciting objects. (James 1890, ii, p. 453)

11 Lotze's Concept of Philosophy

Among other things, Lotze saw philosophy as a kind of *reflection* on the basic concepts of science. This makes it understandable why he began his physiological psychology with an elucidation (*Erläuterung*)—instead of with an explanation—of the basic concepts of physiological psychology.[106] One cannot define the basic concepts but only interpret or elucidate them. If one leaves out the critical *reflection*—one can also talk about *analysis* here—mistakes are preordained. A typical example is the natural philosophy of the German idealists. Fichte and Hegel understood biology as a discipline that differs radically from physics simply because the term "life force" supposedly plays the leading role in it. As we have already seen (in § 3 above), however, Lotze was firmly convinced that the term "life force" explains nothing.

We already know that Lotze adopted Herbart's and Fechner's practice of exploring psychology scientifically. But in contrast to those figures, who tried to get exact results with the help of mathematical methods (§ 3 above), Lotze followed physiology instead—he simply explored the latest results of the physiology of

---

[105] See also Lotze (1852a, pp. 257 ff.).
[106] On the logical difference between elucidation (*Erläuterung*) and explanation (*Erklärung*) see Kant (1800, § 105). The distinction between these two operations of human understanding will later play an important role in the philosophy of logic of Frege and Wittgenstein (Hacker 1975, Geach 1976, and Milkov 2017c, pp. 199 f.).

the mind philosophically. That was actually the main task of Lotze's *Medicinische Psychologie*. One cannot bypass the facts of psychological experience, the phenomena that science collects. However, they must be explained according to the *principles of judgment* (or *criticism*) in order to arrive at a *general philosophical vision*. It cannot be achieved simply through physiological observations, as the positivists claim, but neither with the help of speculation alone, as the German idealists did.

This is also what makes philosophy so important (actually, indispensable) for science. It examines the *connection of things* in science or its ontology (§ 5 above). Philosophy, however, cannot serve as a justification of definite statements. It can only advance an orientation scheme with the help of which one can assess and classify the facts of perception through reflective observation. At the same time, science is indispensable for philosophy as well—it provides the data, the "microscopic" (empirical) observations that are vital for exploring the connection of things.

According to Lotze, philosophy, just like human mind, is a unity. However, one can examine being and reality from different perspectives. In fact, the various schools of philosophy refer to different aspects of being—they are not really antagonistic. One can simply grasp the world from different points of view. Lotze expressed this conception in the following way:

> The hiker who goes around a mountain sees, as he repeatedly goes back and forth, up and down, a number of different profiles of the mountain recur in predictable order. None of them are the true shape of the mountain, but all are valid projections of the same. But the true shape itself, like all those apparent ones, would consist in some sort of mutual arrangement of all its points. This proper form, the real inner connection of the things, can perhaps also be found, and one would then certainly prefer this true objective law of reality to all derived and only valid expressions of it; for the time being we console ourselves with this nature of truth that it makes innumerable apparent forms of itself and a valid back-and-forth of knowledge possible between them. (1864, p. 217; 1885, ii, pp. 334–335)

Let us take as an example Hegel's idealistic and Herbart's realistic conception of philosophy. The realists see the world as a collection of appearances. Furthermore, they believe that beyond appearances one can find a structure that is simple and unchangeable, with junctions that are not related. The idealists, on the other hand, maintain that there is a level in the world that is beyond appearances which alone is the reality. For Lotze, despite the fact that the realists and idealists have different objectives, they can peacefully coexist (2021b, p. 674). The causal view of the world is typical of the realists. The idealists, on the other hand, maintain that the structure of the world is ideal.

Lotze agrees with the Hegelians that the structure of the "subjective mind" is ideal. For him, however, it is not just an idea; it is closely linked to matter—to anatomy and physiology, and thus also to science.[107] At the same time, physiological psychology is broadly based on reflective philosophical observation. It alone can organize the scientific ("microscopic") results in one unit.

In fact, Lotze's perspectivism in relation to polemic philosophical conception (Chapter 1, § 3.3) was nothing new. Already Hegel maintained that "the *history of philosophy* shows ... that the particular *principles* [of different philosophers], one of which was the basis of a system, are only *branches* of one and the same whole" (1830, i, § 13). Be this as it may, one must discriminate Lotze's perspectivism in relation to the historical development of philosophy from Fechner's perspectivism in relation to the mind-body relation—but also from Lotze's dialectics. In Lotze's perspectivism, there are two dimensions of reality that can be explored from two different theoretical points of view—scientific and philosophical. For him, the spiritualistic tendencies are part of the psychological description of reality, "a personal manner of reading things, a poetic intuition of the cosmic life" (Santayana 1889, p. 155). Other parts of his system, e.g., his atomism, were clearly embedded objectivistically in the scientific description of reality (Chapter 1, § 3.2).

12 Logic and Psychology

Today, Lotze is widely recognized as the pioneer of anti-psychologism in philosophy. In short, anti-psychologism claims that logic and philosophy must develop separately from psychology. One can illustrate this position with the help of Frege's dictum: "The psychological should be sharply separated from the logical, the subjective from the objective" (1884, Introduction). As a matter of fact, the position of anti-psychologism was already formulated by Plato and Aristotle and was pronounced in a new form by Kant. However, it was Lotze who made it the leading principle in the philosophy of the *fin de siècle* (Introduction, § 4.2).

Be this as it may, in Lotze's physiological psychology, logic and psychology go hand-in-hand. How can this be explained? Above all, one can do this by reference to Lotze's adoption and further development of Kant's "logicalization" of philosophy (Introduction, § 4.1), by following the method of drawing rigorous ("logical") distinctions in philosophy. Above all, Lotze distinguished between the given and the validity. He assumed that the given *is*; it is opposed to what happens (e.g.,

---

107 Elsewhere in *Medicinische Psychologie*, Lotze wrote: "Causal investigations were therefore not at all in the fairway of this [of Hegel's] philosophizing, and the absurdities that arise so numerous when one looks at his interpretations of the meaning of the phenomena for interpreting their mode of realization, are based on a misunderstanding of the whole intent, of which, however, Hegel himself was now and then guilty" (1852a, p. 157).

events, facts) and what is valid (judgments). Transitions among these three are impossible. In this way, Lotze introduced a radical distinction between genesis and being, between "happened" and "is". The genesis (the devolvement) of thought is examined by psychology, including by experimental psychology, the validity by logic. Lotze himself was not an experimental but more of a "logical" psychologist, although, as already seen (in § 6 above), he also left the door open to experimental psychology.

This position becomes particularly clear when one looks at Lotze's criticism of Herbart's associationism. Following David Hume, Herbart maintained that thinking is produced by connecting (associating) atomic ideas. Lotze saw this view as misleading from both a psychological and from a logical standpoint. The atom in logic is the proposition, not the concept.[108] From a logical standpoint, judgment is not simply an "association of ideas". It is an assertion of a certain relationship among contents,[109] among states of affairs or connection of things (Chapter 1, § 4.5). Psychological associationism cannot explain the fact that human mind grasps goals and projects according to which people can also act (§ 10 above).

Among other things, Lotze's criticism of associationism in psychology helped William James to develop his famous concept of "stream of consciousness":

> The traditional psychology talks like one who should say a river consists of nothing but pailsful, spoonsful, quartpotsful, barrelsful, and other molded forms of water. Even were the pails and the pots all actually standing in the stream, still between them the free water would continue to flow. It is just this free water of consciousness that psychologists resolutely overlook. (James 1890, i, p. 255)

In fact, James' conception was directly influenced by Lotze's term "course of imagination [*Vorstellungslauf*]", which is often used in *Medicinische Psychologie*.

A clear indication that Lotze's physiological psychology was developed in close contact with his logic is the role that the term "sign" plays in it. It suffices to recall here Lotze's theory of local-*signs* (§ 8 above). He also talked about the "transformation" of these signs into others, which ultimately determine our perception and the form of psychological phenomena. In some places (1852a, p. 258) Lotze spoke of the "translation" of the signs as well. In so doing, he was actually following Leibniz's dictum that a system of signs (characters) can be translated into another *salva veritate*.[110]

---

[108] Michael Dummett (1956) called this conception the "context principle".
[109] As we are going to see in Chapters 4 and 5, this conception of Lotze was also adopted by Franz Brentano and Carl Stumpf.
[110] This dictum was later sharply criticized by Willard Quine in his "indeterminacy of translation" thesis (1960).

Chapter 3
Lotze's Philosophical Anthropology

1 Opening

Lotze's philosophical anthropology was best presented in his *Mikrokosmus, Ideas towards a Natural History of Humanity: Essay on Anthropology*. The book was published in three volumes, which appeared in 1856, 1858 and 1864. Soon, it became one of the most widely read philosophy books of the time. In 1866, it was translated into Russian, in 1885/1887, which was followed an English translation, and in 1911/1916, it was translated into Italian.[111] By 1923, the book had been published in six editions in Germany alone.[112] Raymund Schmidt wrote in his Preface to the 6th edition of the book: "Lotze will never be a modern [author] again, we shall never evidence a neo-Lotzeanism or something of the sort, but [his *Mikrokosmus*] will be always read as a part of the education of the young philosophers and for deepening the education of every thinking man" (Schmidt 1923, pp. vii–viii). Unfortunately, this prophecy turned out to be proven false. After the Great War in the English-speaking world and after 1932 in Germany, Lotze's *Mikrokosmus* was almost totally forgotten.

2 Setup

2.1 First Description

The place of *Mikrokosmus* in Lotze's philosophical development was judged in different ways in the literature. Some authors, including J. E. Erdmann and E. W. Orth, believed that this was his most important book. Max Scheler called it "a classical monument of the philosophical literature" (1997, p. 133). Others hold the contrary view (Woodward 2015, p. 283)—the book was mainly a popular statement of Lotze's

---

[111] The Russian translation was done by Evgenij Korsch and published in two volumes with Soldatenkov: Moscow; the English translation was done by Elizabeth Hamilton and E. E. Constance Jones; and the Italian translation (of Vols. I and II only) was done by Francesco Bonatelli and Gaetano Capone Braga, Pavia: Mattei, Speroni, et al. In 1988, a new, abridged Italian translation of the book appeared, which was produced by Luigi Marino and Gianstefano Stella with Unione Tipografico Editrice Torinese: Torino.

[112] The newest (7th) German edition of the book appeared in 2017 (Orth 2018, Vagnetti 2020a).

philosophy, which was developed on a more theoretical level in his "greater" *Logic* (1874) and "greater" *Metaphysic* (1879).

The incidental reader of Lotze's *Mikrokosmus* today will be surprised by its freshness. Its content alone is exciting. It shows a book which often discusses themes that are today almost forgotten, or it puts prima facie alien themes side by side, thus inspiring deep insight. Briefly, in *Mikrokosmus*, Lotze charts a map of philosophy that is rather alien—in an exciting way—to the contemporary philosophy reader.

The three volumes of the book discuss, respectively, the Body, Man, and History—or the individual person, the social person, and society as such. The volume on the individual person (the first volume) explored, in particular, the relation between mind and body (in the second book, pp. 204, 261 f., 264 f., and 432).[113] The volume ends with examination of life in its different forms.

In the second volume on man, first, his relatedness to and differences from other living creatures are investigated. It follows an analysis of mind in which special emphasis is given to the person's sensuality and feeling of pleasure and pain. This analysis prompted Lotze to make consumption (*genießen*) a central concept in anthropology. His discussion of man continues in chapters on language and thinking and on knowing and truth. Finally, the author examines the man in his macrocosmic (terrestrial and cosmic), as well as in her microcosmic (in his relation to other persons in family and society) environment.

In the final, third volume on history, Lotze examined the progress, the different cultures and forms of life, the private and political economy, the different forms of work and leisure, and of art. The volume ends with Lotze's philosophy of religion.

How is this content to be judged? Above all, in *Mikrokosmus*, Lotze tried to fulfill the program for regressive analysis that he adopted as an organon of research effectively (Chapter 1, § 3.3). According to it, in philosophy, analysis is not to start with exploring the latest achievements of mathematics and natural science, nor with investigating human understanding. It is to begin with investigating the "whole culture", with human history. To be more explicit, in the book, Lotze presents the philosophy of history as a completion of his philosophy of psychology (1857, p. 15), which we already discussed in Chapter 2.

Lotze's *Mikrokosmus* is most helpful for obtaining a correct understanding of Lotze's development as a philosopher. It worked out in detail some theses, already formulated in his earlier works, the "lesser" *Metaphysic* (1841) and the "lesser"

---

[113] Here and in what follows, Lotze's *Mikrokosmus* is quoted according to his 7th edition (Lotze 2017).

Logic (1843a), albeit in rudimentary and rough form. In *Mikrokosmus*, Lotze made them thus sophisticated, so that in his *System of Philosophy* (1874/1879), he could use them with elegance and precision. In particular, Lotze elaborated in it the inner connection between philosophical logic and anthropology, thus logicizing many intimate problems of human mind and action. This quite convoluted and intensive program was entangled with so many ideas that it could give inspiration to the leading world-philosophies of the 20th century.

There was also another perspective of the book, however. We have already noted (Introduction, § 5; Chapter 1, § 3.4) that advancing his "theoretical anthropology", Lotze intended to merge the theoretical and the mundane philosophy. This is what he made in *Mikrokosmus*. On the one hand, Lotze developed in it many new points of his theoretical philosophy. At the same time, he tried to tear down the wall between theoretical and mundane philosophy, to build a bridge between them. For this reason, Lotze intentionally wrote the book "in completely popular form" (2017, i, p. 467).

A good illustration of Lotze's *Mikrokosmus* as a book on popular philosophy is his examination of the differences and relatedness between man and woman in it:

> The corporal needs of women are lesser then those of men. Women get accustomed to new environment easier, whereas men eliminate the traces of their early education and formation only with much effort. However, the intellectual capacities of the two genders are not substantially different. Rather, more often than not, they use them for different purposes and with different attitude. Roughly, men's knowledge and will are directed to the general, those of women to the whole. Men like analysis and mechanical explanations, women have a preference for the living, for coziness (*Gemütlichkeit*), for beautiful, closed wholes. Women are good in bringing order in space, men in time. Property is what is important for men, women often live wastefully. To women's heart, the truth has another meaning then for men. Women are inclined to accept appearances; they have a predilection for surrogates (1858, pp. 381–389).

In this way, the book was to present a break with what Schopenhauer had called *Kathederphilosophie*, the university philosophy that dominated post-Kantian Germany. The latter, the "philosopher's philosophy", was rather scholastic, formal, far away from the general conversation of mankind. In fact, Lotze's *Mikrokosmus* can effectively be seen as an attempt to put together the academic philosophy with the looming series of books that mainly discuss *conditio humana* of such authors like Schopenhauer (Introduction, § 5). And since we have already said much about Lotze's theoretical philosophy in Chapters 1 and 2, in this chapter, we shall concentrate mainly on Lotze's philosophy of culture.

2.2 Three Traditions of Microcosmic Studies

Surprisingly enough, the very term *microcosm* (*Mikrokosmus*) was used only three times in the book; furthermore, it was not used in its body but rather (i) in the Introductory Remark to the whole work; (ii) in the Conclusion to Volume I; and (iii) in the Contents of Book VI, Chapter One. In (ii) and (iii) Lotze spoke of the microcosm as "the lesser world". The question which poses itself is: why was Lotze so hesitant to speak of *microcosm*? By way of answer, we should say that, first of all, Lotze was convinced that new terms are rarely to be introduced in philosophy. The only justification for doing so could be the discovery of a totally new concept (1843, p. 25). Secondly, this was a measure against the danger that his work would be associated with the old German tradition of microcosmic studies set out by Paracelsus and Jacob Böhme. In this context, it should be recalled that there are at least three traditions of microcosmic studies in philosophy:

(i) The first one, much more popular than the other two, maintains that men or other "lesser monads" and the universe

> are constructed according to the same harmonic proportions, each sympathetically attuned to the other, each a cosmos ordered according to reason. [Furthermore,] By an imaginative leap, the universe itself [i]s thought to be, like man, living and conscious, a divine creature whose nature it reflected in human existence. (Levy 1967, p. 122)

This conception emphasizes the unity of life and thought in the world. Many philosophers connect the conception of microcosm thus understood with the idea of the World Soul, which, in this way or that, controls or animates particular (lesser) souls. The Orphic, Gnostic, Kabbalistic and Hermetic traditions made use of it, connecting it with the mysticism, pantheism and the occult.

This idea of microcosm was also considered a hallmark of German philosophy, of what was called *philosophia teutonica*. Nicholas of Cusa, Agrippa of Nettesheim, Paracelsus, Leibniz, Herbart, and later also Max Scheler, all of them adopted a kind of micro-cosmology that claimed that the lesser worlds are controlled by the greater world, which, in turn, in one sense or another, leads the life of the lesser words. We would like to say already at this stage that Lotze's project was of a different type.

(ii) *Cosmos* (κόσμος) means *order* in Greek.[114] So, *microcosm* can also signify "any part of a thing, especially a living thing that reflects or represents the whole it belongs to, whenever there is a mirroring relation between the whole and each of its parts" (Levy 1967, p. 122). On this principle are built many sciences—and also

---

[114] In ancient Greek philosophy, cosmos was opposed to chaos (Plato, *Timaios* 27c–29d).

pseudo-sciences. Here, one is immediately reminded of astrology, which claims that the fate of a person, over a period of time, is influenced or even determined by her co-relation to such macro-worlds as planets, stars, or constellations of stars. Today, such microcosmical relations are often discussed in medicine. Two examples: (a) in neurology, parts of the brain can be presented as representing different parts of the body or its abilities (speech, orientation); (b) the main point of acupuncture is that small parts of the surface of human body are representatives of inner organs of the body.

(iii) Finally, in Greek, *cosmos* (κόσμος) also means a *unity* ordered according to certain principle. As we shall see in the following, it is precisely in this sense that Lotze spoke of microcosm. He investigated how the microcosm of the human world —physiological, private, social—is ordered; and he found that it is ordered in a way similar to that the macrocosm is ordered. To elucidate this point further, let us turn back to the history of Lotze's book *Mikrokosmus*.

Before doing so, however, we must mention a puzzling moment in this work which testifies against our interpretation to some degree. In the Conclusion to Volume I, Lotze prima facie mentions the term *microcosm* in sense (i): he speaks about "that perfect picture [*vollkommenes Abbild*] of the big reality, the lesser world, the *microcosm*" (1856a, p. 452). In order to elucidate this place of Lotze's *Mikrokosmus*, we shall compare it with another passage, in which the author specifies that the man is not a picture (*Abbild*) of nature but rather a *living point* that receives a vast amount of information from the world in the form of perceptions; not, however, in order to reflect it in the same form, but in order to be stimulated by it according to his own disposition (*Naturell*) (1858, p. 362) (Chapter 1, §§ 4.3, 4.7).

2.3 History of Lotze's *Mikrokosmus*-Project

The history of Lotze's *Mikrokosmus* is long and well-documented (Pester 1997, pp. 201–202). Already in 1844, the author suggested to his editor, Samuel Hirzel, a book-project for an *Anthropology and Natural History of Human Race*—which would be part of a project for an encyclopedia of medicinal sciences. Soon, however, Lotze abandoned this idea. To be sure, the subject of this project lay between medicine, philosophy, theology and natural science, and so was an unfeasible task. Six years later, in 1850, Hirzel tried to persuade Lotze to bring the project back to life, but Lotze refused again. Surprisingly enough, by the time of his visit to Göttingen in the winter of 1852–1853, i.e., after Lotze had finished his *Allgemeine Physiologie des körperliches Leben* (1851) and *Medicinische Psychologie oder Physiologie der Seele* (1852a) (Chapter 2), Hirzel convinced him to do so.[115] Hirzel's new idea was to end the book with a chapter on the "Developing History of Human Culture". This time, Lotze agreed, and in a letter to his editor dated March 8, 1853, he drew up the first plan for his new book (Lotze 2003, pp. 229–230).[116]

The very title *Mikrokosmus* came later. It appeared first, in relation to this project, in his letter to Hirzel from October 2, 1854, where Lotze also noted: "I am not sure if it [the title] is silly or rather good [*ob er recht dumm oder ziemlich gut ist*]" (Lotze 2003, p. 257). Lotze gradually realized that the analysis of microcosm in the light of the cosmos is more strict and comprehensive than the deduction of the forms of life from the logical forms as accomplished by the speculative natural science of Hegel and Schelling (Pester 1997, p. 150). What was important to him was that the microcosm works according to the *order* of the "macrocosm": they follow the same principles. However, he did not assume that we can make *conclusions* about the microcosm in analogy with the macrocosm, or vice versa (§ 2.2 above).

This approach shows, with formal precision, the way the microcosm repeats the idea of the macrocosm. More to the point, it demonstrates that

> if we understand the organism as a microcosm, then, according to Lotze, we can grasp the importance of life through a trait of its behavior, which must in fact express only a formal expediency of [it …], without to necessarily determine or imagine its content (p. 204; see also pp. 151f.).

This trait of its behavior was its order.

3 Methods

In the preceding two chapters, we have said much about the principles and methods that Lotze followed in his philosophical explorations. These were above all: (i) the second step of logicalization of modern philosophy (Introduction, § 4.1), (ii) the method of regressive analysis (Chapter 1, § 3.1), (iii) the method of teleomechanism;

---

[115] Apparently, this was not accidental. Lotze decided to write on his philosophical anthropology only after he cleared for himself the relation between mind and body.

[116] On the technical side, as Lotze wrote his editor, he accepted to work on this project since "it requires multifarious reflections, and this is very good for someone like me who is habituated to more abstract range of thoughts" (Lotze 2003, p. 230). Apparently, Lotze sought a change in the style of this work in the direction of blending theoretical and mundane philosophy—and this change turned out to be fruitful indeed.

(iv) the method of physical–psychological mechanism; and (v) the principle of occasionalism (Chapter 2, § 6). In this section, we are going to concentrate on the methods that Lotze used specifically in his analysis of human culture.

3.1 Ontological Approach

The concept of social order as part of social ontology plays a prominent role in Lotze's *Mikrokosmus*. In other words, Lotze's book takes a strong ontological stance in the sense that it shows "a concern with ontological structure" (Smith 1994, p. 3; see also Chapter 1, § 4.2), in particular, with the ontological structure of the society. More precisely, in the book, Lotze examines the development of human life according to the type of order or "ontological volume" in which it is involved.

Lotze was a pioneer in adopting this approach in social philosophy. In its full form, it was embraced only in recent years. Its champion in the 20th century was Eric Voegelin, who produced an extensive review (in five volumes) of human history from the point of view of the different levels of order adopted in it (Voegelin 1956/87). Some twenty years later, another author declared the concept of social order, alongside that of social practices, to be central to social philosophy (Schatzki 2002).

There follow some excerpts from Lotze's social ontology:

> The "savage" changes passive, prolonged periods of leisure with extremely intensive strain. In contrast, the settled peasant lives in rhythmic series of small portions of work and leisure. Her heart melts together with the near landscape, making of it a home (*Heimat*). In this way, she becomes more patient since she gets accustomed to wait for the reaping of the crop, following the four seasons rhythm of the nature. Such rhythmic life teaches the mind to feel involved in the consequential, but branched, lawfulness of nature. (1858, p. 428)

> Family life changes the mind further. In a family house (in private economy), the person is isolated from outer perceptions and so concentrates herself on the intensive contact with family members. The walls of the house enclose a new realm of human imagination. A sequence of intertwined periods of joy, suffering, hopes, and memories follows. (1858, p. 429)

> In the wild life of the savage, men and women accomplished their typical work separately: men go hunting, women stay at home to bring up the children. But genders develop and manifest their true abilities—men's power and women's soul—only in their work together: in mutual complementation, which can be realized only in the more developed society.

> Something similar can be said about the different generations. Whereas in the wild life, the new generation separates from the old one immediately after it reaches physical maturity, the new generation of the settled society often develops tasks and projects that were started by the old one. The result is interwoven souls, with common interests but also with different

characters and direction of imagination. This leads to conflicts of the wishes, hopes, and fears but also to spiritual enrichment. It can be no surprise about this point, though: the members of the family have a chorus of endlessly rich interests, only a small part of which come to the surface of consciousness.[117]

The "drama of life", however, would be colorless if the family would remain at home. The family needs glances and evaluations from the outside; it needs the recognition of other families, of society. (1858, p. 435)[118]

3.2 Ecological Stance

Besides the ontological approach, Lotze's *Mikrokosmus* also had specific ecological emphases. In this context, we must not forget that Lotze planned his *Mikrokosmus* as a sequel to Herder's *Ideen zur Geschichte der Menschheit* (1784/1791) and to Alexander von Humboldt's *Cosmos* (1845/1862). Both works were written, at least in part, in geographic terms. The following are excerpts regarding Lotze's ecological stance:

> The shaping (*Gestaltung*) of the ground and the coloring of the sky immediately reflects on the temperament and the national imagination of the denizens of the specific country. On the other hand, all revolutions in human history had as a consequence a radical change in the life of the earth (1858, p. 349). Nevertheless, direct conclusions from the cosmic to the human life, or vice versa, are not reliable. You cannot infer (as Charles Montesquieu did) the alleged underdevelopment of the black race from either the brightness of the sun in Africa or the monotony of the tropical life, the fact that the black continent has too few inlets, too small a number of navigable rivers, or the small number of mountains (p. 353). At the same time, Lotze noted "how advantageous for the heart the simultaneous overview of huge spaces is; what a pleasure is the ability to review a multiplicity of different objects in their reciprocal positions as if they were embedded in a secure mesh of relations" (p. 353). Furthermore, "[o]ne can say the same about the frequent changes of earth and water which help to form our geographic intuition. Geography influences the spiritual disposition (*Naturell*) not by what it is but by how it stimulates the still uneducated heart. Most importantly, examining such influence is to reveal its mediating steps" (p. 356).

Concluding this section, we would like to notice that the ecological approach in social philosophy has been explored only in recent years. According to Barry Smith (1998), a central concept of social philosophy is that of the niche in which the object fits. Another recent author is more concretely ecological. Felipe Fernández-Armes-

---

117 This point of *Mikrokosmus*, repeated in Lotze's later works, made him interesting to the psychoanalysts (Chapter 4, § 3.5).
118 The struggle for recognition was Hegel's theme (1806, pp. 128 ff.), recently rediscovered and further explored by Honneth (1992).

to defines human civilization "as a type of relationship, a relationship to the natural environment, recrafted by the civilizing impulse, to meet human demands" (2001, p. 14). The main thesis of this author is that some civilizations collapsed because they handled their environments so roughly as to break them.

3.3 Theoretical Liberalism

Lotze was opposed to the hasty (and apparent) satisfaction of our theoretical needs and expectations in philosophy through one-sided theories and conclusions. Instead, he introduced a method that involved discussing different views (*Ansichten*) on the subject under scrutiny. He further claimed that his suggested solutions are nothing but views that satisfy the "needs of the heart". The latter phrase, incidentally, had a sense of both a pathological finding as well as of a critical standard (Orth 1983, p. 378). Among other things, it can be comfortably interpreted in the sense of Wittgenstein's claim that philosophical obsessions are similar to mental neuroses, which need therapy (1953, § 133).

The implication of this position is that values are equipollent. In sense of this claim, Lotze treated every epoch of human culture as developed around particular value:[119] "(i) the Orient developed a taste for the colossal; (ii) the Jews for the elevated; (iii) the Greeks for the beautiful; (iv) the Romans for dignity and elegance; (v) Middle Ages for the fantastic and characteristic; (vi) modernity for the critical and inventiveness. These orientations and achievements are on a par with one another" (1864, Book 7, Chapter 5).

Especially in political philosophy, Lotze's acceptance of the plurality of values was rather unusual in the Germany of the time. We can easily find anti-Semitic judgments by Herder (1784/1791, p. 437) and Kant, but not by Lotze. Lotze's theoretical attitude towards women was similar (§ 2.1 above). Incidentally, for that reason, some authors interpret Lotze as a precursor of modern feminism (Woodworth 2015). It is no wonder, then, that, in general, "the admirers of Lotze were on the 'liberal' rather than the 'conservative' side of the political fence" (Kuntz 1971, p. 59).[120]

---

[119] Lotze's examination of the relation between men and women, discussed in § 2 above, shows the same theoretical stance.
[120] From the perspective of his theoretical philosophy, however, Lotze was clearly a conservative thinker (Introduction, § 4.2).

4 Life and Society

4.1 Forms of Life

As already mentioned, Lotze was adamant that we cannot prefer logical forms over facts, as Hegel had once done. In particular, he criticized Hegel's ladder-model of natural history, which claimed that we can deduce the value and importance of every particular species from its place on the ladder of evolution. Instead of formal (logical) rankings of living species, Lotze promoted a comparison of their natural figures or forms (*Gestalten*) (Milkov 2005a). From this perspective he also circumvented Darwin's theory of evolution (Milkov 2017b, § 4.2). In addition, the difference between the mind of animals and that of human beings does not arise because of a difference in the elements which they contain; in fact, both here and there, the same building blocks, or "mosaic-stones" (*Mosaikstifte*), come into play.[121] Rather, that variation results from the *way* in which they are combined and used (1858, p. 266) (Milkov 2020d).

In other words, in contrast to Darwin's evolutionary theory of species based on the principle of natural selection, Lotze focused on the ontological side of biology. As a matter of fact, Lotze discussed Darwin's evolutionary theory only in the third edition of *Mikrokosmus* (1878). This delayed reaction to Darwin's *On the Origin of Species by Means of Natural Selection* is easy to explain, however. Darwin's book was published first in 1859, i.e., three years after Lotze published the 1st volume of his book and a year before the second volume, in which he discussed different forms of life, was published. In his short notes on Darwin's theory made in the third edition of Volume II (2017, ii, pp. 465–467),[122] Lotze did not criticize Darwin but merely stated that Darwin's "struggle for survival" is a genetic and not an ontological theory and thus has little to do with philosophy.[123] This makes Frederick Beiser's claim that Lotze's "failure to treat Darwin in any detail [...] was one of the greatest shortcomings of his mature philosophy" (2016, p. 111) rather problematic.

Lotze also criticized the intellectualism of the German idealists in the philosophy of biology. Against it, he sided with the German Enlightenment's stance by emphasizing the importance of sensuality, of feelings and imagination (*Phantasie*). In this respect, he classified animals not according to their capacity to think (as did

---

121 This point was recently confirmed by genome studies. Humans and chimpanzees have approximately 99% identical DNA.
122 See also Lotze (1879, § 237).
123 Over a century ago, an ontological conception of the biological species, which does not oppose Darwin's theory, was advanced by D. W. Thompson (1917). The latter can help us better understand Lotze's conception of biological species (Milkov 2002b; Rescher 2011).

Herder) but according to their physical performance and forms of consumption (*genießen*). On this point, he was criticized by many of his contemporaries, including his philosophical friends, the "speculative theists" I. H. Fichte and C. H. Weiße. These two figures found in the *Mikrokosmus* too little idealism and too much realism (Weiße 1865, pp. 289 ff.).

It deserves to be noted, however, that this reproach was hardly justified. In fact, Lotze endorsed the essential difference between the human mind and that of other animals. As we already have seen, the difference between them does not exclusively come from the divergence in the constitution of the brain. Rather, the human mind is also formed from within, from the social traditions that find expression in language, science, skills, and morals, as well as in practical habits and in judgments of everyday life (1858, p. 262).[124] In this process, the ability to use the arm, and later also the use of working instruments (tools) was of prime importance. Furthermore, Lotze claimed that "to know man means, above all, to know his vocation [*Bestimmung*], the means which he has in disposition to achieve it, as well as the hindrances that he must overcome in this effort" (p. 72).

4.2 Social Progress

Lotze emphasized the fact that achieving social progress is not a matter of quantitative growth but rather of reaching a "systematic complete harmony" in specific culture. This state could be attained, for example, if the rules of social conduct were conceived of as a system of rights and duties of an objective overall spiritual (*geistiges*) organism (p. 440). Such a society could be considered a work of Nature, "or rather not simply of Nature, but of the Moral World Order [*sittliche Weltordnung*] which is independent of the individual" (p. 443).

Lotze was not convinced that the scientific and technological progress of the human race through the first half of the 19th century had increased its humaneness (*Humanität*). Among other reasons, this is the case since the rise of humanity's power over nature was often accompanied by a proportional increase in our dependence upon it. The new ways of life afforded by developing technologies created new consumption needs. However, many of these new needs were rather superfluous—they were not true needs at all, but superficial desires. Some of them could

---

[124] Years later, Wittgenstein also emphasized the fact that language is a unique human ability embedded in human culture—in the human "form of life". Recent explorations in science confirm this claim (Kenneally 2018).

be also positively harmful.[125] Thus, it is not unreasonable to think that we might have been better-off without the technologies that, although they enabled humanity to solve certain practical problems, created others that were previously unknown.

However, such felt needs or desires cannot be eliminated through mere insight into "truth", e.g., by recognizing that they are superfluous and harmful. The disapproving stance on this matter taken by Diogenes of Sinope or Rousseau, is attractive and convincing mainly as a critique. Indeed, the natural state that they propagated can be seen as a state of innocence but also as one of barbarism.

As a solution to this problem, Lotze adopted the view that there is a *constant human way of life* that repeats itself practically unchanged—its purposes, motives and habits have the same form.[126] This is the "course of the world" (*der Weltlauf*), an ever-green stalk from which the colorful blossoms of history cyclically emerge. In fact, the true goods of our inner life increase either only slowly or perhaps they do not increase at all (1858, p. 345).

Be this as it may, we are inclined to think that there is one direction of progress that leads to final ends. This, however, is not necessarily the case. At least the apparent progress that humanity made in the first half of the 19th century did not achieve this task, maintained Lotze. It is true that the physical world is now clearer to us than five centuries ago. However, the emotional strength with which the heart clings to nature remains the same.

Perhaps the most interesting development of modernity is the introduction of division of work and the new Protestant phenomenon of "profession". An important effect of this phenomenon is that life is now divided into work and leisure (1864, p. 281; pp. 245–247). Every profession stimulates the heart to embody a specific direction of imagination, a perspective on the world, and a way of judging. This development produced different forms of existence (*Existenzarten*), which makes modernity one of the most exiting epochs in human history.[127] The main disadvantage of the professional life, Lotze says, is its monotony (1858, p. 437).

---

125 Think, by way of comparison, of the relation between the various culinary technologies that in the last decades made fast-food possible, the growth of desires or just felt-need for fast-food, and the negative effects of fast-food upon public health.
126 Cf. Wittgenstein's concept of human "form of life" (1953, §§ 19, 23).
127 In contrast, Lotze's age-mate Karl Marx (Marx was only one year younger than Lotze), saw the introduction of professions, of the division of labor in modern Europe, as the cause of the exploitation of one social class (the proletariat) by another (the capitalists) (Marx and Engels 1845/1846).

4.3 Philosophy of History

Social history is a central subject of Lotze's *Mikrokosmus*. Lotze's views on this topic are best presented in contrast to what was then the standard or "mainstream" approach to history of his time which he faulted for lacking realism, and, therefore, for failing to generate genuine historic knowledge. Mainstream history had two chief sources: Hegelianism and what may loosely be described as positivism. Although radically different in their guiding assumptions, these two movements overlapped in terms of their impact on history.

Hegel maintained that history is produced by the movements (1864, pp. 35f.) of an arcane entity called "the world-spirit" (*Weltgeist*) and of its interaction with humanity. Specifically, Hegel believed that the *Weltgeist*'s goal is to bring the human race into the full realization of the *idea* of humanity, i.e., into an ideal state of its being. To this end, it leads certain humans (heroes), by means of which they are unaware, to advance the race in fortunate directions. These are the great figures in history. As Hegel saw it, exactly their evolvements and achievements are of academic interest in history. That is, the task of history is not to describe everything that happens in the society but to portray the great movements that advance humanity toward its ideal, to focus on those events that constitute a substantial realization of the ideal.

In short, the Hegelian approach requires commitment to a contentious idealization of humanity, to an assumption about what counts as the highest realization of human nature. Lotze agreed that such theories have their place in history as a science. But he was afraid that if history is allowed to control the search for its fundamental data, it can skew our perceptions. In Hegel's case, his ideal of humanity led him to neglect both the contributions of women to history (pp. 47ff.)[128] as well as the role played by the mundane aspects of individuals' lives—which, in fact, constitute the lager part of human history (Milkov 2006c).[129]

The positivist approach to history, exemplified by Leopold von Ranke and Johann Gustav Droysen, had similar implications. By focusing too much on "objective" facts and formal considerations and too little on the concrete, embodied, emotional aspects of human life, historically significant but "ordinary" elements of human life receive little consideration.

Lotze rejected both the idealism of Hegel and the demand for "objective faciticity" made by the positivists. Against Hegel, he argued that human progress is

---

[128] See n. 119.
[129] This claim of Lotze shows him to be a precursor of the *nouvelle histoire* school of Marc Bloch, which accentuated discussions in history of past facts of *la vie quotidienne*.

achieved neither linearly nor ladder-wise.[130] In fact, many achievements of human community disappear without a trace, while other fade away for a time, only to be rediscovered and reintroduced by new generations (Milkov 2011b). Rather, Lotze saw humanity as developing in a spiral pattern, in which moments of progress are offset by moments of regress.[131] To be sure, this perspective appears rather gloomy alongside the mainstream approach, but it is clearly more realistic and better suited to teaching humanity about itself.

Lotze agreed with Lessing that the purpose of history is the education (*Bildung*) of humanity.[132] That conception helps draw a more realistic picture of human progress than what Hegelian and positivist history provided. Seeing the discipline of history in didactic terms, Lotze's desiderata for good historical work went together with his ideal for good education. In particular, they were modeled by his conviction that the purpose of human life consists in achieving richness of an education capable to bring in harmony in all the aspects of the concrete, embodied person's life.[133] This is what drove Lotze to reject the positivists' "objective facticity" as inadequate for history.

Lotze's alternative was an aesthetic (poetic) approach to history (1864, p. 46).[134] As he saw it, poetry and history are both creative, setting up new life-worlds. The task of the historian is to present phenomena as they were understood in their original contexts—exactly as they were embraced, felt, and consumed in the past—not anachronistically, as they might be understood in the present through the "lenses" of a new and, to them, alien form of life. This task requires both the focus on empirical fact characteristic of positivist history, but also an element of poetic imagination—for only the latter could add flesh to the dry bones of empirical fact. By combining both modes of cognition, the historian is to determine how the phenomena he explores fit into the total form of life that was characteristic of the period in which they originated—in effect, to re-create the life-world of the humans whose phenomena they were. This line of thought was later followed, among others, by R. G. Collingwood (1946).

---

130 Lotze's criticism of Hegel's philosophy of history is clearly related to his assault against Hegel's deductive logic (Introduction, § 2).
131 A similar position was adopted by Franz Brentano as regards the progress in philosophy (1895). On Brentano's debt to Lotze, see Chapter 4.
132 This point coheres with Lotze's claim, discussed in Chapter 1, §§ 3.2, 3.3, that we can correctly understand philosophy and science only by starting from the history of human education and schooling.
133 Cf. the ancient ideal of *paidea* (παιδεία) (Plato, *Protagoras*, 312b; Jaeger 1945).
134 A similar position was also held by George Trevelyan and, perhaps surprisingly for many, by Bertrand Russell (Stone 2019; Milkov 2019).

4.4 Political Philosophy

Lotze's political philosophy discussed problems like social rationalization, power, bureaucracy, national values, sovereignty, and international relations. He strongly defended the enlightened, hereditary monarchy and distrusted parliamentary representation and party politics. Lotze considered the former as offering "the greatest security for steady development" which, as he saw it, is of greatest value in political life (1864, p. 444).

In more concrete terms, being a philosopher of the concrete, full-blooded man, with his feelings and imagination, Lotze defended paternal patriotism. He preferred love for the concrete fatherland over love for the state with its institutions.[135] Furthermore, Lotze criticized the view (defended, among others, by his contemporary Jacob Burckhardt) that the state should exist for its own sake.

Lotze repudiated Plato's model of the state as an analog of the human person, as a "microcosm", and accepted instead a model of political equilibrium construed as "the result of the reciprocal action of unequal forces" (p. 423). In matters of international law, he was an advocate of a balance of power of sovereign states. Lotze believed that "the increasing relations between the different divisions of humankind changed in great measure the significance of the political boundaries and gave new stimulus to the idea of cosmopolitanism" (p. 436).

Lotze disparaged those critics of modernity who claimed that its proponents only defend their desire for material well-being. Although he did not use the term "liberalism", Lotze adhered to the principles of what we would now call "classical bourgeois liberalism". At the same time, he criticized the "Manchester liberalism"[136] that followed the ideas of such political economists as Thomas Malthus. Lotze referred in that context to what is currently called the "liberal paradox" (Sen 1970)—liberalism fails to show how an isolated human being can be a subject of rights. Indeed, right is a reciprocal and thus collective concept: "one's right is what the others feel for us as a duty" (Lotze 1864, p. 427).

Lotze criticized the concept of natural law employed by the mainstream Western philosophers like Aristotle and Hobbes, who claimed that law is established by nature. Instead, he had sympathies with the historicist conception of law developed by Leopold von Ranke and Friedrich von Savigny who defended the thesis that the notions of law are coined in human practice. Lotze used to say that

---

[135] Over a century later, Jürgen Habermas opposed paternal patriotism with what he calls "constitutional patriotism" (1992).
[136] Cf. the "turbo-capitalism" of the "roaring 1990s".

"the beginning of all legitimacy is illegitimate, although it need not be at the same time illegal" (p. 417).

4.5 Philosophy of Religion

Lotze's philosophical conservatism (n. 120) is especially pronounced in his philosophy of religion. The religion of the modern man was, for Lotze, a feeling of life (*Lebensgefühl*) in which the awareness of the fragility of the human race is connected with a sense of conscience about a lay profession (§ 4.2 above).[137] Men know how modest their life-tasks are and nevertheless are happy to pursue them. This is a feeling, an intuition, that follows the consciousness and the inner voice. Nevertheless, it is exactly as convincing as the knowledge we receive through the senses (1858, pp. 447 f.). We believe in it.

Lotze criticized the claim of the Enlightenment that religion is only a product of human reason. If that is true, then it would be possible to replace religion with philosophy. For Lotze, reason alone is not enough to grasp the religious truth; we can learn it only through *revelation* which can be thought of as the historical *action* of God (1864, p. 546). Lotze specifically criticizes Fries, who compared religion, which starts from unproven truths, to science, which is also ultimately based on unproven axioms that we believe. According to Lotze, whereas the axioms of science are general and hypothetical judgments, the propositions of religion are apodictic.

A leading idea of Lotze's philosophy of religion was that "all the processes in nature are understandable only through the continuing involvement of God; only this involvement arranges the flow of interaction (*Übergang des Wechselwirkungs*) between different parts of the world", for example, between mind and body (p. 364). This claim can best be understood by reference to Lotze's concept of *idealities* that we already discussed (in Chapter 1, §§ 3.2, 3.3). Idealities are values that are identifiable through experience and are constitutive for all academic fields: science, mathematics, and metaphysics. To be more explicit, they help to orient our concepts and studies.

Lotze admitted that he hung the intelligibility of natural processes on the concept of God because of his anthropological stance—because of the central role the concept of humanity played in his philosophy. The important point is that, to him, the concept of humanity does not have a generic character; we can grasp it only in terms of particular individuals (p. 52). This explains why Lotze claimed that the

---

[137] The latter point was extensively discussed by Max Weber (1904/1905).

kind of purposive, creative power seen in the course of nature is thinkable only in relation to a living personality with its will. And, since the course of nature do not emanate from human will, we are doomed to stick to the *person* of God (pp. 587 ff.).

Lotze's use of God as a necessary explanatory category is reminiscent of Kant and has a clear "methodological" quality about it. We cannot *prove* the existence of God, Lotze thought, but we must nonetheless *believe* in Him—simply because our world is ultimately intelligible only this way. This point of Lotze was interpreted by the religious liberals of the *fin de siècle* (by the American Congregationalists, in particular) as supporting the claim that religion is a matter of judgment of the value in the Kingdom of God—a thesis made popular by Lotze's contemporary Albrecht Ritschl (1822–1889), who fought against the conservative-Lutheran and confessional theology of the time.

Ritschl criticized both Luther and Melanchton, who made concessions to the dogmas of the church, losing in this way the moral essence of Christianity. His theology, however, also opposed rationalism and fought for a "positive evangelical teaching" (Neugebauer 2002, p. 27). Ritschl further claimed that reformed this way, theology will be made to correspond to the spiritual needs of modernity.

4.6 Religious Practices

Lotze emphasized the fact that world-religions have started in the Orient with the picture, familiar from the Old Testament, of the world (*die Welt*) as a system that develops according to general laws. Later the West adopted this belief in the form of Christianity. In the Age of Enlightenment, however, the Occident started to look at the universe as something unfinished, giving opportunities to individuals to form it according to their specific purposes. The future was seen as formless in principle, as a chaos—so, that human action can change the world in an absolutely new way (1864, p. 331). Embracing this view, the believers effectively abandoned *vita contemplativa* and embraced *vita activa*. Reducing the horizons of human imagination to the practical tasks of the earthy world, the need to connect it with the transcendental waned. The result was the belief in progress and a turn away from God. From now on, Godhood was considered mainly in moral terms. As a result, dogma and the cult waned.

Pagans, in their most developed form of antiquity, believed in reason, in self-respect, and in the sublime. (Lotze called this stance "heroism of the pure reason".) Unfortunately, pagans failed to foster humaneness. This was the historical achievement of Christianity, which generated a totally new understanding of the moral duties. Of course, pagans recognized moral duties too. However, they understood them as having the same necessity that natural laws have. To be more specific,

Christianity—especially Protestantism—taught its believers to carry out duties following their personal conscience. In consequence, Christianity both established an immediate connection to God and made it possible for individual Christians to pursue their own values of preference, which are independent from the social background of the person and from her actual place in the society. In this way was saved respect for human dignity.

It is beyond doubt that, historically, Christianity generated the best schooling (*Bildung*) ever. However, it is not simply a teaching.[138] It requires faithfulness to the historical God, realized through revelation. That is why dogmatic theology must be preserved and cultivated. Of course, there are many ambiguities in the Holy Scriptures. These, however, result from the fact that the people of the past, those from when these scriptures were written down, had different notions about the world, law, and order than we have today.

Lotze's conclusion was that we must regard dogmatic theology as posing questions about the meaning of human life, not as giving answers. Lotze was confident that every new generation would return to these questions. Of course, dogmatic theology can be criticized. As a matter of fact, historically, Protestant theology was the best example of such criticism. But, according to Lotze, we must not cast dogmatic theology away as substantially obsolete.

---

[138] In contrast, some Lotze's contemporaries, say, Leo Tolstoy, claimed that Christianity is nothing but a moral teaching (Milkov 2004).

Part II: **Lotze and the Descriptive Psychology**

Chapter 4
Lotze and Franz Brentano

1 Brentano and the Neo-Brentanists

Franz Brentano was often presented as a solitary figure who propounded his philosophy in isolation from other contemporary philosophers in Germany. In this chapter, we shall try to correct this picture by establishing that Brentano developed his philosophical psychology while being actively engaged in the rich intellectual-historical and academic context of his time, in particular under the influence of Hermann Lotze.

The misleading image of Brentano as a solitary genius promulgated by the likes of the Neo-Brentanists is analogous to the picture of Gottlob Frege passed off as historical truth by influential Neo-Fregeans—Michael Dummett, for one. In both cases, we find a distinguished thinker portrayed as the reclusive, solitary man of genius. Thanks, however, to the research of Hans Sluga, Gottfried Gabriel, and other scholars, we now know that Frege was an active player in 19th-century German philosophy, in which he propounded the innovations in symbolic logic for which he is famous today. The same holds for Franz Brentano and the elaboration of his philosophical psychology. We shall demonstrate this in the present chapter by probing and assessing the historical, epistolary, and textual evidence.

As opposed to the image of the Neo-Brentanists, Brentano in no way saw himself as an intellectually and institutionally isolated thinker, and he certainly never represented himself as such. In perhaps his most important work, *Psychology from an Empirical Standpoint*, Brentano admitted that "[his] view, at least from one side or the other, had already begun" to be developed by other authors before him (1874, p. 4). In that context, Brentano explicitly referred to John Stuart Mill, Alexander Bain, Gustav Theodor Fechner, Hermann von Helmholtz, and, above all, to Hermann Lotze—each a near contemporary of Brentano—as thinkers to whom he owed his greatest intellectual debts (p. 3).

In fact, Brentano regularly took up and critiqued the doctrines advanced by the philosophers of his time, both German and more widely European. It is not the case, however, as is too often asserted, that he limited contact to empiricists and positivists (such as Auguste Comte). This is clear from the fact that when he traveled to Great Britain in the spring of 1872, he not only planned to pay a visit to J. S. Mill (the visit did not take place because of Mill's unexpected death) but also met with the leading evolutionary theorist and political liberal of the period, Herbert Spencer. In addition, beyond being actively engaged with the broad range of the latest philosophical thinking, Brentano was also a serious, lifelong student of scholastic and classical Greek philosophy.

That the roots of Brentano's "revolution in philosophy" are deeper than has commonly been recognized is further evidenced by what he took for granted in his writings. This is most notably seen when spelling out the ways his positions on various topics related to the views of leading 19th-century German philosophers whose doctrines were so widely familiar in the literature of the time that he felt it unnecessary to identify them by name. A telling example is Jakob Friedrich Fries, who anticipated Brentano's—and, actually, also Lotze's—rejection of the widely held notion that perception consists in a combination of ideas. Fries also anticipated Brentano by identifying "assertions" with perception, a consequential epistemological move that Alfred Kastil first pointed out over a century ago (1912, pp. 52f.), and one we shall take up in due course (in § 3.1 below). It was evidently Lotze again, who was the medium of Fries' influence on Brentano on this count.

Such shared thought-determinations and theoretical outlooks attest to the interrelations among the various currents in 19th-century German philosophy. Multiple lines of influence enabled Kastil, who edited three volumes of Brentano's writings (1921, 1925, and 1933), to trace a variety of similarities between Fries and Brentano, findings which he presented in a book of 352 pages published in the neo-Friesian journal *Abhandlungen der Fries'schen Schule*, New Series (1912).

2 An Overview of the Relationship between Lotze and Brentano

Turning directly to the relationship between Lotze and Brentano, one reads in a recent assessment that between the two philosophers "there was, to be sure, great mutual respect ... as indicated by the fact that Brentano sent two of his pupils, Anton Marty and Carl Stumpf, to study with Lotze, and also by the fact that Lotze played an important role in Brentano's call at the University of Vienna in 1874" (Rollinger 2001, p. 112).[139] Despite the impression that these particulars may convey, however, one hardly finds anything like symmetry in the relationship between Lotze and Brentano. While Lotze certainly was positively disposed toward the younger man, he regarded him as merely one of an entire cohort of rising figures in German philosophy of the time whose professional advancement he, Lotze, felt merited his advocacy. It is true that Lotze endorsed Brentano's effort to secure

---

[139] Brentano also sent another of his students, Johannes Wolff, to study with Lotze (Stumpf 1919, p. 103). Wolff would later become a professor of philosophy at Trier and Freiburg.

an appointment as a professor of philosophy at the University of Vienna. However, one should not read too much into this token of support on Lotze's part. Brentano simply met the intellectual principles that prompted Lotze to help the professional advancement of young philosophers with whom he was personally acquainted. Julius Baumann, Lotze's younger colleague in Göttingen, enumerated Lotze's criteria:

> Has the person the knowledge that is to be presupposed in philosophy today, does he also have a command of the scientific methods, and is he deadly serious in his philosophical interests? On the basis of these criteria, he has, for example, recommended Brentano for Vienna. (Baumann 1909, p. 179)

Lotze's estimate of Brentano was confirmed in person when, in June 1872, Brentano and Carl Stumpf called upon Lotze at his home near Göttingen—the eminent professor's residence, dubbed "The Coffee Grinder" by the students and professional colleagues who gathered there on a regular basis. "Lotze was friendly", Stumpf recalled decades later, "but silent, as so often" (1919, p. 125).

In summary, it is clear that while Brentano benefited a great deal both intellectually and professionally from his knowledge of and interaction with Lotze, the same could hardly be said for the by-then long established and internationally most renowned figure in the German philosophical pantheon of the era. Indeed, twenty-one years Brentano's senior, Lotze saw through to publication the third and final volume of his monumental and widely acclaimed *Mikrokosmus* in 1864 (Chapter 3), two years before Brentano had even secured his *venia legend*—the habilitation.

Lotze's influence on Brentano has previously been noted, if briefly, in the literature. More than three decades ago, E. W. Orth identified Trendelenburg and Lotze as Brentano's "teachers". As Orth put it, "Brentano's philosophical significance consists in that he made the strength of this influence paradigmatically clear in the entire spectrum of its aspects" (1997, p. 18). It is not surprising that Brentano would have learned much from Trendelenburg, having studied with Trendelenburg in Berlin. Among other evidence of Trendelenburg's influence is Brentano's deep and abiding interest in Aristotle, which is reflected in the latter's doctoral dissertation on Aristotle (1862). This was Brentano's first publication, and he dedicated it to Trendelenburg.

But there is also no mystery concerning how Lotze could prove to be a shaping influence on Brentano during the latter's formative period. The young Brentano read widely and deeply, both in the German thinkers of his age and in ancient, medieval, and modern European authors. Hence, early in his philosophical career, Brentano found that, despite "some mistakes" (charges of Brentano that we consider in the sequel), Lotze was unquestionably, on his view, the most brilliant contemporary German philosopher. "Lotze will always show himself to be the most important thinker that he indisputably is", Brentano would write to his former student and close friend Carl Stumpf on June 6, 1868 (Kaiser-el-Safti 2014, p. 16). Surprisingly enough, Brentano came to regard Lotze above his (Brentano's) Berlin mentor, Trendelenburg.

It was Stumpf who cultivated the contact between his two philosophical masters, Lotze and Brentano. Like Stumpf, Brentano, as we have noted, greatly admired Lotze, but his respect went beyond adulation and the promotion of Lotze's thought. In the winter of 1870–1871, Brentano initiated a campaign to recruit Lotze for a professorship in philosophy in Würzburg (Kaiser-el-Safti 2014, pp. 28 f.),[140] an offer which Lotze declined. Of genuine import for the history of philosophy, however, is the fact that during that period, in which Brentano worked on *Psychology from an Empirical Standpoint*, his *magnum opus*, he steeped himself in Lotze's writings. We find clear evidence of this in a letter to Carl Stumpf dated June 8, 1871:

> These days I have read a lot of Lotze, and some passages not without joy and admiration. The *Mikrokosmus*, First Volume, Second Book [*Die Seele*], contains excellent thoughts; especially his argument against the Herbartians is masterly.[141] In fact, I do not regret the praise given to him at the end of my first lectures [in Wurzburg].[142] (Kaiser-el-Safti 2014, p. 48)

That Lotze's *Mikrokosmus* was an animating component of Brentano's thinking as *Psychology from an Empirical Standpoint* took shape is manifest in the passages from Lotze's book that Brentano quotes at several key points and at greater length than he does the work of any other author.[143]

3 Relatedness

As Stumpf would ultimately put it, "Lotze's views [agreed] with those of Brentano only partially [*sehr teilweise*]" (1919, p. 102). This is borne out in a missive Stumpf received from Brentano a half century earlier. The purpose of the note, dated November 11, 1867, was to explain why Brentano had sent him to study with Lotze—because, said Brentano, "[I] couldn't name any other professor of philosophy [other

---

140 Letter from October 29, 1870.
141 See Brentano (1874, p. 113).
142 In 1867/1868, while lecturing in Würzburg, Brentano encouraged Carl Stumpf to study with Lotze; cf. his letter to Stumpf dated November 11, 1867, cited in § 3 below.
143 The citation in Brentano (1874, pp. 209–211) comes from Lotze (1856a, pp. 272–273), while the extended quotation in Brentano (1924b, pp. 16–18) comes from Lotze (1856a, pp. 200–201).

than Lotze] whose teachings I don't consider to be erroneous, and because Lotze is excellent in many ways, in spite of all his failures" (Kaiser-El-Safti 2014, p. 2).

Notwithstanding the highly qualified cast of the foregoing statements, they are consistent with a demonstrable measure of significant, albeit limited overlap between the positions of Lotze and Brentano. Just how significant this overlap is will become clear presently as we trace the following cardinal points of convergence in their position: on the content of judgment (§ 3.1), on the content of perception (§ 3.2), on the concept of intentionality (§ 3.3), on the practice of descriptive psychology (§ 3.4) and on the claim that perception is accompanied by judgment (by knowledge) and emotion (§ 3.5). With regard to these shared views, it is essential to set the record straight, for a number of influential commentators have unwarrantably claimed that it was Brentano who first introduced (or reintroduced) to 19th-century German philosophy various of the notions to which, as their writings attest, both he and Lotze subscribed. While it is true that Lotze mooted them in somewhat different form, the credit unquestionably belongs to him for first contributing to German philosophical literature penetrating treatments of them decades before Brentano.

Beyond the seminal points of convergence just passed in review, Lotze and Brentano also advanced similar philosophical programs on at least two additional fronts, one seen in their effort to recast and pursue philosophy as a rigorous science and the other in their move to introduce a stepwise or "piecemeal" approach to the prosecution of philosophy (§ 4.2 below). Significantly, both methods stood at the foundation of early analytic philosophy (Milkov 2020b, pp. 181–182, 213–214). Moreover, on these methodological scores, just as with the five more circumscribed moments of convergence, Brentano followed Lotze's lead.

3.1 Judgment and Its Content

The concepts of *judgment* and its *content* play a formative role in Lotze's logic, and they do so in Brentano's as well. The first to call attention to this shared element in Lotze and Brentano was Georg Misch, Wilhelm Dilthey's student (and son-in-law). Misch found that Brentano "agrees with Lotze's later doctrine on the main point that judgment—and value judgment [*Werturteil*], treated [by him] in parallel—is related to reality through matter-of-factness [*Sachlichkeit*]" (Misch 1912, p. xvii n.).

Lotze held that judgment is not the result of any "association of ideas", taking issue here not only with the British empiricists Hume and Mill but also with J. F.

Herbart.[144] Rejecting the philosophical logic of these thinkers, Lotze argued that judgment is not a reciprocal relation of ideas but is rather the affirmation[145] of a reciprocal relation of objective content, or of things. Put otherwise, a judgment *asserts* a *state of affairs*.[146] The content of a judgment manifests, on Lotze's view, the structure of the minimal ontological interrelation that obtains among objects (things). Lotze understood this to be the defining moment of a judgment, the thing that makes a judgment a *judgment*. The affirmation alone is what differentiates judgments from mere series (complexes) of concepts, from questions and other language forms.

Brentano also adopted Lotze's conception of the priority of judgment in logic. He reflected that standpoint when declared that "in judging, to a simple idea, a second, fundamentally different relation of consciousness to the object comes to the fore" (Brentano (1924b, p. 39), namely, that the idea is true.[147] In other words, we affirm or assert the idea.

Brentano, however, did not espouse Lotze's concept of the "state of affairs" as the content of judgments—as did Carl Stumpf (Chapter 5, § 7) who, as we have noted, studied first with Brentano and subsequently with Lotze. Instead, Brentano claimed, as did Frege later, that the content of a judgment is an object (Chrudzimski 2004). That said, Brentano, the Aristotelian, also rejected the precept of the old Aristotelian logic that judgments simply put a subject and predicate together as one concept. Here, Brentano again concurred with Lotze; more precisely, he seconded Lotze's highly consequential insistence that concepts are *functions*, not complexes of subject and predicate.

3.2 The Content of Perception

Although Lotze criticized Herbart's logic, he adopted Herbart's epistemological doctrine that the content of perception is the *given* (Chapter 1, § 4.5). Lotze charac-

---

[144] According to Oskar Kraus, Brentano closely followed Lotze's criticism of Herbart's psychology of association of ideas (1974, p. xiii). On Lotze's critique of Herbart in this particular issue, see Brentano (1874, p. 113).
[145] As remarked above (in § 1 above), Lotze inherited this idea from J. F. Fries. Lotze's "affirmation" or assertion is what, under Frege's influence, has come to be termed the "assertoric" force of a judgment.
[146] See Milkov (2002a) for a discussion of the sense in which we owe the concept of state of affairs to Lotze.
[147] The newly conceived role that judgment plays in Lotze's logic went hand-in-hand with a variation of the context-principle: "It is senseless to assert a single term; only a statement that relates the content of one term to another one can be asserted" (Lotze 1864, p. 469).

terized the given as a lived entertainment (*erleben*) of the content of perception. Furthermore, he categorially distinguished the content of perception from the content of judgment. The given, for Lotze, thus stands opposed, on the one hand, to events and facts, which is to say, to what *happens*, and, on the other, to judgments that are *asserted*—or to that whose determinate character is a function of *validity*. Unequivocally differentiating in this manner events and facts from judgments, Lotze derived from the ontological difference that sets events and facts apart from validities a fundamental metaphysical distinction between *genesis* and *being*, between "happens" and "is" (Chapter 2, § 12).

To appreciate the groundbreaking and highly influential nature of Lotze's non-representational epistemology, one may turn, for example, to Oskar Kraus (1974), who called attention to the manifest similarities in the epistemologies of Brentano, Johannes Rehmke (Milkov 2004), and Hans Driesch—all three of whom eschewed the representative (*Abbild*) theory of perception and knowledge. That the three thinkers hardly exhibit complete agreement, however, will become clear if we examine the Lotzean notion of the content of perception. Brentano inherited from Lotze this way of conceiving of acts of perception as having content, whereas Rehmke and Driesch, who evinced little interest in Lotze's writings, did not.

Among other things, Lotze's position that the content of perception is "the given" is no less than the origin, still little-recognized, of the philosophical concept of "sense-data", which historically has been assumed to be an innovation of Anglophone philosophers. In fact, however, it was Lotze's lectures in metaphysics that inspired Josiah Royce to formulate the notion.[148] A short time later, the term "sense-data" acquired currency in the thought and writings of William James, who, like his close friend and Harvard colleague, Royce, nurtured the highest respect for Lotze. Ultimately, however, "sense-data" as a foundational epistemological notion was to receive its greatest impetus in the widely influential early work of G. E. Moore and Bertrand Russell, the founding fathers of analytical philosophy (Milkov 2001) (Chapter 8, § 3). This lineage of a historically formative 20th-century epistemological concept is but one of numerous examples of how Lotze's thought, a catalytic element in Brentano's development and independent philosophical contributions, proved to be seminal in currents of philosophical thinking that otherwise have little in common with Brentano.

Also, Brentano's descriptive psychology builds upon Lotze's view that the acts of perception have specific content. What distinguishes Brentano's position from

---

148 In the spring and summer of 1876, Royce took two courses, one in metaphysics and the other in practical philosophy, with Lotze in Göttingen, whom he deemed "the first in constructive philosophers now living in Germany" (Royce 1970, p. 49) (Introduction, § 3).

that of Lotze in this context is the distinction that Brentano draws between inner and outer experience. The phenomena of Brentano's descriptive psychology are part of our inner experience alone,[149] which he regarded as discrete from outer experience. Phenomena exist, in other words, only in our mind and not in the external world, our contact with the latter occurring by way of outer experience.

This account of Brentano's exhibits only a distant kinship to Lotze's epistemology. As we have already seen (Chapter 2, §§ 8f.), Lotze championed the view that we can acquire empirical knowledge only through the idealities that belong to the mentally given, not to material reality. But idealities require matter in order to become valid. That is why they inhere in our sensible life, as, for instance, in empirically keyed feelings of pleasure and displeasure (§ 3.5 below). This explains why we have no a priori idea of *blue*, for example, or of *sweet* (Lotze 1864, p. 241). We know qualia exclusively in experience.

3.3 Intentionality

A most significant but historically ignored or overlooked fact concerning Brentano's debt to Lotze is that it was Lotze who laid the groundwork for Brentano's signature contribution to philosophy—the (re)introduction of the notion of intentionality.[150] Recently, Frederick Beiser briefly noted that alongside his famed distinction between validity and reality, Lotze had also discriminated between intentionality and existence (2016, p. 87). Regrettably, Beiser does little more than call attention to this key move of Lotze. Some two decades before Beiser, E. W. Orth published a more detailed analysis of Lotze's thinking on this count. Orth pointed out that, alongside Adolf Trendelenburg, Lotze set the stage for Brentano's introduction of the notion of intentionality when he articulated the idea of the evolving (*sich entwickelnden*) mind in philosophy. To be more explicit, Orth rightly recognized as "decisive" in this respect that Trendelenburg and Lotze defended "the absolute incomparability of mental with physical phenomena and of the primacy of the mental phenomena over the physical" (1997, p. 24).

---

[149] Uriah Kriegel emphasizes that intentionality is not the only key concept in Brentano's descriptive psychology. The claim that mental phenomena are objects of inner perception is exactly as important. But while intentionality is the underlying nature of the mental, the inner-perceivability is the "concept's reference-fixer" (2017, p. 197).

[150] Some authors call it "Brentano's Thesis" (Textor 2017). In fact, the notion of intentionality was already used by Plato (*Parm.* 132b), Aristotle, and Aquinas (Milkov 1992, pp. 50–51).

In more concrete terms, of special importance for Brentano's move to (re)introduce the problem of intentionality in the modern philosophical curriculum was Lotze's conception that mental acts have content. In particular, the Lotzean influence is apparent in the way Brentano initially presented that concept, not even employing the term "intentionality" as such, but speaking instead of the "reference to a content" (Poli 1998, p. 4): "Every mental phenomenon is characterized ... by what we shall call ... the relation to a content, the direction toward an object, ... or the immanent objectivity [*Gegenständlichkeit*]"[151] (Brentano 1874, pp. 124–125). But the (re)introduction of the concept of intentionality in philosophy was also prepared by Lotze's conception of substance as an entity "that is capable to effect and to suffer" (Lotze 1879, p. 481) (Chapter 1, § 4.5).

By way of conclusion regarding this topic, we shall adduce Paul Linke's remark made well over sixty years ago that Gottlob Frege discovered "on his own" (i.e., independently of Brentano) the intentional relation of consciousness—this from the standpoint of "the lived experience [*Erlebnis*] of logical thinking" (1961, p. 55; Hill 1998, p. 45). Frege namely contended that the sense of propositions is something that we livingly grasp. *Pace* Linke, we explain this otherwise puzzling affinity between Frege and Brentano's school by reference to the relatedness of Frege's logic to that Lotze's, something that nowadays is an established fact (Gabriel 1989a). If we connect this point with Lotze's relatedness to Brentano—we have already said much about it above—then the genealogical circle of influence gets closed: parts of Frege's logic show relatedness to Brentano and his school only because both Brentano and Frege adopted vital ideas of Lotze.

3.4 Descriptive Psychology

Over a period of decades, Lotze addressed various problems of descriptive psychology that Brentano and his followers made their special field. To distinguish the character of descriptive psychology in this context is to disclose pivotal, yet rarely discussed continuities in the thinking of the two philosophers.

Brentano insisted that we need first to *describe* phenomena before we are in a position to *explain* them or to pursue genetic psychology in general. It is in this regard that Brentano's analysis of the content of mind constitutes a form of de-

---

[151] Brentano discerned in Lotze seven different types of mental relation to a content: (i) sensation, (ii) perception, (iii) relating perception, (iv) space intuition (*Anschauung*), (v) time intuition, (vi) emotions, (vii) will (1988, pp. 59 f.).

scriptive psychology.[152] In other words, Brentano held that description is prior to explanation and, accordingly, to genetic psychology, "which seeks to find the laws of mental event as unfolding in time" (Smith 1994, p. 30). It deserves notice, however, that while descriptive psychology was the prime discipline of Brentano and his school, Lotze, in fact, practiced it for decades. More especially, his analysis of the content of perception was, in fact, a form of descriptive psychology.

Lotze also brought in the distinction between genetic and descriptive science. He strongly distinguished among (i) the given or what is, (ii) what happens (Chapter 2, § 12), e.g., what changes (i.e., what is "genetic"), and (iii) what is valid. In line with this distinction, Lotze also introduced and discussed at length the distinction between what is genetic and the validities. Descriptive psychology is only interested in validities and not in explanatory, genetic accounts of psychical phenomena.

Furthermore, and most germane to modern psychology, Lotze employed the term "mind" throughout his writings as a *terminus technicus:* as "a phenomenological expression that summarizes a series of phenomena" (1850, p. 453; 1852a, pp. 137ff.). He repudiated views of the mind that define it as an individual or as a substance (Chapter 2, § 10). To lift a trope derived from Lotze, one made famous by William James, mind is a "stream of consciousness" constituting nothing but a discrete series of phenomena. In fact, it makes no sense to confine what mind denotes in philosophical psychology to a *single* configuration of psychic phenomena. One can properly approach the variety of mental phenomena only by taking a strictly *descriptive* route which is precisely the methodology that Lotze had in mind *when* he employed the term "*descriptive* psychology" (Orth 1997, p. 22).

Significantly, Brentano introduced the discipline of descriptive psychology as a Cartesian science in an effort to provide sound foundations for both science and philosophy. From this perspective, he severely criticized Kant's epistemology. Roughly, while Kant was more of a constructivist thinker, Brentano was a kind of monolithic philosopher. While Kant developed a particular "predilection for constructions", Brentano intended to explore the "things themselves".[153]

Historically, Brentano opposed Kant based on some ideas of Aristotle.[154] In this context, it is important to note that the picture of Brentano drawn by some histor-

---

[152] On this count, Brentano's descriptive psychology instructively compares with that of Wilhelm Dilthey, upon whose thinking, as was the case with Brentano, Lotze exerted formative influence (Orth 1995/1996). Dilthey developed his ideas on the divide between descriptive and explanatory psychology in (1894).
[153] Husserl adopted this phrase of Brentano and made it the top maxim of his phenomenology.
[154] Ultimately, Brentano's move paralleled Leibniz's turn back to Aristotle (in Leibniz's case, to Aristotle's "substantial forms") as a means of opposing the radically mechanical philosophy of John Locke (Milkov 2006a).

ians, according to which "Brentano's philosophy is part of the Aristotelian Renaissance which began with Bonitz's, Tricot's and Schwegler's works on Aristotle, and continued with Trendelenburg's *Geschichte der Kategorienlehre*" (Libardi 1996, p. 26), is incomplete. In fact, the Aristotelian Renaissance itself was part and parcel of a massive movement against Kant's formalism that was started in Germany by Friedrich Schleiermacher and continued by philosophers and logicians like Trendelenburg, Lotze and Frege. The latter, in particular, insisted that his logic, in contrast to that of George Boole, is not formal but rather a logic of content.

3.5 Perception, Knowledge, and Emotions

Brentano found deeply persuasive Lotze's observation that a feeling of pleasure or displeasure attaches to every idea (*Vorstellung*) we perceive.[155] As he saw it, it was just this discerning perception that led Lotze to find in the concept of "values" a core principle of philosophy (Brentano 1924b, p. 93). Later, it also stimulated the psychoanalysts. Sandor Ferenczi, an early member of Freud's inner circle, declared that "this idea of Lotze's agrees with ideas of psychoanalysis that were achieved through empirical ways to such an extent that we can consider him ... as a predecessor of Freud" (1913, p. 238).

Another of Lotze's findings that Brentano took as a point of departure for his own investigation was that judgments accompany all mental acts (Brentano 1874, p. 195). Lotze, for his part, maintained that perception—including that which distinguishes cognition in imagining, dreaming, and daydreaming—does not only present a "kaleidoscope" of pictures (*Bilder*) (Lotze 1843a, p. 72). It also produces "secondary thoughts" (*Nebengedanken*) that only connect those of the perceived images that intrinsically belong together (Milkov 2002a). Lotze understood this secondary relation or synthesis of perceptual *Bilder* to be the process by means of which we acquire knowledge (Chapter 1, § 4.3; Chapter 2, n. 91).

4 Agreements

Besides the multiple points of convergence that we have traced in Lotze and Brentano—a shared constellation of ideas that testifies to Brentano's profound debt to

---

[155] Indeed, it is precisely in this context that Brentano twice adduced extended passages from Lotze's *Mikrokosmus* in three consecutive pages in his *Psychology from an Empirical Standpoint* (see n. 143).

his senior colleague—there are at least two further, *methodological* aspects of their doctrines that reflect a still deeper meeting of the minds in their most influential work.

4.1 Philosophy as a Rigorous Science

Lotze and Brentano shared the project of establishing philosophy as a rigorous science.

Brentano pursued this end in terms of an "empirical" scientific philosophical psychology. To be more explicit, he spoke about "introspective empiricism", as it was referred to in the literature. The exclusive focus of Brentano's doctrine was the inner experience, on which ground it is arguably possible to build up a scientific psychology that can also serve as a basal science for aesthetics, logic, pedagogy, ethics, and politics.

To put it otherwise, Brentano maintained that descriptive psychology provides sound foundations for all humanities. Its task is to reveal and describe their building blocks and to define their concepts.[156] In a sense, descriptive psychology is thus important to humanities as physics is to natural sciences. This is the case since the only difference of the humanities, when compared to the natural sciences, is that they explore (very) complex mental acts. Theory of knowledge, for its part, makes inquiries into the content of judgments (not of the concepts) and their relation to truth. In other words, it investigates the justification of knowledge.

In fact, humanities all prove mutually consistent, indeed orientationally complementary if approached from the standpoint of introspective empiricism. In contrast, Brentano found that such consistency fails to obtain if one regards them from the stance of metaphysics—which the logical positivists would later dismiss as "pseudoscience".

Basically, Brentano maintained that his novel "empirical psychology" made it possible to fix the basic laws of his sciences with "the same sharpness and precision as the axioms of mathematics do" (1874, p. 67). Furthermore, he conceived his doctrine as "the *science of the future* [...] that would allow a significant influence on practical life" (p. 36). Brentano was convinced, moreover, as was later Frege, that there is only one truth and only a single "realm of truth" (p. 5). That philosophy could develop itself as an independent discipline so late historically, following

---

[156] A related program for renewing all humanities, posing them to realistic foundations that are to be explored by the "linguistic phenomenology" was advanced by J. L. Austin (Milkov 2003, pp. 165–167).

Brentano's project, is something he attributed to the fact that its elements are signally more convoluted than the defining moments of the other sciences—in particular, of the elements, or the "objects", of such exact sciences as mathematics and physics.

It should be clear by now that the mutually commensurate innovations of Brentano and Frege are historically and philosophically pivotal outgrowths of Hermann Lotze's philosophy.[157] Brentano himself perhaps best spelled out what underlies Lotze's formative influence, namely

> the method of his way of doing philosophy, the weight that he places upon experience and observation, the manner in which he uses the results of natural science, the caution and conscientiousness with which he makes his claims.[158] (Kaiser-El-Safti 2014, p. 2)

4.2 Similarity of Philosophical Approach

Most current students of Brentano, indeed of the history of 20th-century philosophy at large, are either unaware of or have failed to credit the cumulative significance of the evidence developed in the foregoing pages. However, the import of our historically substantiated reflections shall become even clearer if we consider in more general terms the striking similarities of approach in the philosophies of Lotze and Brentano. In the century since Brentano's death, his thought has had a growing impact on major currents of Western philosophy. After decades of unwarranted neglect in the end of the nineteenth and the first half of the twentieth centuries, his works ultimately received their due recognition and have inspired generations of descriptive psychologists, phenomenologists, and new ontologists. Oddly enough, for many years during Brentano's lifetime (he died in 1917), philosophical debate centered on the work of his students—Edmund Husserl, Carl Stumpf, Alexius Meinong, Kazimierz Twardowski, and Anton Marty—while virtually ignoring Brentano himself, the founding father of the new philosophical movement. The "Brentano puzzle" and the "Brentano invisibility" are how later historians of philosophy would refer to the unaccountable marginalization or absence of Brentano's name in the leading studies of the time (Poli 1998, p. 1).

If anything, such neglect was to prove even more egregious in the case of Lotze, whom John Passmore aptly described as the "most pillaged philosopher" in 20th-century thought (Introduction, § 4.2). This is a factor that must be laid at

---

[157] In § 3.3 above, we briefly discussed the parallel and independent influence of Lotze on Brentano's and on Frege's conception of intentionality.
[158] Letter from November 3, 1867.

Lotze's own feet, and it is at least partially responsible for his relegation largely to the margins in the literature down our own day. The issue is Lotze's own attitude toward how he wished his philosophical contributions to be exploited by those who found inspiration in his works. In fact, this attitude reflects nothing so much as Lotze's revolutionary break with the encyclopedic systematicity of philosophy, that, culminating with the classic German idealists, held sway until his day as the regulative idea of serious philosophical thought.

Lotze struck out metaphysically in a radically new direction by analyzing philosophical problems on a "piecemeal" basis. Consequently, he addressed the *aporiai* to which he devoted his theoretical energies each on its own grounds and not, as had been the practice of the leading German idealists, by approaching it on the basis of its formal relation to the solution of other philosophical issues. As Passmore rightly discerned, "it was precisely his *lack* of system on which his influence depended" (1966, p. 51). This method would be later adopted by Bertrand Russell, who referred to it as "piecemeal" philosophy (1918b, p. 85). Russell further insisted that only by means of such a methodology could philosophy develop as a rigorous science.[159]

The same holds true for Franz Brentano. Like Lotze, Brentano

> wrote no philosophical system. He discussed certain fundamental problems [of philosophy], just as the scientists contribute to the slowly developing science, by making relatively finite investigations of particular laws.[160] (Puglisi 1913, pp. 16–17)

5 Differences between Lotze and Brentano

Despite the highly significant points of convergence with Lotze that we have reviewed thus far, Brentano was without question an independent thinker. The independence of his mind is unmistakable in the explicit criticism that he leveled at Lotze. What must count as one of the most hard-hitting examples of this criticism occurs in the letter to his former student and friend Carl Stumpf from March 3, 1867:

> I am far from approving [Lotze's] opinions throughout. [He is] too much influenced by Kant's criticism. ... That he does not know the [philosophy of the] Middle Ages and therefore does not appreciate it,[161] cannot be a surprise to you. It also seems to me that he has very limited knowledge of the ancient philosophy.[162] (Kaiser-El-Safti 2014, p. 2)

---

159 For an account of Lotze's influence on Russell, see Chapter 6.
160 See § 3 above.
161 In contrast to Brentano, Husserl spoke about Lotze's "scholastic realism" (Introduction, § 2).

Two of the more specific objections that Brentano raised against Lotze target the latter's local-signs theory of perception and his atomism. Brentano dismissed these as constructivist doctrines and hence as, in his view, retrogressively Kantian. At any rate, Lotze's atomism and his doctrine of local-signs are in no way descriptive, and on that count, they are epistemologically antithetical to Brentano's "nativist" psychology (Chapter 2, § 8). Moreover, Brentano's radical form of nativism, according to which mental phenomena are innate, made him leery of Lotze's advocacy of experimental investigations in psychology. Tellingly, it was on precisely these grounds that Brentano would ultimately find himself at cross purposes with his student Carl Stumpf, who undertook to combine nativist psychology with experimental psychology (Chapter 5, § 4). As a matter of fact, Stumpf became a champion of experimental psychology under the influence of his PhD and habilitation supervisor Lotze. Needless to say, Stumpf's venture left Brentano cold.

More generally, Brentano repudiated what he detected as lingering elements of German Idealism in Lotze. One such holdover that struck him as particularly unacceptable was Lotze's principle of teleomechanism (Chapter 2, § 4). Brentano saw it as a concession to Hegel. In this context, he found it exasperating that "in spite of all [his] sciences" Lotze failed "to overcome even the Hegel disease" (Brentano 1989, pp. 7f.).[163] Brentano complained, moreover, that while Lotze's writings commence along promising and compelling lines, they often trail off "in a most foggy swindle". He found it a pity that in Lotze, over and over again, "something [that] begins so sober, ends so drunken and hypnagogically blurred" (pp. 7f.).

Unsurprisingly, Brentano also rejected Lotze's tripartite classification of mental phenomena into imagination, emotional excitement, and striving (will), which the latter apparently adopted from Kant (1924b, p. 22).[164] Brentano found this taxonomy hopelessly abstract, objecting that not only does it fail to credit the differences among diverse phenomena; in addition, more fundamentally, it fails to discriminate the different ways that the mind refers to its objects. Brentano, for his part, divided mental phenomena into ideas, judgments, and emotions (the phenomena of hate and love) (p. 33).

---

[162] That Brentano was mistaken on this account shows Husserl's assessment of Lotze's Platonism (Introduction, § 2).
[163] Letter to Stumpf from February 15, 1868.
[164] Brentano mistakenly assumed that Lotze inherited this classification from William Hamilton.

Chapter 5
Lotze and Carl Stumpf

1 Introduction

Carl Stumpf was a key figure in *fin de siècle* Germanophone philosophy. Unfortunately, after the Second World War, interest in Stumpf as a philosopher waned. The authors of Stumpf's *Festshrift*, dedicated to him on his 75th birthday (Koffka 1923), were not philosophers but mainly psychologists from the Berlin Institute of Psychology, founded by Stumpf in 1906, including the leading Gestalt-psychologists Max Wertheimer, Wolfgang Köhler and Kurt Lewin.

The interest in Carl Stumpf's philosophy has only been revived over the last twenty years. The Neo-Brentanists were of great service in this development. But while the association of Carl Stumpf with Franz Brentano has fostered Stumpf studies,[165] it also gave rise to one-sided interpretations of Stumpf as a philosopher. In this way, many facets of his importance and idiosyncrasy as philosopher remained in the shadows. In this context, it deserves notice that before the Second World War, Carl Stumpf was considered to be an autonomous, philosophically oriented psychologist, not simply another member of Franz Brentano's school (Moog 1922, pp. 157–161; Lehmann 1943, pp. 107–113).

One of the objectives of this chapter is to free Stumpf from Brentano—to try to see him as an autonomous philosopher. There is no better means of achieving this task than study of the relatedness between Carl Stumpf and his doctoral and habilitation dissertation supervisor Hermann Lotze.

2 Biographical Notes

Carl Stumpf was born on April 21, 1848, in the municipality of Wiesentheid, Franconia. Between 1859 and 1865, he attended the gymnasium in Bamberg and in Aschaffenburg. In 1865, Stumpf matriculated at the University of Würzburg. The next year, he began attending Franz Brentano's lectures. One year later, following Brentano's advice, Stumpf started post-graduate study with Hermann Lotze in Göttingen. In 1867/1868, he wrote his PhD thesis on "The Relation of Plato's God to the Idea of Good" (1868). In the same year, Stumpf returned to Würzburg in order to continue studying with Brentano. In 1870, however, he went back to Göttingen,

---

165 In 2010, the Carl Stumpf Society was founded in Germany.

where he wrote the second dissertation (*Habilitation*), "On the Basic Laws of Mathematics", once again under Lotze's supervision. Supported by Lotze's recommendation, between 1870 and 1973, Stumpf was appointed an adjunct professor (*Privatdozent*) in Göttingen. Later, he remembered that while in Göttingen, Lotze became his devoted fatherly adviser (1917, p. 5). It cannot be a surprise, therefore, that Stumpf's first book, *Über den psychologischen Ursprung der Raumvorstellung* (1873), which was praised by such figures as William James and Bertrand Russell, was dedicated to Lotze. Lotze and Stumpf remained in close contact even after the latter left Göttingen in 1873.

Stumpf, however, was explicit that Brentano played a central role in his philosophical development. Later, he remembered: "My whole understanding of philosophy, the correct and mistaken methods of philosophizing, the basic and essential doctrines of logic and epistemology, psychology, ethics and metaphysics, which I still maintain today, are his doctrines" (1919, p. 144). But Stumpf also noted that "[Lotze's] way of thinking had influenced my own more than Brentano wanted it to be the case, despite the fact that the outline of my epistemology remained that of Brentano" (1924, pp. 4–5). Apparently, Stumpf was under the formative influence of both Brentano and Lotze. Unfortunately, Brentano was an authoritative teacher who could not stand theoretical dissents on the part of his students. The effect of this side of his academic character was clearly negative for Stumpf—it narrowed the scope of his philosophical explorations (§ 6 below).

In 1873, at the age of 25, Stumpf was already a full professor in philosophy in Würzburg as successor of Brentano who moved to Vienna (Lotze was instrumental for this appointment again). There followed a series of professorships that Stumpf changed every five years—from 1879 until 1884 in Prague, until 1889 in Halle, and until 1894 in Munich. In that year, Stumpf became professor at the Friedrich Wilhelm University in Berlin, where he remained until the end of his days. Between 1907 and 1909, he was a chancellor of that University. In 1878, Stumpf married Hermine Biedermann (1849–1930). He died on December 25, 1936.

These facts suggest that Carl Stumpf was a key figure in *fin de siècle* Germanophone philosophy. As already mentioned, after the First World War, interest in him as a philosopher waned. One reason for this was that in the 1920s, the attention of the mainstream philosophers shifted in the direction of the rising rivalry between analytic and continental philosophy. Besides, Stumpf worked not only in philosophy but also in general psychology, in comparative musicology, and in ethnomusicology. Furthermore, in contrast to his professor Brentano but similar to his other professor, Lotze, Stumpf did not set up his own philosophical school (§ 6, (ii) below). His endeavor was only to motivate his students to make their own explorations in a scientific spirit. Finally, because of the outbreak of the Second World War, his major work, *Theory of Knowledge* (1939/1940), remained widely ignored.

In his long academic career, Stumpf supervised 23 PhD dissertations. Most prominent were his Berlin doctoral students, the upcoming gestalt psychologists Kurt Koffka, Wolfgang Köhler, and Kurt Lewin as well as the novelist Robert Musil. Stumpf also supervised Edmund Husserl's second dissertation (habilitation) *On the Concept of Number* (1887). In a sign of gratitude, Husserl dedicated his groundwork, *Logical Investigations* (1900/1901), to Stumpf. Stumpf had a wide circle of friends and colleagues. While in Göttingen, alongside his close friend, the mathematician Felix Klein, he set up the "Eskimo Society". This was an interdisciplinary society of young Göttingen dons, in which scholars of philosophy, physics, chemistry and mineralogy were presented. While in Prague, he was close friends with another student of Brentano and Lotze, Anton Marty, and had contact with Ernst Mach and Ewald Hering (§ 4 below). In Halle, Stumpf was often together with Georg Cantor and Johann Eduard Erdmann. Starting in 1882, Stumpf had a number of meetings with William James while the latter was in Germany. The two maintained a vivid mail correspondence for years (1928).

As a young philosopher, Stumpf was seriously working in philosophy of mathematics, which, as already mentioned, was the subject of his habilitation (1870). In it, he followed Lotze's idea that mathematics (not only arithmetic, as another student of Lotze, Gottlob Frege, maintained) can be reduced to logic. In this context, Stumpf held to Lotze's belief that non-Euclidean geometry is "nonsense". Soon, however, Felix Klein convinced him that new developments in mathematics made this position problematic. In consequence, Stumpf decided not to publish his habilitation.[166] It is also probable that Stumpf met Frege in Göttingen, who, between 1871 and 1873, was a doctoral student in mathematics there. This is indicated by the close similarities between Stumpf's 1870 arguments against Mill's philosophy of mathematics and these of Frege in his *The Foundations of Arithmetic* (1884), to say the least.[167] In contrast, it is a matter of fact that Stumpf gave Frege the nod to write this non-technical book (*The Foundations*) after he published *Begriffschrift* (1879), which remained widely unnoticed or misunderstood in Germany.

---

[166] It was only published in 2008.
[167] In fact, the title of Stumpf's habilitation, *Die Grundsätze der Mathematik* (*The Basic Laws of Mathematics*) (1870), already reveals its relatedness to Frege's philosophy of mathematics, the title of its main work being *Die Grundgesetze der Arithmetik* (*The Basic Laws of Arithmetic*) (1893/1903).

3 Zeitgeist

Traditionally, philosophers are classified in groups and circles according to the countries in which they were born, received their educations, and made academic careers. But it can also be insightful to put together philosophers who were born in the same year. If we follow this approach, we shall notice that many influential European philosophers were born in 1848: the year of sweeping political revolutions all over Europe. Besides Carl Stumpf, in that year were also born Gottlob Frege, Wilhelm Windelband, Hermann Diels, Johannes Rehmke, and Johannes Volkelt, in Germany as well as Arthur Balfour and Bernard Bosanquet in the United Kingdom were born. The question arises: what shaped the philosophical formation of this group of philosophers?

Undoubtedly, an important factor in the intellectual development of these philosophers was the outstanding figure of Hermann Lotze. At least four of these authors, Windelband, Frege, Stumpf, and Bonsanquet, were directly influenced by Lotze: Windelband was his doctoral student and closest follower, Frege visited Lotze's lectures and later tried to digest Lotze's "greater" *Logic* in his "17 Key Sentences to Logic", and Bosanquet was instrumental in the translation of the same book of Lotze and also his "greater" *Metaphysic* into English (1884–1885) (Introduction, § 2). The present chapter will show that Lotze considerably influenced Carl Stumpf as well.

Of course, there were also other philosophers of the time who considerably influenced the philosophers born in 1848. One of them was Lotze's oldest ally in the fight against subjectivism in philosophy, Adolf Trendelenburg. Another figure from the same epoch was Otto Liebmann, whose famous book *Kant und die Epigonen* (1865) gave birth to the movement of Neo-Kantianism.

A legion of other scientifically oriented philosophers also inspired and educated the generation of 1848: Fries, Herbart, and Fechner, among others. This point speaks against the claim that "the years from 1830 to 1870 circa were a period of a crisis and decline for philosophy in Germany" (Libardi 1996, p. 31). Exactly the opposite was the case. Between 1840 and 1870, German philosophy was on the rise, so that, a little bit later, it could prompt the emergence of Neo-Kantianism, analytic philosophy, and phenomenology. The historical mission of the generation of 1848 was that it realized (materialized) its achievements. Unfortunately, many of these developments remained in the shadows until today.

4 Stumpf's Descriptive Psychology

The crucial point on which Lotze, Brentano and Stumpf agreed was that philosophy is to be developed together with science. Stumpf in particular maintained that it is a very general science. It thus forms a continuum with science. One can also say that philosophy is "after-science" (*Nachwissenschaft*); it investigates the common laws of all sciences. It is a theory of the world (*Welttheorie*) (Stumpf 1906, p. 43). For this purpose, it also uses the achievements of the so called "neutral sciences"—phenomenology, theory of forms (*Eidologie*), and general theory of relations, which serve as *organon* of sciences (Stumpf 1906, pp. 26 ff.).

In more specific terms, Stumpf held that both Lotze and Brentano explored "structural characteristics of mental functions" (1924, p. 46).[168] The point is that in the realm of phenomena, there are such things as "immanent laws of structure" that are rather different from the causal laws—the latter are not valid in this realm (1906, p. 28). The "laws of structure" are mainly of two types: those explored by descriptive psychology, and those explored by, what we have already called (Introduction, § 4.3) "philosophical logic". We are going to discuss the former in the remainder of this section and the latter in § 5 below.

Closely following Brentano, in his epistemology, Stumpf severely criticized Kant's formalism. Kant did not adopt the distinction between form and qualia based on scientific (psychological) discussion but through voided a priori logical deliberations. The point is that "nothing can be epistemologically true and psychologically false" (1891, p. 482). Kant's formalism was patently detrimental to the development of both philosophy and psychology. Against Kant's constructivism, Brentano and Stumpf introduced the discipline of descriptive psychology, which explores the ultimate phenomena of human mind. It is a Cartesian science. The phenomena themselves, such as perceptions, are either the content of mental acts or its functions. Indeed, space, time, and causality, declared by Kant to be a priori forms of human reason, are nothing but contents of consciousness, each of them with specific multiplicity (p. 485).

Following the physiologist Ewald Hering, Carl Stumpf considered the descriptive psychology *nativist*—it explores the origin of our mental states: "Nativists are called those [scientists] who assume the initial [*Ursprüngliche*], [and] empiricists, those who embrace genetic explanations" (1883, p. 96). In other words, Stumpf identified "empirical psychology" with "genetic psychology". Brentano, in contrast, understood descriptive psychology as empiricist psychology.

---

[168] In other places, Stumpf identifies "Lotze and Brentano [as] the great masters of analytic psychology and introspection" (1928, p. 28).

But did Brentano and Stumpf defend radically different positions on this matter? In order to answer this question, we shall, first, underline that both Lotze and Stumpf combined nativism and experimental psychology. In other words, in contrast to Brentano, Stumpf was both a descriptive psychologist and, at the same time, an external (non-introspective) experiential psychologist who checked the results he achieved in his nativist descriptions with experiments, without, however, committing a "genetic fallacy": without becoming a genetic psychologist. Brentano's psychology, for its part, "was empirical without being experimental" (Libardi 1996, p. 36). In fact, Brentano advanced a new kind of empiricism that can be also called "introspective empiricism".

Furthermore, exactly like Lotze, Stumpf was not only a philosopher but also a scientist. In contrast, despite the fact that in his dissertation, Brentano declared that "the true method of philosophy is none other than that of the natural science", he never did "real science" (Ewen 2008, p. 21).[169] In particular, Brentano was never occupied with psychological experiments, preferring instead to do introspective armchair psychological research.

In this context, it deserves notice that in his address to the Friedrich Wilhelm University of Berlin as its Rector in 1907, "The Renaissance of Philosophy", Stumpf repeatedly referred to Fechner and Lotze as his predecessors, not to Brentano. Some authors explain this with the "confessional biases of that epoch" in Germany, keeping in mind that Stumpf read his address at the Prussian and Protestant Berlin University (Münch 2006, p. 57, n. 21). In truth, it refers, at least to some extent, to a serious divergence between Carl Stumpf's and Franz Brentano's philosophy.[170]

Indeed, compared with Brentano, "Stumpf had a drastically different idea of what scientific methodology actually is. Unlike Brentano, he left no place for any prominence of inner perception and its alleged evidence" (Martinelli 2006, p. 82). This gave Ricardo Martinelli sufficient reason to call him an "empiricist".[171] As we already have seen, however, Carl Stumpf understood himself as a nativist, not as an empiricist. But what Stumpf meant when he criticized empiricism was, in fact, the "genetic" approach in psychology, as practised by colleagues of his like Wilhelm Wundt, with whom Stumpf was engaged in heated polemic (1891).

Be this as it may, Stumpf magisterially institutionalized his experimental stance. In 1890, he launched the prestigious journal *Zeitschrift für Psychologie und Physiologie der Sinnesorgane*, and in 1898, he founded the journal *Beiträge zur Akustik und Musikwissenschaft*. In 1900, Stumpf founded the Institute of Psy-

---

[169] Among other things, this point found expression in Brentano's negative attitude to Einstein's Theory of Relativity—he found it "incoherent", as did his acolyte Oskar Kraus (1925).
[170] We shall address this point again in § 6 below.
[171] Schuhmann (2000/1), pp. 63 ff. did the same.

chology in Berlin (he directed it until 1922) and also The Society for Child Psychology. In 1912–1913, he established a station for anthropoids in Tenerife and made his former student Wolfgang Köhler its first director.

We have already noted (in Chapter 4, § 5) that Brentano openly criticized Lotze's theory of local-signs. To remind the reader (Chapter 2, § 8), Stumpf joined Brentano in this criticism (1917, p. 5). Above all, Brentano and Stumpf were against the increased role that Lotze's theory of judgment assigned to the free will. In other words, they were against the involvement of a will-informed action that constitutes our reality. In fact, Lotze embraced this theory following an idea of J. G. Fichte (Chapter 2, § 9). In other words, it was a trace of German Idealism in his philosophy—a trace that both Brentano and Stumpf felt to be alien to their supra-objectivist intuitions.

At the same time, against Brentano and Husserl but following Lotze, Stumpf criticized Fechner's conception of psychophysical parallelism, according to which mind and matter are aspects of one and the same reality (stuff) (Chapter 2, § 3). Instead, he adopted a dualist position of interaction of mind and body (1919).

5 Stumpf's Analytic Method

Stumpf's extensive use of experimental methods in descriptive psychology was only possible because he, following Lotze once again, took an idiosyncratic analytic method as the starting point of descriptive psychology. In short, Stumpf's analytic psychology held that

> through analysis [Zergliederung] of "impressions", we reach the ultimate elements of concepts that we use in the ordinary thinking; elements that in the scientific thinking are combined in different ways, according to their needs. (1891, p. 491)

In contrast, following his transcendental argument, Kant was not interested in the origins (Ursprunge) of space, time, and causality but rather in what these concepts contribute to the scientific discourse. Besides, Kant failed to analyse what he meant under "intuitions", so they remain complex ideas. According to him, space, for example, is perceived through different senses that grasp different parts of it: place, magnitude, etc.

Stumpf's final objective was to illuminate the "absolute contents" of our mind, especially our ideas of space and time. In this context, he argued against the conception of relativity of perception, defended by Fechner again. According to the latter, every perception receives its meaning through connection with other perceptions. In contrast, Stumpf held that tones, smells, colors, and tastes are absolute qualities (1883, p. 137).

Furthermore, Stumpf explored the psychological origins of our ideas by way of analysing complex ideas to their constituents. The decisive point is that the complex is not just a sum, but it is also not an "organic unity".[172] The relation between complexes and elements is a relation between parts and whole. However, there are parts that are independent from the whole, and there also parts that are "ontologically dependent" on it.

Of course, Brentano's descriptive psychology was also analytic psychology.[173] However, Stumpf added to it important new elements. To be more explicit, his analytic psychology presents a way of disclosing immanent laws of structure alternative to that of descriptive psychology. This venue of exploration was another of Stumpf's debts to Hermann Lotze, in particular to his philosophical logic (Introduction, § 4.3). The prime example of Lotze's philosophical logic was his method of recasting specific problems of German Idealism in a refined, logical form. Stumpf's most important discovery in this area was that a kind of space is already given with the idea of quality: we cannot imagine space without a color, nor a color without space. This idea of Stumpf profoundly influenced Edmund Husserl's theory of grounding (*fundieren*)—there are concepts that exist autonomously, and there are other kind of concepts that are grounded on the autonomous concepts. Husserl himself loudly acknowledged his debt to Stumpf on this point (Husserl 1900/1901, p. 780).

At the end of this section, we would like to point out that Stumpf's analytic psychology was unexpectedly close to some leading ideas of the founding fathers of analytic philosophy. Above all, the program for investigating "absolute contents", as developed in *Tonpsychologie* (1883/1890), was intimately related to the ontology of Russell's logical atomism. Besides, Stumpf's conception of judgment was close to that of Frege as developed in his famous paper "On Sense and Reference" (1892). Indeed, Stumpf was explicit that judgment plays a central role not only in the art or in politics, "but already in the most elementary spontaneous [*unwillkürlicher*] comprehension and interpretation of sense-impressions" (1899, p. 5). In fact, it is active in every space orientation. A related position is defended in *Tonpsychologie:*

> Judging, as we understand it, does not always consist in deliberations and is not always connected with language, even not with inner speech. In many situations, it is immediately and instantly connected with sense impressions. (Stumpf 1883, p. 4)

---

172 Cf. Lotze's analysis of the unity discussed in Chapter 1, § 4.2.
173 Cf. George Stout's *Analytic Psychology* (1886), written under Brentano's influence.

Similarly, Frege claimed that with every thought that we entertain "seriously", i.e., we have when we are awake (i.e., not in a game or a daydream), for example, "It's raining now!"—we already judge a situation as true or false: "the step from the level of thought to the level of reference (the objective) is already done [in it]" (1892, p. 34).

6 Further Points of Relatedness Between Lotze and Stumpf

We have already noted that although Stumpf started his philosophical development as a devoted Brentanist, he gradually dissociated himself from the theoretical position of his teacher—despite the fact that, emotionally, he remained Brentano's loyal devotee. Furthermore, most of Stumpf's deviations from Brentano were a result of his apprenticeship with Lotze. In the lines above we already have mentioned some specific ideas that Stumpf inherited from Lotze. In this section, we are going to add other points of influence that can only be expressed in more general terms:

(i) *Stumpf as Non-Dogmatic Philosopher.* Like Lotze and in contrast to Franz Brentano (Chapter 4, § 5), Carl Stumpf was not a dogmatic philosopher. He was convinced that exactly like science, philosophy is to be a cooperative study and not merely a matter of schools and sects (Stumpf 1907, p. 194; Münch 2006, p. 14).

A good example of this stance, as developed by Lotze, was that even Stumpf's open criticism of his theory of logical-signs (§ 3 above) did not harm the personal friendship between teacher and student. Exactly the opposite was the attitude of Franz Brentano toward his students. A prominent case was Stumpf's discussion with Brentano concerning the question of whether or not pleasure has a content. Specifically, Stumpf criticized Brentano's position that sense perceptions (bodily pain, pleasure, etc.) have content. Among feelings, content have only emotions in form of particular states of affairs. Furthermore, Stumpf maintained that whereas emotions are passive feelings, desire and will are active and have as their content values, not states of affairs. Typically, Brentano fiercely attacked Stumpf's position in letters and in print until the end of his life:

> [Brentano] blamed Stumpf in a bitter tone for his deviations from the original doctrine, and suggested, as wrote Stumpf in his Preface, "that I seemed to be a dissident for him". ... There followed a long controversy in the correspondence and in a series of published papers, which lasted until Brentano's death in 1917. (Fisette 2011, pp. 40–41)

The effect of this attitude of his teacher was clearly negative for Stumpf's intellectual development. Above all, it narrowed the scope of his philosophical explorations. Later, Stumpf remembered:

> I admit that this was one of my motives for developing a considerable amount of time to the area of the psychology of sound and acoustical observation. There I could hope to achieve something useful without taking a position of agreement or dissent with regard to a great number of unpublished views of the teacher. It was the same with Marty in philosophy of language and Kraus in philosophy of law. (Stumpf 1919, p. 145)

(ii) *Stumpf Did Not Set Up His Own Philosophical School.* One upshot of Lotze's theoretical liberalism was that he did not set up his own philosophical school. This was out of the question exactly because of the "exceptional considerate liberality [of Lotze] in relation to every personal development. The individual person was for him an untouchable sanctity" (1917, p. 10).

Like Lotze and in contrast to Brentano, Stumpf never set up a school of philosophers, despite the fact that his pupils included such prominent figures as Edmund Husserl, Wolfgang Köhler and Kurt Lewin.[174] Apparently, this was also the main reason why in the mid-20th century, Stumpf the philosopher was delivered to oblivion for decades (§ 1 above)—a fate he shared with his teacher in philosophy, Hermann Lotze.

We further maintain that the difference in method of teaching, dogmatic or liberal, was not simply a William Jamesian matter of temperament. It reflected the difference in the philosophical method employed by Brentano, on the one hand, and Lotze and Stumpf, on the other hand. While the "empirical" philosophy of Brentano was also deductive and synoptic,[175] the philosophy of Lotze–Stumpf proceeded in a bottom-up manner and was developed step-by-step, piecemeal.

It cannot be a surprise, therefore, that Brentano was also close to other philosophers that explored "truths in themselves", like Husserl and Frege, in another respect: he was dogmatic in regard to any further elaboration of his philosophy. Closer to Lotze–Stumpf, in contrast, were some empirically oriented philosophers, such like Russell and Carnap, who practiced an "open door policy", encouraging correction of their own philosophy by their students (Milkov 2012; 2020b, § 10 below).

(iii) *Theoretical Integrity.* Finally, Lotze and Stumpf were also related since they both did not change their position in philosophy throughout their lives. In contrast, Brentano's philosophy had its Part One and Part Two. While the early Brentano

---

[174] To some extent, Stumpf can only be considered the father of the Berlin school of Gestaltpsychology (§ 2 above).
[175] Stumpf himself maintained that "[Brentano's] advantage was in the deductive part of the [nativist] method, in the set-up of most general perspectives" (1919, p. 147).

was a descriptive psychologist, in his second, ontologically-oriented phase, he developed an idiosyncratic reistic position in philosophy.

7 Stumpf's Ontology

An important characteristic of Carl Stumpf as a philosopher was that he inherited Lotze's interest in quantitative subjects: a stance that put space, time and numbers at centre of his philosophy. Among other things, this point is supported by the fact that in his Göttingen years (1868–1873), Stumpf was also on good terms with the philosopher Julius Baumann, to which the concepts of space, time and numbers were of prime importance.[176] Unfortunately, Stumpf did not develop his ontological interests in full. As a young philosopher, he was seriously working in the theory of numbers and, as already noted (in § 2 above), he even wrote his habilitation thesis on this subject (1870). Soon, however, he lost interest in it. As regards the philosophy of time, apparently, Stumpf was hampered in exploring it because of the paralyzing effect of Brentano on his students discussed (§ 6, (i) above): indeed, Brentano himself worked on the psychology of time perception.

Be this as it may, the only areas in which Stumpf developed his ontological intuitions in full were the philosophy of space and the concept of states of affairs:

(i) *Space*. As pointed out in Chapter 2, § 9, following Kant, Lotze held that space and time are forms of intuition that make our knowledge possible. In contrast to Kant, however, he discriminated between extension and place/moment. Extension is a conceptual (formal) notion and refers to an infinite multiplicity of possible directions. Only a place in space or a moment in time, however, makes them reality. With the help of this conception, Lotze tried to preserve the objective character of space and time, opposing in this way Kant's subjectivism.

Stumpf developed Lotze's objective conception of space and time further into the idea that places and moments are perceptual contents (*Sinnesinhalte*) (Russell 1897a, p. 196). These are psychological *phenomena*. He further maintained that "a perceived space is not composed of many identical impressions, but [is] a unity in which we can discern [through analysis] different parts" (1873, p. 126). Stumpf added that the order is ontologically dependent on content: indeed, "there is no order which is not based on an absolute content" (1873, p. 275).

---

[176] Baumann's *Die Lehren von Raum, Zeit und Mathematik in der neueren Philosophie* (1869) was the book to which Frege referred most often in his *Grundlagen der Arithmetik* (1884)—it was Frege's main source of historical information in philosophy of arithmetic.

(ii) *States of Affairs*. Following Smith (1992) and Stumpf himself, many philosophers today maintain that the concept of states of affairs was introduced in Stumpf's manuscript lectures on logic (1888). Beatrice Centi had recently added to this that Stumpf also "uses the term *Sachverhalt* before the year 1888, in a less technical but not less significant sense due to its generality, in the same way as he uses the term series" (2011, p. 77). More particularly, Stumpf's later concept of states of affairs as well as his concept of judgment were "rooted in a wider concept of state of affairs expressing the intrinsic and totally subject-independent relationality of reality" (p. 78). Indeed, Stumpf constantly explored how contents relate to one another: "how does space and quality relate to one another [*sich zueinander verhalten*]?" (1873, pp. 107, 114). This was actually the tenor of his *Raumbuch*.

In fact, however, the use of the concept of state of affairs in the *Raumbuch*, to which Centi refers in support of her claim, is made neither in the sense of the content of judgment nor in the sense of contents related to one another. Rather, it is used in the trivial sense of a *case* (*casus*) that is also popular in the ordinary German today, in particular, in legal discourse. In contrast, in his "great" *Logic* (1874), i.e., long before 1888, Lotze repeatedly referred to the concept of states of affairs in the sense of content of judgment (Chapter 1, § 4.5). Some Neo-Brentanists are reluctant to recognize this because they fail to realize that Lotze already introduced the concept of content of judgment as well as that of the content of perception in philosophy. Otherwise, it is really the case that the concept of states of affairs is rooted in the connectionist (relationist) ontology—in the connectionist ontology of Lotze (Chapter 1, § 4.3), however, that was developed much earlier and genealogically preceded that of Carl Stumpf. Indeed, Lotze spoke about contents that relate to one another already in his "lesser" *Logic* (1843, p. 25).

8 Carl Stumpf's Philosophical Acolytes

Regarding Carl Stumpf simply as another member of the Brentano's school, some authors raise the question: "Was Stumpf, who received his repute as experimental psychologist, a philosopher at all?" (Münch 2006, p. 12) The author of these lines, Dieter Münch, eventually answers his question in the affirmative. But the very fact that it was posed says much about the state of Stumpf studies today.

One of the arguments for denying Stumpf the status of a philosopher is that, "apparently, Stumpf lacks the philosophical ambition that characterizes Brentano and his school. He had neither Brentano's sense of mission nor the relentless defending stance typical of Marty, Kraus and other followers of Brentano" (Münch 2006, p. 13). We consider this view mistaken. Stumpf had both strong philosophical interests and a clear philosophical message. These, however, did not look in the direction of the mainstream members of Brentano's school.

One of the reasons for questioning Stumpf's status as philosopher is that, allegedly, he had just one philosophical acolyte—Edmund Husserl. This claim is not true either. In fact, Stumpf also exerted a formative influence on the Berlin Group around Hans Reichenbach (1928–1933) that had a program parallel to but at the same time clearly different from the program of the Vienna Circle.[177]

To be more exact, Stumpf influenced the Berlin Group mainly (but, as we are going to see later, not exclusively) through his closest pupils Kurt Lewin and Wolfgang Köhler, who were also members of the board of the Berlin Society for Scientific Philosophy (1927–1935) led by the Belin Group (Milkov 2021b). Lewin and Köhler also took part in the first Conference of Exact Philosophy in Erlangen in March 1923 (Thiel 1993) and were instrumental in establishing the *Zeitschrift für exakte Philosophie* in 1923. Unfortunately, that journal never appeared (Milkov 2011a, p. xiv). Later, both of them contributed papers to its more fortunate successor, the legendary journal of scientific philosophy *Erkenntnis* (1930–1939). Köhler also acted as a reader of the doctoral theses of the core members of the Berlin Group Walter Dubislav and Carl Hempel. Between 1920 and 1929, Kurt Lewin, on his side, worked closely together with Hans Reichenbach and Paul Oppenheim. Furthermore, Rudolf Carnap, in *The Logical Construction of the World* (1928), and Hans Reichenbach, in *Philosophy of Space and Time* (1928) and *The Direction of Time* (1956), made extensive use of Kurt Lewin's term of *genidentity* (Padovani 2013). Finally, another core member of the Berlin Group, Kurt Grelling, explored (partly alongside Paul Oppenheim) the logical aspects of Gestalt theory (Milkov 2021a).

That Carl Stumpf's philosophy is related to the scientific philosophy as developed in the second half of the 19th century is also clear from a number of claims he made. We have already noted (in § 5 above) that Stumpf repeatedly spoke about the "catastrophe" resulting from the supremacy of the philosophy of German Idealism between 1790 and 1840.[178] The "Renaissance of philosophy" started in the mid-19th century following the (re)introduction of special sciences, especially the introduction of psychology, into it.

Reading some of Stumpf's papers, one gets the impression that what Bertrand Russell and Hans Reichenbach later called the "rise of scientific philosophy" in fact already took place in the 1850s and 1860s in Germany thanks to such scientifically oriented philosophers as Fechner and Lotze. Both of them were not only philoso-

---

[177] In short, while the Vienna Circle defended logical positivism, the Berlin Group defended the philosophy of logical empiricism (Milkov 2013a).
[178] Lotze, for his part, maintained that the "large part of Hegel's views or, more exactly, the whole, in the form in which it is put, is totally untenable [*unhaltbar*]" (1857, p. 7).

phers but scientists as well: Lotze was also a professor of medicine, and Fechner was also a physicist. This is how the rebirth of philosophy came into being. Following these examples, to Stumpf, it is important that "philosophers learn and are trained in a specific craft [*Handwerk*] which means that they have to have experience in some concrete area of either humanities [*Gesisteswissenschaften*] or natural sciences" (1907, p. 179). Only experts trained in this way can produce "a philosophy which has an exact concept-formation [Chapter 9] and strict proofs" (1907, p. 180). This way of working also made Leibniz a great philosopher.[179]

But Carl Stumpf's program for renewal of philosophy was very close to that of Hans Reichenbach, not only in the direction it followed but also in its content. Indeed, Stumpf advanced a kind of empirical philosophy (*Erfahrungsphilosophie*) that progresses step by step and whose aim is to achieve a "relative conclusion", so that "every higher step [of science] conveys new life-impulses [to philosophy]" (Stumpf 1907, p. 170). Similarly, according to Reichenbach, every significant scientific discovery and theory is to be explored logically in order to distill the constitutive principles of the renewed science. Instead, relying on Kant's a priori principles of science, one is to explore the relative a priori of all sciences (Milkov 2011a, p. ix).[180]

Regarding this connection, it deserves notice that Reichenbach was Carl Stumpf's student at the University of Berlin. Apparently, Stumpf's lectures did not remain without a trace for Reichenbach's formation as a philosopher. The main reason why the relation between Stumpf and Reichenbach did not develop in full was ideological rather than theoretical. At the beginning of the 20th century, namely, Carl Stumpf was conceived of by his students as a *politically* conservative philosopher, while, for Reichenbach, the revolution in philosophy was part and parcel of the social revolution (Milkov 2013a, § 1.5). In more detail, being a Chancellor of the Friedrich Wilhelm University in Berlin, Stumpf was engaged in a conflict (he himself spoke of a "war") with the left-wing "free student movement" (1908); ultimately, he dissolved that society. After Stumpf retired from his position, the society was restored and, understandably, its members saw Stumpf as another old-fashioned "bourgeois" philistine. Significantly, at the beginning of the 1910s, Hans Reichenbach was a very engaged member of the free student movement and, by all accounts, adopted a negative attitude toward his philosophy professor from the older fellow-students. It also deserves notice that psychologically, Reich-

---

[179] Carl Stumpf started the German Leibniz Academic edition (1923/Present), writing for it an enthusiastic Preface. The edition is still unfinished (http://www.leibniz-edition.de/).
[180] Recently, the concept of the "relative a priori" was revived by Michael Friedman (2001). Our analysis above made it understandable why Friedman's main point of inspiration by elaborating this concept was the scientific philosophy of the early Hans Reichenbach.

enbach was very sensitive regarded who supported his endeavors and who, he believed, was against them.

This short digression on Carl Stumpf's cryptic influence on Hans Reichenbach indicates that the two philosophers were only two links in a genealogical chain, the first member of which was Hermann Lotze. We shall explicate in due course the connection between Lotze and the logical empiricists in Chapter 9.

Part III: **Lotze and Bertrand Russell**

Chapter 6
Lotze and Bertrand Russell

1 Russell: Hegelian or Lotzean?

Many contemporary historians of analytic philosophy find the early philosophy of Moore and Russell to be much more Hegelian than used to be believed. Thomas Baldwin, for example, speaks of "a Hegelian origin of analytic philosophy" (1991, p. 49). What is even more striking is that Russell himself insisted that between 1894 and 1899, he was a Hegelian. Furthermore, "wherever Kant and Hegel were in conflict, [he] sided with Hegel" (Russell 1959, p. 42).

We can explain this belief of Russell and his exegetes by reference to the fact that Russell's notion of Hegelianism was communicated to him mainly by his senior friend in Trinity College, Cambridge, John Ellis McTaggart, in particular, by McTaggart's first book, *Studies in Hegelian Dialectic* (1896), which was published precisely when Russell took his first steps toward articulating his own philosophy. This makes understandable why Russell dedicated his *Essay on the Foundations of Geometry* (1897a) to McTaggart.

These observations substantiate the starting claim of the present chapter, which is that the influence of Hegel on Russell in the mid-1890s was rather vague and general. We can trace it mainly through four elements of Russell's thought:

i. The adoption of the ontological argument for God's existence.
ii. The project for a dialectical transition from one science into another and for an encyclopedia of sciences. The idea was that, when sciences are developed in isolation, they are incomplete and enmeshed in contradictions. That incompleteness can be overcome only through a dialectical transition to a broader science.
iii. Russell's penchant for paradoxes that, among other things, led him to discover the "paradox of classes" (Milkov 2003, p. 56; 2016b).
iv. Also, Russell's main task as a philosopher was set out in Hegelian terms. He strove to solve some of the problems of Hegel's (bad) logic and mathematics —to put it aright with the help of ideas from Cantor, Dedekind and Weierstrass.

This, however, was a very loose form of Hegelianism indeed. It only set up the general direction of Russell's philosophy at the *fin de siècle*, its broad shape, not its content. The thesis of this chapter is that with respect to content, the influence of Hermann Lotze was much more powerful. Briefly stated, Lotze gave Russell both the specific themes and problems of his philosophy as well as theoretical means to deal with them.

One sees this borne out by the prominent role of Lotze's thinking in all three books of Russell's theoretical philosophy from the turn of the century: *An Essay on the Foundations of Geometry* (1897a), *A Critical Exposition of the Philosophy of Leibniz* (1900a), and *The Principles of Mathematics* (1903). In the *Essay*, in particular, a special section (pp. 93–109) was dedicated to the analysis of Lotze's philosophy of space, which is more extensive and more developed than the sections dedicated to other philosophers and mathematicians. In *Leibniz*, Lotze, not Bradley, was the most frequently quoted 19th-century philosopher. Further, the only philosopher of the same century to whom Russell dedicates a whole chapter in the *Principles* was once again Lotze: in Chapter LI, Russell discussed Lotze's theory of space and substance.

It should be observed, however, that Russell was rather picky by following Lotze's original approach. While he adopted the central role that relations play in Lotze's philosophy as well as the objective content of judgments (propositions) (§ 7 below) and of sense perceptions (sense-data), at the same time, he rejected Lotze's overall philosophical "system",[181] in particular his anthropological stance (Chapter 1, § 3.2).

2 Lotze and Russell: An Overview

That connectionism and Lotze-style relationism[182] (Chapter 1, §§ 1, 4.3) lies at the bottom of Russell's project for New Philosophy, is clearly seen in Russell's *The Principles of Mathematics*. Indeed, a Lotzean subtitle "A Philosophical Study of Order" could properly be applied to the latter, given its focus on the order in space (Part VI) and the order in time (Part VII). The only leading theme of the work that was not explicitly discussed by Lotze is the order in mathematics. The reason for this is simple. While Lotze, similarly to Russell later, maintained that logic establishes the foundations of mathematics,[183] he was against the formalization of logic. Lotze saw

---

[181] Importantly enough, Lotze's "system", in strong opposition to that of Hegel, was formed of different, autonomous parts. In other words, it had no monolithic character.
[182] Russell embraced Lotze's relationism, which was also central to T. H. Green and F. H. Bradley, already in *An Essay in the Foundations of Geometry*. In it, Russell adopted the view of "space as relational and of spatial figures as relations" (1897a, p. 96).
[183] For Lotze, "mathematics develops as a branch of general logic [...], so that] the fundamental ideas and propositions of mathematics have their systematic place in logic" (1874, § 18). Sluga

in it an "addiction of thinking" that is attractive not because of the value of the scientific results themselves but because of the exactness of the results to which it leads (1843a, p. 2).[184] For this position, he was harshly criticized by Russell in *An Essay in the Foundations of Geometry* (1897a, p. 96).

In fact, the connection between Lotze's ontological and cosmological conception of order and mathematics was made by the leading German mathematicians of the time Richard Dedekind and Georg Cantor. Both of them visited Lotze's lectures in Göttingen. In the summer term of 1852, Dedekind diligently wrote down Lotze's lectures on the "History of the Newest German Philosophy" (Woodward 2015, p. 244). In 1866, Georg Cantor attended Lotze's lectures in Göttingen as well (Ferreirós 2004, p. 67). Importantly enough, both exercised a decisive influence on Russell's philosophy of mathematics.

That, like the British Idealists (Introduction, § 3), Russell was more Neo-Lotzean than Neo-Hegelian in the last years of the 19th century is further supported by these two facts:

(i) The thinking of the German philosophers who directly influenced Russell most during this period—Helmholtz, Stumpf, Benno Erdmann—was significantly shaped by Lotze, not by Hegel. Russell also subscribed to many of the ideas of Lotze's teachers Herbart and, ultimately, Kant.

(ii) Russell already embraced Bradley's anti-psychologism in his first printed review (1895).[185] We must remember, however, that the father of the criticism of psychologism in philosophy was neither Bradley nor Frege but Lotze (Gabriel 1989b, p. ix; Introduction, §§ 3, 4.2).[186] In fact, Lotze's anti-psychologistic views were already mature in 1841–1843 (they were articulated in his "lesser" *Logic* and "lesser" *Metaphysic*), before Bradley was even born.

3 Lotze's First Impact on Russell (1896)

The first metaphysical (cosmological) concept that Russell made central to his philosophy under Lotze's influence was that of spatial and temporal order. In the

---

sees in this position an ancestor of Frege's logicism: "Among the many things that Frege owes to Lotze, the most important is perhaps the idea of logicism" (1980, p. 57).

184 Similar argument was later used by Husserl (Hamacher-Hermes 1994). In support of the non-formal exposition of logic, Lotze explicitly referred to Trendelenburg.

185 Today, it is widely accepted that "Bradley's attack on psychologism was [...] by far and away [his] most important contribution to modern logic" (Griffin 1996, p. 216).

186 Up to the end of the 19th century, Bolzano's anti-psychologism in logic remained largely unknown.

Essay of the Foundations of Geometry,[187] Russell explored it at length and found Lotze's discussion of space and time "excellent in many respects" (1897a, § 85).

Most fundamentally, Russell adopted Lotze's transcendental argument that in order for thinking to be possible at all, its objects must be complex[188]—they must consist of clearly different elements. Indeed, a simple thing, argued Russell, "is unthinkable [unintelligible], since every object of thought can only be thought by means of some complexity" (1896, p. 564); it is also indefinable. But complexity can be achieved only when referring to unique individuals (terms), which are different from any other individual.

In fact, here, Russell followed Lotze's dictum, which we already discussed in Chapter 1, § 1, that "the proposition 'things exist' has no intelligible meaning except that they stand in relations to each other" (1887a, p. 186). Around 1890, Bradley extensively discussed this principle of Lotze, transforming it into its negation. Bradley's final dictum was that the very idea of a plurality of objects standing in relations is unintelligible (1893, Chapter 3). As we just saw, Russell embraced here Lotze's position, not Bradley's.

Russell found differentiation (complexity) to be a key element of perception itself. In perception, there must be "at least one 'principle of differentiation', an element, that is, by which the things presented are distinguished as various" (1897a, § 128).[189] Russell called this a priori element "a form of externality". His reason here was similar to his argument in defense of complex objects of thinking. The objects of perception must be complex since in order to perceive them, we must differentiate their parts; and in order to differentiate and then relate them, they must be external one to another.

For human beings' forms of externality, space and time are indispensable. These forms of intuition make our knowledge, the intelligibility of the world (of the being), possible. Following Kant, Russell maintained that they are given to us a priori and so are most fundamental. Furthermore, Russell underlined the uniqueness of the moments of time as compared to events. His argument was that two moments in time can be different only when they are mutually external; in contrast, two events can happen together in time.

This was a central assumption of Russell's early philosophy, which entailed placing a considerable weight on the concepts of space and time in all periods of his philosophical development. This point was ingeniously underlined by Paul

---

[187] The book was finished in October 1896 and published in May 1897.
[188] Lotze also maintained that in order to think and also to say something reasonable at all, we must grasp objects or terms *in relation* to each other.
[189] Typically, Russell himself believed that this is an idea of Bradley and Bosanquet (1897a, §§ 187 f.). In fact, it was Lotze's idea, which was adopted by Bradley and Bosanquet.

Hager, who insisted that "space and time theories are absolutely central to Russell's philosophy" (1994, p. xii); so that when Russell revised his philosophy, this involved, as a rule, a change in his position on space and time.

Furthermore, Russell discriminated between empty space and spatial order. More specifically, he understood empty space as the *possibility* of the relations between and in spatial figures, which secures their form of externality (1897a, § 197). It is purely conceptual.

Empty space is only differentiated through matter. Its simplest unit of differentiation is the atom. The atoms are unextended, so they have no spatial characteristics; they are points which are connected through spatial relations to other atoms. Straight lines, planes and volumes are spatial relations between two, three and four atoms, respectively. Roughly, spatial order is an aggregate of spatial relations that are immediately presented to us. Questions about "parts of space, or spatial figures, arise", said Russell, "only by reference to some differentiating matter, and thus belong rather to spatial order than to empty space" (1897a, § 204). Once again, the spatial order of matter is different from empty space.

It should be noted that this theory of space is compelling evidence of the influence of two ideas of Lotze's on Russell. First of all, Russell's distinction between empty space and spatial order followed Lotze's distinction between extension and place/moment, which appears already in his "lesser" *Metaphysic* (1841). There was no such distinction in Kant. Secondly, and more specifically, Lotze claimed that extension refers to an infinite multiplicity of possible directions; only a place in space and a moment in time make these possibilities actual reality (Chapter 2, § 9).

This conception of Lotze's was, in fact, motivated by his objectivism (Chapter 1, § 1)—by his wish to preserve the objective character of space, in opposition to Kant's claim that space is a form of subjective intuition.[190] In particular, Lotze's argument was that if space is only our form of intuition, to which there is no analogue in the objective world, as Kant claimed, then other beings may have radically different concepts of space. These spaces, however, can be never presented to us—at least, not as spatial relations (1841, pp. 232 ff.; 1887b, pp. 195 ff.). Lotze's conclusion was that space and its objective counterpart have at least the same multiplicity.

Russell was impressed with this argument of Lotze's and adopted the view that it is possible to learn something from subjective intuition about "the manner in which what appears to us as space *must* appear to any beings with our laws of

---

190 The criticism of the subjectivity of space and time in Kant in the mid-19th century started with the publication of the *Logical Investigations* by Adolf Trendelenburg (1840) mentioned above and continued until the end of the century (Adair-Toteff 1994).

thought" (Russell 1897a, § 86). He understood the empty space as conceptual precisely in order to preserve the objective character of human knowledge of space. Indeed, Kant's claim that space is intuitive leads to radical subjectivism.

Another idea of Lotze's that Russell followed in the *Essay* was his atomism. In fact, Russell defended a Lotzean-style atomistic philosophy of science already when reviewing Hannequin (1895). Lotze, incidentally, introduced this conception of atomism in his philosophy of space and time around 1840 when criticizing Jacob Fries' notion that matter is interplay of powers (2003, pp. 85 ff.). According to Lotze, atoms are the ultimate building blocks of the universe—they are idiosyncratic and remain unmodified in all compositions in which they come. Lotze's atoms are thus different from the atoms of antiquity (Chapter 3, § 9), which were understood as last elements of reality which have different forms but the same substance (1856a, p. 39; 1885, p. 34). As already mentioned, Lotze's atoms are "punctual" (*unräumlich*), without extension. After all, extension is only possible where there are many points which can be easily identified and differentiated (1879, §§ 188 ff.; Milkov 2017b, § 3.5).

4 Lotze's Second Impact on Russell (1897)

After Russell put his *Essay* into print in October 1896, he travelled for three months to the USA, where he lectured at Bryn Mawr and John Hopkins Universities. Later, he remembered: "Contact with academic Americans, especially mathematicians, led me to realize the superiority of Germany to England in almost all academic matters" (1967, i, p. 197). Back in Britain, in March 1897, he read (in German) Hegel's *Wissenschaft der Logik* for the first time, only to find that it deviated radically from his own standards of exactness. Looking for a new philosophical inspiration, Russell read Lotze's *Metaphysic* once again in May 1897 (Chapter 7, Introduction).

The first fruit of this new reading of Lotze's was not late in coming; it found expression in the paper "Why Do We Regard Time, But Not Space, as Necessarily a Plenum?" (1897b), that Russell wrote in June 1897. Nicholas Griffin speaks of it as "in many ways an enigmatic little paper"—its brevity belies its importance (1991, p. 331). The paper would not appear thus enigmatic, however, if one reads it with the knowledge that Russell wrote it under Lotze's influence. This is clear, among other things, from the notes "Can We Make a Dialectical Transition from Punctual Matter to the Plenum?" (1897c), written immediately before the paper, in which Russell refers expressly and positively to Lotze.

In "Why Do We Regard Time, But Not Space, as Necessarily a Plenum?", Russell tried a new start in philosophy, laying more stress on the logical discussion of metaphysical problems, putting in this way logic and metaphysics together and drawing up a program that he was to realize in full only in *Leibniz* and in *The Principles*. First of all, Russell distinguished between two concepts of space and time: (i) as consisting of relations; (ii) as adjectives to the absolute. Secondly, Russell insisted that, for logical reasons, space and time need to be treated in the same way—either as relational or as adjectival. Thirdly, he claimed that, if accepted, "an adjectival treatment of space and time would imply both that space and time were plena and that monism was true. On the other hand, a relational treatment would entail that space and time were punctual and that pluralism was true." (Griffin 1991, pp. 328–329) In short, with this claim Russell assumed that "the question whether space and time are relational or adjectival will decide the issue of monism versus pluralism" (1991, p. 331). Fourthly, the paper also outlined the conception that relations are irreducible to properties, and this makes monism problematic; indeed, the very formulation of the question of relations or adjectives tacitly implies as much (Imaguire 2001, p. 69).

Characteristically, the paper offered no solution to the problems it raised. It did something more important though—it outlined the logical scheme in which Russell was to discuss the problems of space and time, monism and pluralism, etc., for years to come.

5 Lotze's Third Impact on Russell (1898)

Early in 1898, Russell experienced an influence of Lotze even stronger than the first and the second ones. A central claim of this chapter is that this influence was largely responsible for Russell's turn of 1898, when he, in his own words, abandoned British Idealism and monism for (Platonic) realism and pluralism.

Here is the whole story, delivered in some detail. In the Lent term (January–February) 1898, Russell attended McTaggart's lectures on Lotze (Chapter 7). The lectures gave Russell an opportunity to thoroughly acquaint himself with the overall system of Lotze's philosophy—including with its anthropological part. The changes in Russell's thinking caused by this third encounter with Lotze's ideas, are fairly perceptible in the manuscript "An Analysis of Mathematical Reasoning", which he started to write on April 1, 1898. Most notably, in the paper's "Introduction", Russell adopted an idea which later became leading in the *Principles:* "Whatever can be a logical subject I call a *term*" (1903, § 47). Terms are all those things which can be counted; they have a being. This idea became the cornerstone of Russell's new theory of propositions, which many authors consider the kernel of his philosophy

(Imaguire 2001; Stevens 2005).[191] Our hunch is that it was based on Lotze's assertion that judgments have an objective content—they relate things (*sie verhalten Sachen in Sachverhalten*) that distinguish one from another with necessity (Misch 1912, p. lviii) (Chapters 4 and 5).

An idea radically different from "being" is that of "existence", which is a predicate.[192] If a term has this predicate, it is called an *existent*. The basic class of existents is composed out of the various parts of space and time—of places and moments. Being "forms of externality", places and moments are different from other existents, more specifically, from the things which are in them (Russell 1898, p. 171). On this view, space and time are series of possible moments and places; the real particular moments and places are *in* the possible ones (Milkov 2005b).

The decision to subscribe to this theory of space and time was further evidence for the groundbreaking changes in Russell's philosophy in April–June 1898, immediately after he attended McTaggart's lectures on Lotze. More specifically, it shows Russell's new theory of judgment as theoretically underlying his theory of space and time.[193] To be more explicit, the (*ontological*) conception that judgment consists of relating substantially different elements, served as a model for the (*cosmological*) conception that space and time consist of relating substantially different moments/places.

Of importance was also Russell's insistence in "An Analysis of Mathematical Reasoning" that the terms in the "universe of discourse" are immutable and eternally self-identical, and that they are the constituents of judgments/propositions (Griffin 1991, pp. 297 f.). In the Preface to the *Principles*, Russell called this position "pluralism which regards the world ... as composed of an infinite number of mutually independent entities, with relations that are ultimate, and not reducible to adjectives of their terms or of the whole which these compose" (1903, p. xviii). The only thing that he did not elaborate in explicit form in 1898 was his new theory of relations (§ 8 below).

Immediately after Russell attended McTaggart's lectures on Lotze, in March 1898, he started to study Whitehead's *A Treatise on Universal Algebra* (1898) and, in April, Dedekind's *Nature and Meaning of Numbers* (1888). In consequence, he ceased to believe that mathematics investigates quantities; instead, Russell adopted

---

191 Russell changed the term "judgment" to "proposition" only in "The Classification of Relations" (Russell 1899). The paper was read in January 1899. It summarizes the implications of his March–April 1898 turn.
192 "Being" is explored in ontology, "existence" in cosmology (Chapter 1, § 4.2).
193 Two years later, Russell was explicit on this point (1900b, p. 225).

the view that it explores "extensive magnitudes" and their structures.[194] In short, "from Dedekind's book he learned to regard the notion of *order*, rather that of quantity, as the central notion in the definition of number" (Monk 1996, p. 116; italics added). In this way he eliminated the contradictions of quantity that played central role in Hegel's philosophy of mathematics.[195]

This turn confronted Russell with the task of laying "the philosophical foundations of a theory of manifolds" (Griffin 1991, p. 280). To be more specific, the intensive examination of Lotze's philosophy in January and February helped Russell most to change his position in the philosophy of mathematics. Russell did this with the help of his new theory of judgment, which was eventually transformed into a new theory of propositions.

We see, then, that in the first half of 1898, Russell underwent two turns. On the one hand, he abandoned the Kantian synthetic approach to mathematics based on intuition[196] and adopted the view that mathematics is reducible to logic, a position also assumed by Lotze (§ 2 above). This shift started when Russell read Whitehead and Dedekind in March–April 1898 and ended at the beginning of July the same year, after his exchange of thoughts with Couturat and Poincare in an intensive correspondence (Milkov 2003, p. 49). On the other hand, with his theory of propositions and the method of analysis of propositions, Russell's philosophy took a turn to Platonic realism.[197] It is essential to emphasize that the second turn was supportive of the first one, in the sense that it was a philosophical underpinning of the theory of manifolds (of classes) that was central to the first turn. We are going to see how it did this in the following section.

6 Lotze and Russell's Philosophical Logic

In the Introduction, § 4.1, we have already seen that according to Lotze, idealities are indispensable in philosophy. In this section, we shall consider how two such

---

[194] To Russell, "intensive magnitudes" are aesthetic perceptions (qualities) like pleasures (1903, § 171).
[195] It is important to notice that Dedekind's new approach to numbers can be easily seen as supplementing Lotze's theory of order, but in the realm of mathematics. As already mentioned in § 2 above, Lotze refused to do this since he was reluctant to blend metaphysical studies with the *formal* (technical) methods of mathematics.
[196] Alberto Coffa (1981) and Gregory Landini support the opposing position. They maintain that "logic is a general synthetic a priori science" (Landini 2019, p. 207).
[197] On Lotze's Platonism, see Introduction, § 2.

idealities—individuals and series—made their appearance in Russell's philosophical logic in the spring of 1898.[198]

(i) *Individuals*. In the *Principles* as well as in *Principia Mathematica*, Russell advanced a program for a symbolic language that is governed by a "philosophical grammar"—language with logically proper names and a strict syntax. This program also entailed an ontology, whereby "there are 'things' [individuals] which have properties and have, also, relations to other 'things'" (1959, p. 158). Things are not simply the sum of their properties, however. They are units without parts.

In fact, Russell had embraced this principle in the already discussed Chapter I of "An Analysis of Mathematical Reasoning", where he insisted that each term is identical with itself and different from all other terms. He called this kind of difference the "difference of being" (1898, p. 168) or "form of externality" (§ 3 above). "It is", notes Griffin, "the kind of difference that numeration depends upon, and it is in virtue of their difference of being that all terms can be counted" (1991, p. 280). Lotze, for his part, introduced an idea very close to Russell's "difference of being" already in *Mikrokosmus*, where he maintained that the being consists of independent members ordered in a series or in a "tissue of series" (*Gewebe von Reihen*) (1864, p. 474).

This notion was arguably nothing less than a fundamental metaphysical (ontological) principle incorporated into Russell's logical symbolism. Russell adopted it only because he was convinced that without it, we cannot understand how human knowledge is possible. One has good reason to maintain that Russell's individuals, which give orientation to his *calculus universalis*—Russell's counterpart of Lotze's mechanism—pertained to what Lotze saw as the "highest and essential being".

(ii) *Series*. Russell held that the concept of individuals is also indispensable by discussing series.[199] Following his transcendental argument, he held that series are crucial for clarifying mathematics, physics, and other sciences. Russell put special stress on the fact that the rejection of individuals, for example, in the form of rejection of the identity of indiscernibles, would make counting impossible.[200] Indeed, "if *a* and *b* have all their properties in common, you can never mention *a* without mentioning *b* or count *a* without at the same time counting *b*, not as a sep-

---

[198] We discussed Russell's philosophical logic in Milkov (2022a).
[199] Lotze called the requirement that we cannot justify series if we do not assume individuals "law of juxtaposition" (*Gesetz des Nebeneinander*) (1864, p. 491).
[200] We see here again a most important characteristic of Russell's philosophy of mathematics and of his logic in general—he connected it inextricably with the real world (van Heijenoort 1967).

arate item but in the same act of counting" (1959, p. 115).[201] Counting is only possible when the elements counted are different. Only thus can they form a series. What is more, the rejection of the identity of indiscernibles would also make the measurement of magnitudes impossible. Indeed, for measurement to be possible at all, each unit-quantity must be different from all the others.

There are different kinds of series: numbers, points in space, moments in time, and causal series of events. Across such domains, Russell claimed that the construction of series—in space, time, colors, and numbers—depends upon mutual incompatibility or a real difference in the constitutive elements (individuals). He thus insisted that the elements of the series must not only be related to one another; they must also differ from one another, in such a way that even indiscernibles should not be conceived as identical. Russell's final claim was—he made it explicitly only in "The Classification of Relations" (1899)—that this requirement can be only achieved if there is an asymmetric transitive relationship between the individuals of every serial order.

7 Russell Misinterprets his own Philosophical Development

Bertrand Russell produced many documents that recount how his philosophy developed. Unfortunately, they were often misleading. We already have noted one such self-misinterpretation at the beginning of the present chapter—Russell always stressed that in the period from 1894 through 1898, he was a neo-Hegelian. The evidence, however, suggests otherwise—he was influenced more by Hermann Lotze then by Hegel. Furthermore, Russell reported that "towards the end of 1898", he and Moore rebelled against both idealism and monism. The latter claim is mistaken as well. Russell, as Griffin rightly observes, "was always a pluralist" and never a monist (1991, p. 306), not even in the *Essay*. Moreover, Russell's contention that he rejected idealism in 1898 is at least controversial: Russell's turn was from a (Kantian) transcendental idealism to (Lotzean) Platonic realism (Introduction, § 4.2). To be more precise, it was a form of *realistic idealism* that Russell abandoned only after he met Wittgenstein. As the analysis we made in § 5 above, clearly show, there are sound reasons to rename Russell's turn of 1898 a "turn towards a new theory of judgment/propositions".[202]

---

201 In his *Tractatus* (5.5303), Wittgenstein, who lacked Russell's "idealistic apprenticeship", refused to follow this argument. Apparently, here Wittgenstein followed the assumptions that mathematics is simply "a logical method" (6.2) and that logic is tautological.
202 Russell's theory of judgment is to be discussed in detail in Chapter 8, § 4.2.

In the present section, we are going to see how misleading Russell's recollections are concerning when he exactly made his dramatic turn to a new theory of judgment/proposition, and also who impelled him to take it. Russell's answer was that (i) it happened in the second half of 1898 and (ii) that it happened under Moore's influence.

The first thing to note is that this claim contradicts what Moore himself wrote on this issue. Moore only spoke about "mutual influence" between Russell and himself (1942, p. 15) in elaborating closely related theories of judgment that were later developed in a joint theory of propositions.

But how did Russell and Moore come to their closely related positions? By way of an answer, we shall point to the fact that Moore derived his realist theory of judgment from Franz Brentano, via Brentano's Cambridge acolytes, above all George Stout (Bell 1999). This, however, is not the end of the story. Brentano's theory of judgment, in its turn, only remixed Lotze's realistic theory of judgment (Chapter 4, § 3.1). As we already have seen, Russell, for his part, borrowed his theory of judgment directly from Lotze.

Russell doubtlessly told the truth when he reported his experience in November 1898, when he read for the first time Moore's "On the Nature of Judgment", in which Moore spelled out his relational theory of judgment—it appeared to him as a revelation. Russell only misinterpreted the reasons for this. He did not learn that theory from Moore but rather saw in it his own new theory of judgment from April–June 1898, but expressed in a most clear and precise way.

This claim can be supported by reference to two more facts already cited in the literature:

(i) There is

> an unmistakable similarity of approach between the "[An] Analysis [of Mathematical Reasoning]" and these works of Moore ["The Nature of Judgment" and his second dissertation]. Yet Russell had written the 'Analysis' before he read Moore's Fellowship dissertation of 1898. (Griffin and Lewis 1990, p. 159)

Russell read it in November 1898. Moreover, "the theory of judgment in the 'Analysis' is very much more elaborate than that in either Moore's second dissertation or 'The Nature of Judgment'" (p. 160).

Drawing the ineludible conclusions from these facts, Nicholas Griffin declared that Moore's two dissertations of 1897 and 1898 as well as his paper "The Nature of Judgment" could not be the source of the changes in Russell's logic in April 1898 (1991, pp. 298 f.). Unfortunately, Griffin did not explore other possible sources that may have prompted the change of Russell's mind, viz. Hermann Lotze—despite the fact that Griffin was the first to note that "Russell had a Lotzean phase in 1897–8" (p. 37, n. 44).

(ii) Russell met Moore in 1898 for discussion first on May 10, i.e., when a good deal of "Analysis" was already written. Moreover, some published letters of Russell's make it clear that in these discussions it was Russell who brought ideas to Moore, not vice versa: "[Russell was] talking mainly to Moore, who seemed on the whole inclined to assent to what [he] had to say" (Griffin and Lewis 1990, p. 159). The same happened at their second discussion on June 18: "He [Moore] was not at all discouraging" to what Russell told him (Griffin and Lewis 1990, p. 160).

8 Russell's Supposed Disagreement with Lotze

In the discussion above, we have already seen that in the first years of his philosophical development Russell was considerably influenced by Lotze's philosophy. It is true that, apart from Lotze's anthropological stance and his spiritualism, Russell also rejected certain core theses of Lotze's ontology and natural philosophy (cosmology), as the two salient examples that follow illustrate. As we are going to show, however, he did so without fully grasping the position of the German philosopher.

(i) Russell's most general disagreement with Lotze's concerned the latter's alleged doctrine that the points are factual, not absolute. As a consequence, Russell charged, Lotze did not accept autonomous relations but claimed that relations are functions of the points between which they stand. Russell further contended that this view arose "from neglect to observe the eternal self-identity of all terms and logical concepts, which alone form the constituents of propositions" (1903, § 426).

Lotze's actual position on this matter was not, however, as one-sided as Russell understood it to be. Following his perspectivism, metaphysically, to be more precise (Chapter 1, § 4.2), cosmologically, i.e., in respect of what is real (*wirklich*), Lotze *did* assume that external relations have priority over the things they connect. From the perspective of the philosophical logic, however, in respect of what is possible,[203] he adopted, just as Russell later did (§ 3 above), a form of atomism. Significantly, this interpretation was adopted by those commentators who read Lotze as an atomist, for example Harald Høffding (1896, ii, pp. 574 ff.) and Anthony Manser. On Manser's

---

[203] On the difference between metaphysical and logical perspective by Lotze, see Gabriel and Schlotter (2017, pp. 178 f.).

reading, Lotze held that "what is complex in our mental life must be constructed out of simple atoms" (1983, p. 309).[204]

(ii) A second example that illustrates how Russell's criticism trades on an oversimplified representation of Lotze's thinking concerns the question: "Are there absolute points of space and moments of time?" Lotze claimed that the things are "the fixed points to which is attached, in whatever way, the varying course of events" (1864, p. 466; 1885, ii, p. 579). Their independence as fixed points of the ontological discourse is at hand, however, only logically—"up to the moment of their [of individual things] being again perceived by us.[205] This being perceived is itself nothing but a new relation which is added to, or dissolves, the old ones" (p. 467; ii, p. 580).

All in all, it can be said that, to Lotze, the priority of things over the relations in which they enter is logical, while the priority of the relations over the things is metaphysical (cosmological): "In order to think the existence of things [as different from perceiving them] one must grasp [them as independent]" (p. 471; ii, p. 584). However, this does not mean that they *are* independent. In this sense, Lotze observed that "the existence of everything presupposes the existence of some other to which it must be related" (p. 472; p. 585). Things, to Lotze's way of thinking, are in the net of these potential relations, in a "vault [*Gewölbe*] of mutually related things" (1864, p. 469).

Apparently, in these two cases, Russell was trapped by the subtlety of Lotze's dialectics. As we already have noted (Chapter 1, § 3.3), in his writings Lotze often and deliberately presented alternative points of view in an attempt to mediate between them. He managed at that to remain logically consistent. In contrast, "Russell characteristically preferred his philosophical types unmixed: if it were monism, then Hegel, if pluralism, then Leibniz; but not 'monadism–monism'" (Kunz 1971, p. 57). This explains why he often presented Lotze as one-sidedly adopting at the same time many of his central positions.

---

[204] Manser is, of course, wrong when he claims that Lotze did not accept the context principle since the latter allegedly contradicted his atomism (1983, p. 310).

[205] Cf. Werner Heisenberg's "uncertainty principle" in quantum mechanics, according to which the more precisely the position of a particle is determined, the less precisely its momentum can be predicted.

Chapter 7
Bertrand Russell's Notes on McTaggart's Lectures on Lotze

1 Introduction

Bertrand Russell's conspectus on J. E. McTaggart's Lent term 1897/1898 lectures on Lotze was written at a very important moment of his philosophical development. Russell always insisted that between 1894 and 1898, he was "a full-fledged Hegelian". In fact, he became acquainted with Hegel only through his elder friend McTaggart (Chapter 6, § 1). To be sure, in these years, Russell worked closely together with McTaggart, in a way similar to his work associations with Moore in 1898–1900, with Whitehead in 1903–1909, and with Wittgenstein in 1912–1913 (Milkov 2013b). Apparently, this was Russell's *modus operandi* in both theoretical philosophy and in mathematical logic.

Russell read Hegel (his *Logic*) for the first time in March 1897 (Chapter 6, § 4), after he returned from his trip to the USA, and was deeply disappointed. As a consequence, he urgently started to look for a discussion with McTaggart. As a matter of fact, in late March 1897, McTaggart visited Russell for a few days (Griffin and Lewis 1990, p. xxxvi). It goes without saying that the two men discussed problems of Hegel's *Logic* and Russell's way out. It is also likely that in this meeting, McTaggart directed Russell's attention towards Lotze. This cannot be a surprise, however. As already mentioned (Introduction, § 2), in these years, both Oxford and Cambridge were under Lotze's sway. In fact, at this point in time, Russell already knew Lotze well—he discussed Lotze's *Metaphysic* at large in his *Geometry* (1897a) (Chapter 6, § 3). Following McTaggart's advice, however, in May 1897, Russell read Lotze's *Metaphysic* for the second time (Chapter 6, § 4).

Importantly enough, precisely in these months, McTaggart was elected as a lecturer in Moral Sciences at Trinity College, Cambridge. In Michaelmas term 1897/1898, he started lecturing on Leibniz and in Lent term on Lotze. One can only guess that this choice was dictated by his discussions with Russell in March 1897.

This story shows that the received view that at this point in time McTaggart "usually lectured on Leibniz at Cambridge" (Monk 1996, p. 118) is incorrect. McTaggart lectured in the Michaelmas term 1897/1898 on Leibniz and in Lent term on Lotze for the first time and due to his own preference. It was not a matter of his academic duties or convenience. This claim is supported by the fact that between 1899 and 1901, McTaggart lectured on the British empiricists and not on the German atomists and occasionalists Leibniz and Lotze.[206] Also, McTaggart's trip to New Zealand in 1899, during which Russell replaced him as a lecturer at Trinity College, was not unexpected but planned. As a matter of fact, "beginning in 1891, McTaggart took a number of trips to New Zealand to visit his mother" (Thomas 2012).

It is of special importance for our study that Russell chose to attend McTaggart's lectures on Lotze and not on Leibniz. Apparently, he believed that these lectures could shed more light on points that remained unclear in his mind after he abandoned Hegel as a leading authority and read Lotze's *Metaphysic* for the second time. To understand the importance of this decision, it should be observed that the careful recording of McTaggart's lectures was rather an unusual act for Russell of 1898. As a student, he kept notes on lectures by Stout, Sidgwick, and Ward bur never after 1894.[207] Apparently, Russell had his reasons for doing this.

Let us examine McTaggart's Lotze lectures in more detail. In the Lent term 1898, he read 16 lectures on Lotze's philosophy that were based on three books: (i) on Lotze's *Logic* (Lectures I–IV), (ii) on his *Metaphysic* (Lectures V–XII), (iii) and on Book IX of his *Mikrokosmus* (Lectures XIII–XVI), which discuss problems of metaphysics, more precisely, of ontology and cosmology. In this context, it should be observed that, following an old tradition in Western (above all German) philosophy, Lotze's *Metaphysic* consists of three parts: (a) "general metaphysic" or "ontology"; it explores the interconnection of individuals, or things (*Dinge*); (b) philosophy of nature or "cosmology". It investigates space, time, motion (mechanism, gravitation, electricity, chemistry, biology), and matter; (b) philosophy of mind (Chapter 1, § 4.2).

It deserves notice that Russell skipped the first three lectures on Lotze's *Logic* but subsequently visited the next 13 and took copious notes on them. It can be concluded that his interest in these months was above all in Lotze's metaphysics—to be more exact, in his ontology and cosmology. This is supported by the fact that in his path-breaking, paradigm-changing work *The Principles of Mathematics*, Russell put together problems of the philosophy of language, mathematical logic, and the philosophy of mathematics (of arithmetic and geometry) and explored them by referring to ideas of Lotze's ontology (above all, Lotze's theory of order and his theory or relations). The book also discussed themes of Lotze's cosmology. Part VI explored problems of space and part VII those of matter and motion, with chapters on "Matter" (LIII), "Motion" (LIV), and "Causality" (LV).

---

[206] We have this information from Mr. Adam Green, Senior Assistant Archivist, Trinity College Library, Cambridge (England).
[207] We have this information from Kenneth Blackwell.

After clearing up important problems of metaphysics (of ontology and cosmology) with Lotze's help, Russell directed his attention to Leibniz. To be sure, this cannot be a surprise—the philosophical views of Leibniz were clearly related to those of Lotze (Chapter 1, § 2.1). In Lent term 1898/1899, Russell delivered the lectures on "The Philosophy of Leibniz" on which also his book *Leibniz* (1900a) was based. It is fairly likely that Russell decided to do this following McTaggart's advice—as we already know, McTaggart had already lectured on Leibniz in Michaelmas term 1897/ 1898. Russell at least discussed Leibniz with McTaggart.

As we already have noted (in Chapter 6, § 1), in Russell's books on theoretical philosophy published between 1897 and 1903 (in *Essay*, *Leibniz* and *Principles*), Lotze, not Bradley was the most frequently quoted 19th-century philosopher. Importantly enough, it can be conclusively demonstrated (something that we are not going to do here) that in his writings of that period, Russell often confused Lotze's position with that of Leibniz. In other words, he often spoke about Leibniz while he in fact expounded Lotze's position.

* * *

In what follows, the reader will find Russell's notes on McTaggart's lectures on Hermann Lotze as transcribed and expanded by Arlene Duncan and Kenneth Blackwell from Texas microfilm Rec. Acq. 385, file 4; box 6.50. The footnotes are composed by Kenneth Blackwell. We added to them commentary (§ 3) in form of endnotes.

2 Lectures on Lotze

fol. 98

MacTaggart. Lent Term 1898.

LOGIC. Book II.

⟨*Lecture*⟩ IV.[208] Disparate sensations: not only in different senses, but red and blue also disparate. Not so of musical notes, according to Lotze: could imagine intermediate notes if had heard two.ⁱ Cases where comparative terms accurate only:

---

208 The lectures are transcribed from a microfilm printout of an unfoliated notebook in the Morrell papers, Ransom Center, Texas (RA Rec. Acq. 385, box 6.50). Lecture divisions were made uniform and symbols italicized; double underlines became small caps. Square brackets are Russell's (Blackwell 2015); "G.A." for "God Almighty" is retained. "effected" *replaced* "affected" at pp. 126, 128 (twice) and 129 (twice). "Rot" is a common exclamation in Russell's marginalia and notes. It means something that is no good at all.

hotter and bigger e.g. Antinomies of motion: Zeno's arrow destroys rest as well as motion. Therefore leads to scepticism. Argument denies community between moments, which is essential to rest. Fallacy is in regarding time as discrete.

In Mathematics, how know of all triangles what proved of one? Not owing to nature of space but because can set aside all irrelevant properties. Lotze here sets aside problem, which is: Why have geometrical propositions this peculiarity? Why is not life of German Emperor essential? We are à priori certain that it isn't, which is peculiar to Mathematics. [McT. has no solution to offer].

Probability, says Lotze, subjective:[ii] has to do with our rational expectation. No event improbable after it has happened. Therefore don't need *higher* cause for what was formerly unlikely, if it happens, than for anything else. This not valuable remark. If double 6's happen often, dice may have been loaded for that purpose, which is *different* cause, if not *higher*.

Book III. *Scepticism:* presupposes truth:[iii] can't say you aren't getting truth, unless there is truth you aren't getting. Besides scepticism asserts propositions. Can't say properly we can know nothing, for this is knowledge. But suppose we say all the same that there is truth, but we can't get it. Why should sceptic believe there *is* truth? Therefore this modified scepticism also unsound.—Even if what we know are phenomena, shouldn't say we *only* know phenomena, for this suggests noumena[209] better.

fol. 99

What mean by saying a thing *real?* Lotze objects to *Setzung* (positing) as implying action. Takes *Wirklichkeit* (reality). Three stages, Being, Becoming and Validity.[iv] These three irreducible to each other. Events real, though can't say they *are.* Validity (∴) reality which belongs to Propositions. Propositions about triangles valid though there are none: therefore proposition valid independent of Being.—Concept can't be valid, only judgment.[v]—In empirical cases this obvious: not in Philosophy. Nevertheless McT. admits it in Philosophy too: mistake in Kantian categories.

Can't have anything absolutely passive: effects always partly due to nature of effected.

Law of "like cause like effect" can't be proved by experience, nor even shown to be probable: for apart from law, future needn't resemble past.

Relation between two ideas is a third idea therefore can't be explained away.[vi] —Talk of relations *between* things or *between* things and ideas. Correct to speak of relation *between* ideas, not *between* things.[vii] Whatever holds here is in each. If a relation exists, something different from if relation didn't exist. In case of ideas, difference is difference of mind, not of ideas. Therefore relation may be *between* ideas. But in case of things, relation can't hang in air: only thing to be changed

---

209 "noumena" *written over deleted* "phen'a".

is the things related. Relation between things means correlated changes. Of course ideas *are* affected by relation, but relation is not *merely* in this affection.—As regards things, we have change in *A*, and change in *B*. Seem to have made things independent, and lost relation. This developed in Metaphysics by unity of things, M.[viii] —*Universals* valid, not existent. But Lotze doesn't mean ultimate reality (is) particular things as such: individuals exist only by virtue of universals.[ix]—Processes like classification purely subjective, but may bring out objective truth. McT. thinks this question of detail in each case, whether such processes have happened.—Ultimate propositions must be self-evident[x] but not identical or analytic. Test not contradiction but absurdity of negative. McT. thinks ultimate truths not necessarily self-evident, but got by induction.

(*Lecture*) V. METAPHYSIC. Distinction between Metaphysics and Logic that Metaphysics has for object Reality as opposed to Possibility. For Lotze, follows that Metaphysics deals with change, which Logic doesn't.—All Reality interconnected: can't be proved but involved in all proof.[xi] Explanation assumes things are connected, by cause and effect. Causation can't be proved by experience. Things wouldn't require explanation unless universe interconnected. Apart from this, things wouldn't seem reasonable or unreasonable, therefore no explanation sought for. Explanation due to interconnection, as well as presupposing it.—Can't base metaphysics on Psychology because Psychology involves Metaphysics. Final evidence in any case immediate evidence of Propositions: also talk in Psychology of Reality, causation etc., which involve Metaphysics if need explanation: if don't need explanation, no Metaphysics required, psychological or other.—Metaphysics says Lotze, against Hegel, can only supply general laws, not tell where or how realized.—Lotze emphasizes importance of idea of *Plan:* higher than Law. Plan means unity capable per se of producing difference.[xii] Lotze doubtful if we can get it.—Can't suppose only one ultimate Law: moreover these must have data given to them. Laws and matter not in unity: each exists independently. Idea of plan differs: all laws fused in a system by plan, and moreover data not indifferent to plan. In what sense fused into a whole? Not *mere* unity: difference too. Lotze says unity aesthetic.[xiii] This only analogy, but important.[xiv] In picture, no contradiction in things being different, and yet there is a unity. This what Lotze means. No *logical* reason why things not different, but harmony would be spoilt if it were. Lotze doesn't think this ideal can be proved, unless on religious grounds.—Hegel shouldn't have deduced facts he *didn't* know from dialectic[xv]—Didn't, says McT.—Dialectic doesn't give Temporal succession.—Hegel didn't say there was sequence corresponding to dialectic, says McT.

Start from common sense.[xvi] Three books: Ontology, Cosmology, Rational Psychology. First book: What is Being of things?[xvii] Not analyze difference between Reality and Non-Reality, because unanalyzable.—Being of THINGS: four classes, things, qualities, occurrences and relations. Consider things as opposed to other three here. Common sense says: From sensations get conclusion there are things behind them. Therefore sensation evidence for things. But common sense regards things as permanent. Common sense regards things as persisting in relations in which ⟨they⟩ would be perceived if we were there. What mean by saying THINGS exist? is a question with a meaning.—Some say things are so because they have quality of Pure Being. Lotze's criticism same as Hegel's, that this is Nothing.—Others say things are things owing to *Setzung.* Lotze says mere positing ⟨is⟩ nothing: must now what and where you are positing. May posit a quality or even a contradiction in terms.—Lotze says, against Herbart, Being not necessarily permanent. Argument later on, where says some Being not eternal. Can't put Being in things not in relation but afterwards entering into relations. If a thing once isolated, must remain so.—What we mean by a thing being is that it is in relations with other things.[xviii] What qualities must things have in order to be in relations.—May mean common quality or principle of individuation.—Things change: this fact ultimate.—Two senses of identity: material identity and identity of content. Have to find things which have first sort of identity. Keep *Identität* and lose *Gleichheit* (equality). Therefore a thing can't be a simple quality: this must change wholly or not at all. No meaning in blueness turning into redness or sweetness. (Hegel remarks Identität without Gleichheit *begins* with quantity.) Both Lotze and Hegel say conscious spirit only thing which can change without losing identity.—Can't regard Reals as changeless, and grouping alone to change, as Herbart did. For *we* at any rate change when we perceive a change, and we are reals. [?] Changes therefore may be *in* reals. But predicates *are* unchangeable: this postulate, and involved in our knowledge of change.

fol. 102   Relations between things: is essence in composition or behaviour? Must be latter, since in simple things can't be former. But essence *per se* can't give thing as opposed to idea of it: have essence in our minds. Some difference therefore between essence in things and in us. What is it? Can't have indeterminate matter with essence superposed, for couldn't get any particular essence. Cause can't act on effect without effected thing's cooperation, which involves effected thing having a nature.—If matter and qualities have always necessarily coexisted, matter can't explain essence, since mere abstraction impossible without essence.—Reality not a stuff to fill out images with, but just whole nature of things as they are. Can't say essence plus abstract quality Reality makes thing. Things are real when behave as such, says Lotze. What mean? (1) Remain identical with itself. (2) Centre of influence. (3) Must change with some definite actions and reactions. (3) suggests thing is a law. Can't find subject, but only these marks. Law not necessarily general law. Thus thing only law of actions and reactions.[xix]

⟨*Lecture*⟩ VI. Ended with thing may be a law. Common sense says: *conforms* to law. But know nothing else, therefore thing not left over. If it were left, would have no reason to obey the law. *May* call thing *realized law*, though both words bad.—A law must allow for change. There are unchanging ideas, but *also* changing things. *Substance mode of behaviour of things.*[xx] Combination of change and regularity is what induces us to look for things. Lotze thinks entirely irregular change unknowable. Partial regularity is what makes us look for things to explain change.—Law leads us to *becoming*: ultimate fact.[xxi] Can't be got out of Being and Not-Being. Lotze means Becoming in Time is ultimate idea. Hegel's Becoming not necessarily in time says McT. [?] Can't have Law without Becoming, but can't have law if you have *mere* Becoming, for wouldn't have connection between a and b.

Thing is conceived as having some permanence: Law persists. *fol.* 103

Changes predicated by Law are hypothetical: conditions may not be realized. Laws give potentialities. What makes thing melt when conditions occur? Not logical necessity, for why should thing bother about Logic? Ultimate nature of things is only answer: thing is law.[xxii]—But how about cases where thing influenced by outside things? Internal action in A must set up ditto in B. Relation can't be *between* things, but must be quality of something. How possible change *in* A produce one *in* B? Not more mysterious than producing change in itself, but seems so: take internal action as ultimate. How can a thing have states at all? How thing same still? Put off this question. Degrees of Being possible, says Lotze: measured by power of thing: influences others, not itself influenced much: Spinozistic. Not like Degrees of Reality in Bradley.—All transeunt action[xxiii] requires plurality of causes: A, the external cause, and B, the thing effected, whose nature is relevant: therefore two at least. Lotze doesn't use cause and effect as parallel terms: Cause is thing, effect is change in thing effected. A and B *causes*, a state of A which brings about β, the *effect* in B. V⟨ide⟩ § 52, *Metaphysik*. Cause can be counteracted, ground can't. [?]—Something must happen to causes to make them produce effect. Herbart thinks coexistence in space. Lotze says, no reason to suppose causes *do* touch one another, and no reason why if they did they should cooperate more than distant things.—What mean by an influence passing from A to B? How does it exist while passing? Only a *thing* can pass. But relations between | things in this case *fol.* 104 causality, and thus problem breaks out again. Identity of cause and effect, as Lotze points out, extraordinary confusion. Is causation transference of state from A to B? No, for (1) cause and effect not same state. (2) Can't transfer state, for can't exist during transference. (3) Why should state go to B? Causal connexion, ex hypothesi, begins when state gets to B, therefore why get there? Need new cause, and so ad infinitum.—Shall we get rid of transeunt action altogether? Criticism of Leibnitz: Absolute predetermination necessary, or states of A and B may cease to correspond. What difference whether predetermined world exists or only imagined by God? None unless parts of world all conscious. (This no difference to Leibnitz, since admitted consciousness everywhere.)—Determinism involved morally repugnant says Lotze, but only *asserts* it.—How is it monads develope at right rates? a, α in A, b, β in B: why α and β simultaneous? May be more intermediate stages in one case than in the other. (Leibnitz would deny this: same number of stages between a, α and b, β.) Nothing in Leibnitz, says Lotze, to necessitate laws. Those without laws, says Lotze, prohibited by God's wisdom, those with, except actual one, by his goodness. (But this unfair to Leibnitz.)—Transeunt action or determinism thus remain alternatives.

fol. 105 ⟨*Lecture*⟩ VII. Lotze's solution of difference of causality. Inexplicability of immanent causality less objectionable than that of transeunt ditto. That change in x should produce another change in x is fact in which reason can rest. All transeunt action can become immanent by regarding everything as one thing, M. M = $\phi(ABR)$: A, B any two things, R rest of reality.[xxiv] Equality here means identity. All changes are in M, and therefore all causality immanent. M preserves its own nature when affected, but reacts only against itself. Substantial unity essence of Lotze's M, and deduced by him from interaction. M ought to determine Lotze's whole view of Absolute, but doesn't quite. M both one and many of course. Reality, says Lotze, larger than thought: can't understand Becoming, how then Absolute? (McT. makes obvious retorts.) (McT. says Lotze should have said *formal* thought: mustn't say "either—or" too much.)—Since only one substance, all relations fall within it, and are relations of adjectives.—On this theory of causality, says Lotze, we can save Free Will: for an unmotived change could start fresh series in M: uncaused cause can have effects [Blasted rot!].[xxv]—Two sorts of relations: between, which only affect ideas; in, which affect things. (Latter can only be causal. Similarity, e.g., doesn't seem to affect things.) Does likeness only exist in us, not in things? Lotze would say: In so far as relation affects things, would be found as independent quality in each. Doesn't say this explicitly, but should.—Why does M change at all? Why was first change what it was? Lotze says these questions ultimate and unanswerable. Answers, if known, might satisfy mind though not Logic.—No possibilities to which M must submit. (Proper reasons given.) Lotze admits Hegel saw this, but several post-Hegelians did not. Schelling's later works e.g. thought pure thought could only lay down possibilities: pure thought tells Reality it may be A, B or C, but not D: Reality then chooses A.—Lotze points out that this is ROT.—If say: M = $\phi(ABR)$, Idealism: if say $\phi(ABR)$ = M, Realism, says Lotze. Difference depends on which we emphasize.[xxvi] Lotze thinks neither form best: can't do without

fol. 106 either unity or differentiation to start with: neither comes out of other.

Differential form, says Lotze, better for Science. (McT. objects.) But Realism, says Lotze, doesn't enough emphasize aesthetic unity among ultimate laws.—

Been talking of M having *states*. What mean by this? Lotze takes it with a jump. Says Self only thing we conceive to remain a unity while changing. Thing must be more than thing: can only be distinct from states, if it distinguishes itself from its states. Lotze gives no proof and can't: says what is true, that we *do* conceive of ourselves as things, but can't show we can conceive nothing else so. To be thing, must be object for Self. Mere beginning of feeling is therefore enough. [Why?] Reality needn't all be rational, but must all be sentient, says Lotze.[xxvii] [Rot! Only by assuming rationality has he got sentience]. [His ground is that sentience necessary to make *things* intelligible]. A finite thing not conscious of itself, says Lotze, can't be distinguished from M, which is its ground: only self-consciousness makes things distinct.—Lotze not monadist: merges everything in M.[xxviii] Nevertheless approaches Leibnitz in finding conscious selves everywhere. Lotze says later M must be person,[xxix] for otherwise couldn't have states. (This too sudden, says McT. very justly. But idea is new that mere fact of coexistence of change and unity in one being involves its spiritual nature as a Self.)—Here Ontology ends. Cosmology deals with matter, beginning with space. Thinks space purely subjective. Space sui generis, not thing, nor property, nor relation, nor arrangement. Lotze doesn't even subsume space under idea of form of intuition. Parts of space not instances of genus space, because all spaces interconnected.

⟨Lecture⟩ VIII. *Lotze's Theory of Space:* fundamentally like Kant's:[xxx] space only way of perceiving things. Lotze objects to Kant that ⟨you⟩ don't get rid of all differences by saying space phenomenal. If things *appear* in space, must have something which causes them so to appear: unlike Kant, Lotze says must be corresponding properties of things in themselves. Lotze's doctrine improvement on Kant: avoids Kant's duality. Form must have some connection with matter. Why put squareness into some things, roundness into others, if neither has any relation to things themselves? Must be something in sensations that has to do with space. Space-relations our phenomenal way of viewing certain non-spatial qualities of things in themselves.—Antinomies: (1) World infinite in space: Kant says infinitely *extensible*, not extended. Lotze says can't be aware of empty space, therefore if extensible, things must be capable of giving infinite number of sensations, therefore difficulty remains, for *matter* of experience somehow referred to things in themselves. Kant would have done better, says Lotze, to suppose finite amount of matter, with phenomenal empty space beyond. (2) Infinitive divisibility: here too don't get out of difficulty by saying space phenomenal, for wherever we do divide space, there must be some content, therefore infinite divisibility, even if space phenomenal, implies infinitely divided things in themselves.—Lotze's arguments for supposing space subjective: (1) can't suppose hole in space, but if real, we could imagine a hole [Why?]. If space only made by unbroken movement of our impressions, gap becomes impossible. [?]. (This argument seems weak in second part.) [What does a gap mean, except empty space?] Space must be constituted by relations between empty points,[xxxi] if real, since objects move in space, and therefore do not constitute points of empty space. Can't imagine two different kinds of relations between empty points: all such relations must be exactly alike. [Why?] But this won't do. Can't argue space must be outside ourselves because we perceive it: same would prove toothache exists outside us. For both, however, must be external causes, only not like effects.—If space somehow real, say a piece of matter π was in point p. What mean? Matter postulates π being at p makes no difference to either. But what then is relation between π and p? Change of relation must change related terms. Again: p has no influence on π's nature. But if κ approaches π, π will be more strongly attracted. How account for this? κ and its place q just what they were. Where is the change which results in increased attraction? No place for it.

fol. 108   Can we deduce space? Lotze says no, but can show must be some form of space. Says Hegel knew this: didn't deduce space as it is, but showed it filled necessary form of space, which more abstract. Are there non-Euclidean spaces? etc.[xxxii]

Time. Misleading to regard time as having one dimension as opposed to three. All parts of a line equally real, but past and future, if real, differently so from present. Time not parallel with space. Gives time more validity: must, since Becoming, to Lotze, ultimate fact. Can't conceive time as separate from events. Not empty time which causes things to change.[xxxiii] But if time and events change independently, might take opposite orders. No reason why correlated.—Lotze not frightened of endlessness of time: not disputed by Kant, who only shows if so we can't sum it. Why, says Lotze, *should* we be able to sum it? Why not have a real infinity, if necessary? He says we can certainly have *valid* infinite, as in Trigonometry. (But doesn't follow can have *real* infinite.) (I agree don't see why real infinite shouldn't exist.[xxxiv] Hegel says destroys connection of our thoughts, for can't determine anything, owing to endless regress. This only means rejection of real infinite as interfering with complete determinism.) Did Lotze regard God as coeternal[210] with finite world and as in time? McT. thinks not.—Perceptions of space not in space, but perceptions of time are in time. Therefore even if time effect of perceptions, time is still time. (Kant ought to have seen importance of this difference: time form of all perceptions) [No!] (May be *involved* in space something more fundamental than time, though space itself less fundamental than time.) (This view not Lotze's.)—Mere lapse of time can't turn ground into consequent. How then explain their succession? Ultimate fact. Time as whole merely subjective: almost a mistake.

---

210 "coeternal" *written over deleted* "coexistent".

Could we get time out of anything timeless? Mere systematic relations couldn't give present, past and future. These are unique. World might, however, have timeless relations appearing to us temporal, but these real timeless relations would have to contain something corresponding to present past and future. Lotze doesn't, however, believe world is like this: thinks it in time, but puts argument as against Kant. If things have *no* relation to time, why appear in definite series? (Same argument as in space.) Lotze's final view common sense view: Time as a whole abstraction, but lapse of events real and can't be transformed into anything else.—Present for Lotze, mere point of time. Lotze *says* we shrink from this for moral and religious reasons. G.A., at any rate, the only thing Lotze could regard as timeless.

⟨Lecture⟩ IX. *Motion.* What reality behind motion? Something in time but not in space. Approach should indicate closer relation between two things: must be change in relation of consciousnesses. (Must mean some particular sort of relation.) Are changes necessarily continuous? Yes says Lotze, but objects to Kant's view that can change continuously from something to nothing. Can't partake of reality in varying degrees.—Cause and effect must be simultaneous, otherwise would be interval of empty time between, and effect need never happen. Effect must itself contain stages, each simultaneous with its cause.—(Hegel points out change must be discrete as well as continuous: not incompatible with Lotze, but positive to him.) (At some instant a man passes suddenly from alive to not alive, which is discrete: qualitative changes must always be in some way discrete.)—Persistence of motion: untenable that motion *diminishes* by time, since involves persistence of part not annihilated. More logical to suppose motion annihilated at instant of creation—Proof of first law: If travel under force any distance, force in question ceases as soon as any motion has happened. Therefore unless assume motion to continue after force stopped, would never get any motion (§ 163) [Rot!]. Absolute motion: § 154 seq. Accepts absolute motion.—What noumenally corresponds to persistence of motion? Seems to argue some self-perpetuating change in Reality. (Don't see necessity: motion purely abstraction, don't say any motion *will* go on for ever.) [Rot!] *fol.* 109

Matter. Is it homogenous throughout or not? Lotze doesn't decide: no reason to assume complete homogeneity, he says.—Mustn't conceive position depends on attraction and repulsion: position depends on its nature, attractions etc. are its efforts at self-conservation.[211] (Conservation bad word, since suggests change not real.) (Word probably inconsistent remnant of Herbart.) All motion must be effect of action at a distance. [Assumes there are many things].

---

211 "conservation" *replaced* "preservation".

fol. 110   *Atoms.* Atomic view convenient for stinks[212] says Lotze. Presumption in its favour because can cut things up small.—If atoms have finite size, forces must pass through them instantaneously and lose nothing by transmission. Hence doesn't believe in extended atom. Atom like Herbart's not extended, and qualitatively different from each other.[xxxv] This atom has for Herbart[213] the awkwardness of not explaining contact action or any other action. (Pity Lotze doesn't make atoms selves.)—Relations of multiplicity to unity: not relation of incompatibility. Unity systematic, or aesthetic.[xxxvi] Also calls it dialectic unity, meaning the kind of unity proved by dialectic to be true of the world. Says Hegel failed from applying to details of fact principles which can only give a general direction to our thought.—Nothing to prevent one thing from appearing as several atoms in different parts of space.—Unextended atom may be divisible, though not spatially.

⟨Lecture⟩ X. No à priori reason why force diminish with distance. But doesn't agree with Herbart: if admit action at distance, force should diminish as more nearly satisfied. Lotze says this unjustifiable analogy from some neutral facts.—Continuity of change necessary to account for time. All action reciprocal however, therefore force can't take time to act. Time comes from fact that cause and effect each take some time, though they are simultaneous: they are coexisting series.[xxxvii]— Can number of elements be increased or diminished? (Should have waited till elements are treated as souls.) Number of elements may vary according as idea to be realized wants more or less of them. (This point as Lotze puts it not *specially* applicable to matter.—From this point of view, Lotze more of a monist than Hegel.[xxxviii] Hegel less definite as to differences than Lotze is in this passage. Never said elements *not* as ultimate as whole. According to Lotze, Smith is not an end in himself. I believe his arrangement is responsible for result: shouldn't have treated element of matter as same as element of spirit.) No à priori reason to suppose processes of nature convertible. World *might* have a purpose.—No meaning in say-
fol. 111 ing psychological and physical energy equal or unequal. | —Can never reduce qualitative to quantitative differences, though may find causal connections between them.—Principle of nature's parsimony meaningless.—*Value of Science:* (a) Rubbish of Hegel: took Universe as too small a thing. In spite of Copernicus, thought Absolute developed itself only on the shores of the Mediterranean. (This only true of application of theory to practice, not of theory itself.) (Hegel assumed no religion lower than fetishism, none higher than Prussian Evangelicalism.) (b) Though ideas of physical science inconsistent, they work. Lotze thinks it not edify-

---

212 "stinks" *nickname for* "science".
213 "has for Herbart" *after deleted* "is like Lotze's thing:"

ing to emphasize inconsistency. (c) Mechanics versus activity. All activity regulated by mechanical laws: forces at most can only be *directed* by activity. All action mechanical, but none *purely* mechanical.[xxxix] Nothing passive recipient of influences: its nature always manifested in its deeds. [What does a thing's *nature* mean?]—*Life:* If anything special, not vital *force* but vital *impulse.*[xl] Not force in mechanical sense. Life always dependent on inorganic things, and mechanism of body indistinguishable from that of inorganic matter. Can't rest distinction on view that in organism whole before part: whole brought together in time from the parts. (Might help with eternal existence, where whole has always existed.)—Can suppose individual things have tendency not only to self-preservation, but to self-improvement [McT. approves. Rot!].—Creation and preservation same thing, says Lotze.—Unconscious may pursue an end, but then no reason to call it a soul.

⟨Lecture⟩ XI. *Psychology.* Lotze believes in simplicity of soul,[214] but not on account *fol.* 112 of Freedom. Only à priori to suppose bodies haven't freedom: therefore freedom doesn't prove a thing psychological. Can't prove immortality from inconvertibility of psychological and physical. This only proves the ultimate elements of which we are composed as having a psychological aspect. Lotze's objection to our being so composed is derived from unity of consciousness:[xli] this proves a unity of substance. Shouldn't set out from existence of sensations, but from a subject which has sensations. Any comparison of ideas presupposes absolute unity of subject which compares. Hence Lotze derives substantiality of soul. (This seems to me a valid ground.) Lotze is not denying soul may be *effect*, but if it is, it is heterogeneous from cause.[xlii] Unity is like that of a particular, in virtue of which, when two forces act on a particular, they coalesce into one. (I should say can't say they really do coalesce in this case: resultant not combination of forces.) Can't have sensation without subject, (nor yet thoughts, though Green attempted these. If God's thoughts, then not ours). [McT. regards this as reductio ad absurdum: doesn't see denial of Self involved, and therefore all thoughts *simply* God's]—Lotze's argument not from inspection, but from analysis. To see soul *at all* proves that soul is simple: Lotze does not argue that it *is* simple because it *appears* simple. Lotze thinks an indivisible unity, if it is God, can be divided.

Lotze disbelieves in immortality: says, to begin with, pre-existence strangely *fol.* 113 improbable, as also immortality of animals. Says M produces new souls as required. (How can M require sometimes more, sometimes less? Could substantival diversity be created?) If M used to do without us, can do without us again. Therefore no immortality. (Can't metaphysically make a difference between past and fu-

---

214 "simplicity of soul" *written above deleted* "immortality".

ture in this respect.) Lotze says immortality not question for metaphysics. (Lotze illustrates that Kant wrong in thinking G.A. and immortality stand and fall together: on the contrary, they are opposed to each other. If we believe in G.A., impossible to prove by pure thought that we are immortal, since G.A. supplies the necessary permanence of the universe.)—No bond required between body and soul: nothing but interaction.[xliii] Heterogeneous things can interact. Personality lies in soul alone, not in body and soul together. Soul not ubiquitous in body. No difficulty in supposing soul to have position in space. But soul may occupy several discrete points, and may travel about the brain.—Secondary qualities, we *know*, are not in the objects.—Chemistry of ideas should be distrusted.[xliv] No reason to suppose there is such a thing.

fol. 114 ⟨*Lecture*⟩ XII. Unconscious ideas self-contradictory: we *mean*, states of the soul arising from ideas, and capable of again producing ideas. (Questionable whether "unconscious state of the soul" is any better. If soul indivisible unity, as Lotze says, what mean by an unconscious state which coexists with conscious ideas?)—*Association of ideas:* None by similarity: only contiguity, in time or space.—Psychological mechanism[xlv] just as dangerous as chemistry of ideas. Theory is: all ideas aroused by reaction against outside stimulus. But reactions are qualitatively dissimilar, which goes beyond mechanism.—Universal conception can't arise by cancelling peculiarities of particulars: particular images would have to disappear if this were so, and we should not see relation of universal to particular.—How get notion of space? Assume for simplicity ordinary view of space as something outside us. Soul itself non-spatial: how then get ideas representing spatial extension? Local signs (Psychology).[xlvi] [McT. characterizes this as ordinary view in Psychology now-a-days.]—*Mind and Brain:* needn't assume special vital force.[xlvii]—Why not say last atom of nerve actually presses on soul? Can't touch, but no more do two atoms. Inner state in one affects ditto in other, in both cases. — No reason to suppose soul ubiquitous in body on ground of immediate consciousness, since have ditto of other objects.—Lotze thinks not all mental phenomena connected with brain by correlation.—Memory can't be stored in brain, says Lotze. Argues that every atom would have to have many impressions, since same thing may appear in many points of retina.—What happens to soul when unconscious? Doesn't exist, says Lotze. Is born again when you're called in the morning.—Sums up Metaphysics by saying ground of what is should be sought in what should be: Metaphysics should be based on Ethics.[xlviii] (McT. objects this should be result, not postulate, as with Lotze. Lotze's position absolutely unjustifiable.)—Find out Lotze's views on religion from Emil Walter Mayer.[xlix]

fol. 115   *MICROCOSMOS.* Bk. IX. The Real is Thought, i.e. content of thought.[l] (This conclusion has been got in previous books.) Can't be *mere* thought, because active. All contents are states of an infinite being: minds are the only reality. How about tables and chairs? Leibnitz and Fichte. May argue no minds but people and animals: table merely coherent dream of all minds: Fichte. *Or* may suppose table has reality, but this reality is one or more minds. Lotze takes Leibnitz's view. We say: All that is real is mind:[li] we take all we commonly suppose real, and call it mental.—Nothing not self-conscious can be external to G.A. (G.A. is still M.[lii]) [Why the limitation?] Conscious being unity for himself, and therefore has some being not merely God's. Distinguish between *Realität* and *Wirklichkeit. Realität* applies only to things as opposed to qualities and truths.[liii] *Realität* has degrees: in proportion as thing detaches itself from G.A. and is more self-conscious, it has more *Realität*. (Means well, says McT.: means, a thing can be a thorough unity for itself, and yet be part of another unity. More real, more intimately connected with other things. Shouldn't have talked of "detaching itself from infinite".) Soul ultimate: can't be explained in other terms. Fact that soul becomes contradictory in Sciences is due to their defects, not its.—Shouldn't say Soul real *in virtue* of self-existence: Reality and self-existence identical.

⟨*Lecture*⟩ XIII. *Religious ideas*. Can't be certain of religious truths as of laws of thought: latter give hypotheticals, religion makes assertions of matters of fact. Is religious truth like sense-perception? No! Mere sensations not knowledge; when knowledge, no longer certain. *Arguments for G.A.*[liv] Reserve ontological. *Cosmological:* may prove *real* being, not *necessary* one: necessary would imply dependence on something else. Can only infer: *unnecessitated:* this doesn't amount to G.A. *Physico-theological:* Design: Can at best only prove a probability. Moreover, *does* the world show signs of design? A great deal of it doesn't. Might suppose there is a powerful purpose struggling against opposition. This would give a G. not A., who would be no use.—Moreover can't be sure the purposes we see served in nature as good. Might easily get as much harmony as we have owing to purely mechanical laws.

fol. 116

Ontological: Two forms: one wholly worthless, the other only logically. Scholastic form worthless: proved G.A. because existence one of G.A.'s predicates. Cruder but better form that of Anselm: that which exists both in reality and thought greater than one who only exists in thought. But G.A. greatest of Beings, therefore exists. Lotze admits Kant valid logically, because needn't imagine G.A. But says argument suggests following: (vol. ii, p. 670). Immediate certainty that greatest in thought must be real, because intolerable to suppose our ideals non-existent. (Is this mere assertion, or argument? No right to suppose world *not* intolerable. Lotze *might* of course say, immediate certainty, and won't argue about it.)

fol. 117   The morally intolerable cannot be, says Lotze. This is principle of his religion. Follows that G.A. must be a Person ["The Blessed Truth" of M. Arnold.²¹⁵] The Good must exist as a Person, because Lotze's soul longs for this belief. (This is all Lotze's ground for thinking G.A. a Person.ˡᵛ)—Difficulty concerning personality of G.A.: come from his being *all* reality: (1) No Ego without a soul. Says Ego must have a nature independent of non-Ego, for otherwise couldn't tell them apart. Therefore possible to have Ego-nature alone. (But we haven't got to put together Universe out of separate bits: bits together to start with. Ego and non-Ego in relation to begin with: no meaning apart from one another, though meanings not wholly relations to each other.) (2) No good pressing reflection: needn't have things reflected on non-Ego. (This argument right. Lotze wouldn't think necessarily that G.A. can think, but he must feel pleasure and pain.) (3) G.A. could be personal by apprehending himself in opposition to his states and as having states. (This valid, if changing states possible without anything external.) (4) If reason in world, and G.A. not person, reason unconscious. (Might retort, if can't strip off consciousness from reason, can't strip off finitude from consciousness either. Reason *in* finite beings, though no one of them.) (5) Want a God who can suffer (i.e. feel pleasure and pain probably, not necessarily pain). (We know of no change apart from outside causes.) [But you accepted Lotze's account of M's function in causality, which makes gross inconsistency].—G.A. more personal than we are. We have ragged edges; Person is self- explaining unity. (McT. says we are less and less self-explaining unities as we get higher. Lotze has confused *self-contained* with *self-centred.* Former only Universe. Latter person. Pre-Kantians—Leibnitz and Spinoza—thought a thing real in proportion as isolated. This was the root of their difficulty.

fol. 118   ⟨*Lecture*⟩ XIV. Every self-conscious mind for Lotze indivisible unity: but all are parts of G.A. who is also self-conscious. (Confuses self-centred and self-contained. Can M on Lotze's plan be self-conscious?) M must be as real as its difference. (But, can M be what we might call a *punctual* unity?) Comparison presupposes indivisible unity of comparer. (Can one indivisible unity be inside another? G.A. has a mind, and so have I. Therefore my mind is G.A.'s. That can't be all his mind. Therefore I am part of G.A., who is therefore not indivisible.) So truth and goodness depend on God's will, or are they conditions he conforms to? Truth can't be prior to G.A. in any sense. Can't say G.A. can't will a contradiction in terms, if contradiction supposed independent of G.A. For truth not antecedent to all Reality, i.e. to M.ˡᵛⁱ Truths and realities only conditioned by wider realities, therefore no truth which conditions

---

215 "[T]hat favourite doctrine of our theologians, 'the blessed truth that the God of the universe is a Person'" (Arnold 1873, p. 242).

all reality. Equally absurd to say truth is true because G.A. wills it. His existence and volition implies that there is already truth: can't have reality without truth. Can't say truth follows logically from God's nature, for logical sequence presupposes truth. Impossible to say benevolence *might* be bad, for possibility nonsense as applied to M.—Leibnitz didn't imply that God was in doubt which world he should choose: God was completely determined by his goodness.—God can have will, since fundamental nature of will is approval and disapproval, not removal of evil.[lvii] Thus, though God is timeless, may have will. (Lotze has said there must be movement in God: the contradiction here seems unavoidable.)—G.A. does not foresee our future actions: he timelessly regards them as real. (This seems equally to destroy our free will. If we are determined to be demoralized, Lotze's doctrine is as good an excuse as any other.)

Supreme Good. No moral judgment can be passed on mind which doesn't feel pleasure or pain. If no sacrifice in choosing Good, couldn't pass moral judgment on such person (Mistake, says McT.: if a person belongs to a class capable of evil, he deserves praise for feeling no desire to do so) [Don't see the point.]—Goodness, says Lotze, must be some one's happiness. Best Good is love which seeks happiness of all. (Is love, or happiness produced, the good? If the love, is it good as making lover or beloved happy?)

⟨*Lecture*⟩ XV. *Nature of G.A.* Religious feeling objects to notion that world proceeds necessarily from G.A.: thinks proceeds freely. (Don't know what *freely* means in case of perfect Being.) Creation, not emanation: but not creation in time.—Indemonstrable belief in freedom of will: he demonstrates it all the same, only points out the proof *logically* unsound. Rejects Herbart's sense of freedom: means by freedom absence of determination. Proves freedom from penitence, having indemonstrable conviction that proof is sound.—Kant's solution won't do, for moral action is in time and phenomenal. If, as actions in time, they are determined, don't get freedom which Lotze's soul requires.—A priori necessity of causality doubtful, because leads to infinite regress. (If difficulty about infinite regress, must suppose *every* chain of consequences started by free will of some finite being.) Can't bring in G.A., or don't need human freedom. Miracles not impossible. (True: General laws not everything: plan essential, and plan may sometimes dispense with law.[lviii])—Says miracles don't withdraw things from laws, but put them under special laws. (Rot! What law a thing comes under, equally depends on law.) Has the world as a whole a purpose? Speculating can't prove it, but religious feeling proves it. End must be Blessedness. No moral law can have force unless obedience pleases some one. (No proof possible or required: ultimate proposition with regard to values.)—Dogmas are symbols:[lix] if worth while to express your convictions by any set of symbols, then should belong to church which uses them.—Jesus Christ's relation

fol. 120 ("119" being a poor duplicate printout)

to G.A. *may* have been unique: don't know. *Son of God* shouldn't be expressing unique relation. Lotze's views are at most Arian.—Redemption faith which rescues us from wretchedness of Creation. *Practical Philosophy:* includes rules of prudence as well as Ethics. Says moral laws must be obvious. (Don't see why he should say so, since he has a morality of ends, not of laws like Kant.) This is conscience.—Can't *simply* take pleasure as good, because can't be certain of more than our pleasure at moment.

Different pleasures have different qualitative values.[lx] (How know this? Is it immediate, like perception of quantity of pleasures? Wish conscience would speak clearly.)—Supreme idea of Ethics is Benevolence: but Supreme Good is a form of pleasure.[lxi] Benevolence is a means. But value lies in particular actions, not in principle.

fol. 121 ⟨*Lecture*⟩ XVI. Active, not contemplative, life is ideal: depends on Lotze's Hedonism. Doesn't care about work for work's sake. Not like Carlyle, who thinks man not entitled to pleasure or anything else.—Lotze not so much given to à priori proofs of ethical propositions which can only be settled empirically: compare his treatment of divorce or private property. Doesn't emphasize supremacy of man over woman as all other German philosophers do, especially Kant.[lxii]—The end *does* justify the means: [Jesuit in disguise!]: everybody thinks so in case of G.A.: the evil in the world being justified by its happy issue.—As to State, Lotze is individualist empirically: society is not an organism.[lxiii] State is an institution for mere earthly prosperity.—Defends vindictive justice: injured person not compensated by mere restoration of injury, therefore since it is agreeable to see the thief punished, we have a right to punish him. (Fallacious, since impulse to enjoy others' pain not good.)— *Aesthetics.* The agreeable merely pleases *me:* the beautiful gives me a pleasure for which I claim universal validity. Judgment of beauty claims objectivity. Beauty must be something which agrees with something common to all of us. (This seems to show that everybody is right in his aesthetic judgments, which impossible, since people contradict each other about beauty, and yet claim objectivity. Might say objectivity a mistake.) Lotze denies we can drop objectivity without losing the value of beauty. (Don't agree.) Beauty can't be *Anschauung* or *Begriff:* must be *Idee:* defined by end to be reached. Three things in Universe: laws, substances, and *plan.* Cognition can't quite conjoin these three. But occasionally the unity of the three appears to our immediate intuition: when this happens, we get Beauty. For this, the means must be spontaneously active for the end in one object.—Lotze says human body most beautiful thing in world, and proves it fallaciously.—Music expresses Reality as a whole better than other arts, because it can't express anything particular.

3 Commentary

i This argument of Lotze was adopted by Carl Stumpf (Chapter 5, § 5). It shows Lotze to be an adept of descriptive psychology who produces taxonomies of phenomena.
ii Lotze adopted the subjective treatment of probability (1874, Book IX) from J. F. Fries and E. F. Apelt and was followed in this by his student Carl Stumpf (Milkov 2020a).
iii Lotze disproved philosophical skepticism by referring to the principle of self-confidence of reason (1874, § 303) that he adopted from J. F. Fries via E. F. Apelt once again. See on this topic the work of the Neo-Friesian Leonard Nelson (2015).
iv The distinctions among being, becoming (genesis) and validity (1874, § 316) (Chapter 1, § 4.2) represented one of the main theses of Lotze's logic on which also his anti-psychologism was based.
v This is a clear statement of the context principle also adopted by Frege, Husserl, and Russell.
vi Here, Lotze argues for the existence of relation. After 1898, Russell consequently defended them as well.
vii See (Lotze 1874, § 316). Between things take place either "correlated changes", or causation. This position was repeated in *Metaphysic* (1879, § 109) and served Russell as starting point in developing his conception of propositional attitudes (Chapter 8, § 4). In 1898–1905, Russell revolted against it, but he adopted it afterwards.
viii On Lotze's concept of "unity of things" see Chapter 1, § 4.2. Its formula is presented in fol. 105 (p. 130). Russell himself spoke about the "unity of propositions" (1903, p. 466).
ix The relation between universals and individuals (particulars) (*das Allgemeine* und *die Einzeldinge* (Lotze 1874, §§ 319, 340) will become central topic of Russell's philosophy (1911a).
x Cf. Lotze (1874, § 358). The self-evident truths were a central topic in Russell's writings between 1898 and 1919.
xi This claim refers to Lotze's principle that "to exist means to be in a relation" (Chapter 1, § 1) and to Lotze's transcendental argument that we cannot prove this proposition but are to quit science in case we decide to abandon it (Chapter 6, §§ 3, 6).
xii On Lotze's discussion of the emergence of something new according to *plan*, see Lotze (1879, § 67) (see also Chapter 2, § 7). On his concept of plan as higher than law, see Lotze (1879, § x). On contemporary discussion of emergence, see https://iep.utm.edu/emergenc/ (last accessed on December 3, 2022).
xiii See Lotze (1879, § 59). This is a typical merging of metaphysics (of ontology) with aesthetics by Lotze we discussed in Chapter 1, § 4.1.
xiv On the importance of scientific metaphors in philosophy for Lotze, see Chapter 1, § 4.6.
xv Lotze maintained that Hegel's philosophy of nature, in particular, "is a complete failure and because of this a totally abortive member of his system" (1882, § 54). Russell followed him on this.
xvi G. E. Moore shook hands with Lotze on this point (Milkov 2000, § 7).
xvii Lotze's ontology examines *being qua being* (Aristotle, *Met.*, 1003a21) or what is valid in all possible worlds. It investigates the principles of everything thinkable (intelligible). In contrast, cosmology philosophically explores the real world.
xviii "The proposition 'things exist' has no intelligible meaning except that they stand in relations to each other" (1887a, p. 186) (Chapter 1, § 1).
xix Lotze's claim that individuals (things) are laws (1879, §§ 32 ff.) is connected with his insistence that concepts are functions. Later this position was adopted by Ernst Cassirer, among others (Chapter 9, § 6).
xx According to Lotze, things can be seen, *metaphorically speaking*, as something alive. Their relations to other things can be seen as their "behavior" (Chapter 1, § 4.6) (Milkov 2002a, § 7).

xxi See en. xii.

xxii See en. xix.

xxiii See Chapter 1, § 4.2.

xxiv Lotze's formula "M = ϕ(ABR)" renders the relation between whole and its parts. It plays a leading role in his ontology (1879, §§ 89, 92) (Chapter 1, § 4.2).

xxv According to Russell, the conception of spontaneous emergence of new causal chains is the main drawback of Lotze's ontology (see en. xii).

xxvi On Lotze's perspectivism, see Chapter 1, § 3.1, Chapter 2, § 11.

xxvii This position of Lotze only seems to be panpsychical. Lotze spoke about reality as sentient only metaphorically.

xxviii This interpretation of McTaggart is mistaken. As an implication of Lotze's perspectivism, Lotze can be correctly interpreted both as a monadist and as a holist. It depends on whether we are considering the problem from metaphysical (cosmological) or from the logical point of view (Chapter 6, § 7). It is also incorrect to interpret Lotze's "absolute" as Lotze's "M" (en. xxiv).

xxix On Lotze's argument for God as a person, see Chapter 3, § 4.5.

xxx Russell's statement two lines above that Lotze did not "subsume space under idea of form or intuition" shows that Lotze's conception of space was not "fundamentally like Kant's".

xxxi See Chapter 2, § 9.

xxxii Lotze repeatedly argued against the notion of non-Euclidean space (1879, § 137). Carl Stumpf, his former student, followed Lotze on this in his habilitation (second doctoral) thesis (1870) but later came to the conclusion that this is a mistake (Chapter 5, § 2).

xxxiii In his argument against empty time, Lotze shook hands with Leibniz and turned against Newton (Chapter 2, § 9).

xxxiv This is one of Lotze's key arguments. It deserves notice that Richard Dedekind and Georg Cantor, who helped Russell to "solve" the problem of infinity (Milkov 2016b), were among Lotze's students (Chapter 6, § 2).

xxxv See Chapter 2, § 9.

xxxvi See en. xiii.

xxxvii Cause and effect are, according to Lotze, coexisting in a way similar to that matter and mind are coexisting (Chapter 2, § 6).

xxxviii See en. xxviii.

xxxix Actions, according to Lotze, have teleological-mechanical character (Chapter 2, § 4).

xl On Lotze's critique of vitalism see Chapter 2, § 4.

xli Lotze maintained that soul is an organic unity (Chapter 2, § 10). Russell, on his part (e.g., in *Theory of Knowledge*, 1913), understood the "I" as a substance.

xlii This is the position of Lotze's physical-psychological mechanism (Chapter 2, § 5).

xliii This is the thesis of Lotze's occasionalism (Chapter 2, § 6).

xliv Lotze criticizes Hume's and Herbart's understandings of thinking as association of ideas also called "chemistry of ideas": it goes against Lotze's context principle (Introduction, §§ 4.2, 4.3; en. v).

xlv Under "psychical mechanism", McTaggart meant Fechner's identity theory of mind and matter (Chapter 2, § 3).

xlvi Lotze discussed the local-signs (*Localzeichen*) in (1879, §§ 279 ff.) (Chapter 2, § 8).

xlvii Cf. en. xl.

xlviii See our interpretation of this claim of Lotze in Chapter 1, § 4.1.

xlix Emil Walter Mayer (1854–1927) was an obscure German philosopher who, among other things, authored the paper "Christliche Moral in ihrem Verhältnis zum (staatlichen) Recht"

(1892). In it, Mayer did not refer directly to Lotze's view on religion but rather to that of Lotze's prominent student Albrecht Ritschl.

l See Chapter 4, § 3.1; Chapter 5, § 7.

li "All that is real is mind [*Geistigkeit*]" is the title of § 3 of Chapter Three, "The Real and the Mind", Book Nine, of Lotze's *Mikrokosmus*. Lotze's alleged idealism was main problem for Russell and explains his reluctance to accept Lotze as his master and to correctly appreciate the role Lotze played in his philosophical development. As already seen in Chapter 2, § 3, however, Lotze did not maintain that reality can be *reduced* to the *Geistigkeit*. In fact, he was more of a Platonic realist than an idealist (Chapter 6, § 5).

lii Lotze *did not* see God Almighty as "M" (en. xxviii). This was McTaggart's interpretation.

liii See Chapter 1, n. 43.

liv Lotze discussed the proofs for the existence of God in (1864, pp. 549–558).

lv See en. xxix.

lvi See en. lii.

lvii Frege, who attended Lotze's lectures on philosophy of religion, closely connected the approval (assertion) and disapproval (negation) of propositions with human will (Milkov 2015b).

lviii See en. xii.

lix For Lotze's defense of dogmas in religion see Chapter 3, § 4.6.

lx Cf. Chapter 6, n. 194.

lxi On Lotze's hedonistic ethics, see Chapter 1, § 4.1.

lxii On Lotze as the allegedly first feminist philosopher, see Woodward (2015, pp. 284).

lxiii On Lotze as defender of the classical bourgeois liberalism, see Chapter 3, § 4.4.

Chapter 8
Lotze, William James, and Bertrand Russell

1 Opening

Between 1905 and 1919, Russell was critical of pragmatism. In two essays written in 1908–1909, he sharply attacked the pragmatist theory of truth, emphasizing that truth is not relative to human practice. At the same time, however, Russell was clearly indebted to the pragmatists, in particular to William James. He borrowed from James two key concepts of his epistemology: sense-data and the distinction between knowledge by acquaintance and knowledge by description (Milkov 2001).

In this chapter, we shall try to provide a reasonable explanation of this ambiguity. We are going to demonstrate that, historically, Russell's logical realism and James' pragmatism have, at least to a certain extent, the same roots—some ideas of Hermann Lotze. To be more explicit, we are going to explore the fact that in 1905, reflecting on some ideas of Lotze, Russell married propositions with beliefs. This, however, is only the first part of our story. A few years later, Russell embraced the theory of truth-making that had its roots in James and, ultimately, in Lotze once again.

2 William James as a Philosopher

A great predicament in assessing a particular philosopher of about 1900 is the later split of Western philosophy into analytic and continental (Introduction, § 1). William James is especially difficult to place in the pigeonholes of this divide. On the one hand, he was clearly a voluntarist. To be sure, for James, human practice ranges higher than theoretical reason.[216] On the other hand, however, James was an anti-speculative, "concrete" philosopher. He understood himself as a "radical empiricist". This explains why in the Manifesto of the Vienna Circle, James was listed amongst those philosophers who embraced the scientific world-view (Hahn, Neurath, and Carnap 1929, p. 9). Indeed, James was an anti-transcendentalist and a defender of experience and experiment. To him, every form of transcendentalism was a remnant of the philosophical scholastic. Following this maxim, he also fought the abstractness of the "radical intellectualism" of Russell and Moore.

---

[216] This point was first made by Susan Stebbing (1914).

3 James' Direct Influence on Russell

Russell first met James in the autumn of 1896, during his first trip to North America, when he and his wife Alys paid a visit to James and his wife in Boston. Soon, Russell developed a genuine affection for his American host, which also found expression in his writings. He borrowed from James important ideas of his new philosophy. Here are four of them:

(i) James introduced the concept of "sense-data" in *The Principles of Psychology* (1890, ii, pp. 146, 184, 620). In 1898–1900, Russell embraced James' term. Soon, however, after his logical turn of 1900 (Milkov 2016b), he abandoned it. A decade later, though, in *The Problems of Philosophy* (1912a), Russell reintroduced this concept in his philosophy, this time following a hint of G. E. Moore (Milkov 2001).

(ii) James made a sharp distinction between "knowledge of acquaintance" and "knowledge about" in his *Psychology: Brief Course* (1892, p. 19). Russell adopted this distinction in "On Denoting" (1905a) but made an exact distinction between these two concepts only in "Knowledge by Acquaintance and Knowledge by Description" (1911b). Importantly enough, Russell maintained that the concepts of sense-data and knowledge by acquaintance are closely connected. Indeed, according to his epistemology of 1913–1914, we know by acquaintance sense-data, universals, and logical forms.

(iii) Russell borrowed from James' *The Varieties of Religious Experience* (1902) the distinction between "mysticism" and "logic" that he explored in (1918b).

(iv) After close examination of James' conception of "neutral monism" in *Theory of Knowledge* (1913, Chapter 2), Russell adopted it in "On Propositions" (1919) and in *The Analysis of Mind* (1921).

4 James' and Russell's Debt to Lotze

The main claim of this chapter is that the theoretical relatedness between James and Russell can be successfully explained if we pass in review the historical roots of their philosophy. Then we shall see that at the origins of their relatedness was the German philosopher, psychologist, and logician Hermann Lotze.

4.1 Lotze and William James

William James' philosophy was greatly influenced by Hermann Lotze (Poggi and Vagnetti 2015). James met Lotze in Göttingen in person during his study trip in Germany in 1867–1868. But he was really influenced by the German philosopher much later, which occurred in two waves. The first wave began in 1879 when James studied Lotze's basic works *Medicinische Psychologie* (1852a), *Mikrokosmus* (1856– 1864), his "greater" *Logic* (1874), and his "greater" *Metaphysic* (1879). In a letter from 1881, James wrote: "[Lotze] seems to me the most exquisite of contemporary minds" (1995, p. 181). Lotze's influence on James found first expression in James' *The Principles of Psychology* (1890). The second wave of Lotze's influence on James extended from the turn of the century until James' death in 1910. It is clearly perceptible in *The Varieties of Religious Experience* (1902) (Kraushaar 1940, p. 442).

James borrowed at least two doctrines from Lotze:

i. The introduction of immediate data of reality in human understanding: both the data of perception as its content.[217] Starting exactly from this point, James developed the concept of "sense-data" and of the data (the content) of judgments and beliefs.[218]

ii. The primacy of practical reason over theoretical. In fact, this idea was leading in the German philosophy after Kant (Murphey 1968). However, "Lotze goes even further than Kant in the defence of practical reason, for he claims priority not only for formal principles but for values as well" (Kraushaar 1940, p. 446). This means that the question "what can I know?" cannot be answered in the abstract, as Kant did.[219] It is only to be responded anthropologically in terms of embodied persons who are situated in concrete socio-historical context. Only when we adopt this position, Lotze thought, can we also grasp the depth and the importance of the metaphysical problems. Importantly enough, William James followed the principle of primacy of the practical reason over the theoretical in its Lotzean form, not in its Kantian form. This becomes fairly clear when we examine his theory of truth-making (§ 7 below).[220]

4.2 Hermann Lotze and Bertrand Russell: Propositions are Believed

We have already discussed Lotze's influence on Russell in detail in Chapters 6 and 7. Here, we are going to concentrate only on Russell's debt to Lotze by introducing the concepts of "believing propositions" or that of "propositional attitudes" in his philosophy.

---

[217] Lotze influenced Brentano and Stumpf in a similar way (Chapters 4 and 5).
[218] As already pointed out in § 3 above, Russell, in his turn, adopted the concept of sense-data from James.
[219] The abstractness of Kant's transcendental philosophy was main point of criticism of Brentano and Stumpf as well.
[220] On Lotze's influence on William James, see also Chapter 2, §§ 10, 12.

It is a matter of fact that Russell introduced the understanding that we believe propositions when working on Lotze. To be more specific, he first mentioned the concept "belief in proposition" in the paper "The Notion of Order and Absolute Position in Space and Time", delivered on August 2, 1900, in French, at the International Congress of Philosophy in Paris (1901a, 1901b, 1901c). In it, Russell discussed Lotze's conception of relations, in particular Lotze's claim that "relations are either presentations [*Vorstellungen*] in a relating mind or inner conditions of the elements of reality" (Lotze 1879, § 109, p. 208). Furthermore, Lotze insisted that it is "correct to speak of relations *between* ideas, not *between* things" (Chapter 7, fol. 99). Russell commented that "these presentations [which are in the relating mind], we must suppose, are *beliefs in propositions* which assert relations between the terms which appear related to one another" (1901a, p. 250; italics added).[221]

In an attempt to explain why Russell introduced this concept, we would like to remind the reader that at that point in time, Russell assumed that the world consists of concepts and complexes of concepts, or propositions. To be more precise, Russell adapted Lotze's insistence that judgments are directed to objective content (Introduction, § 2). In his logic, Russell expressed this understanding with the words that the world can be referred to by terms and propositions. In fact, Russell's claim from (1901a) that instead of presentations, we can speak about beliefs in propositions, followed this position. In that specific paper, Russell rejected this position. It conflicted with his "robust sense of reality". Relations are not beliefs in propositions. They are denizens of the external world that have "independence of any knowing mind" (Russell 1903, p. xviii).

It should be noted, however, that in this particular criticism of Lotze, Russell fell victim to Lotze's perspectivism again (Chapter 6, § 8). It is true that Lotze maintained that relations are between ideas (or between "beliefs in propositions"). However, he meant this only from what he saw as a logical (ontological) point of view. From the metaphysical (cosmological) perspective, Lotze maintained that the real (*wirkliche*) world consists of interrelated objects. In fact, Russell adopted the latter—cosmological—position of Lotze (Chapter 6, § 6) but rejected its logical (ontological) perspective.

Be this as it may, as an implication of these discussions, the expression "belief in proposition" found solid place in Russell's head. It should be not a surprise, therefore, that in "The Nature of Truth", written while preparing "On Denoting" and read at the Jowett Society in Oxford on June 10, 1905, Russell readily adopted it. Now he held that "it is the things which are or may be *objects of belief* that I call *propositions*" (Russell

---

[221] Clearly, Russell followed here the method of treating philosophical problems in logical terms that he introduced in his book on Leibniz (1900a). As we already have seen in the Introduction, § 4.1, however, this position was also assumed by Lotze.

1905b, p. 494). We only believe propositions, not ideas; moreover, propositions absolutely require beliefs. Russell's main enemy now was the concept of judgment—he replaced it with belief.[222] The problem was that "the notion that truth is concerned with judgments is derived from the notion that truth consists in the *correspondence of our ideas with facts*" (Russell 1905b, p. 492; italics added), and the latter notion is problematic.[223] Against it, Russell (as well as the Moore of this period) maintained the famous "identity theory of truth", according to which "truth lies not in the correspondence of our ideas with facts, but in the fact itself" (Russell 1905b, p. 492).[224]

As an implication of his Theory of Description (1905a), however, put down only a month and a half after he delivered "The Nature of Truth", Russell radically revised his theory of judgment. In "On the Nature of Truth" (1907b), he maintained that belief is identical with judgment. Moreover, a belief differs "from an idea or presentation by the fact that it consists of several interrelated terms" (p. 46). This was the first variant of Russell's famous Multiple Relation Theory of Judgment (of Belief)[225] according to which "propositions are incomplete symbols that require the context of judging mind in order to achieve a meaning" (Stevens 2005, p. 79). Belief, or judgment, is a multiple relation of the believing/judging person to a complex. At the same time, however, Russell continued to speak about "believing propositions".

Importantly enough, this understanding was supported by the concept of "state of affairs", also introduced by Lotze (Chapter 1, § 4.5, Chapter 4, § 7), according to which the individuals of a whole reciprocally relate to one another and also to the whole. Despite the fact that Russell never made use of this concept, it neatly fits his Multiple Relation Theory of Judgment. This is supported by the fact that the concept of "states of affairs" was used by his student and associate Ludwig Wittgenstein, with whom Russell worked on a joint program in March–November 1912 (Milkov 2013b). In more concrete terms, Wittgenstein took it over from the phenomenologists (to be more exact, from Adolf Reinach—see McGuinness 2002, p. 171), who were greatly indebted to Lotze as well (Introduction, § 2).

---

222 Until that point in time, Russell assumed that judgments and beliefs are one and the same thing (Chapter 6, n. 191).
223 Both Lotze (1874, § 304) and Frege criticized the correspondence theory of truth.
224 On the identity theory of truth, see Baldwin (1991).
225 Russell only abandoned it in 1919 as an implication of Wittgenstein's criticism of his *Theory of Knowledge*. Because of this criticism, Russell did not finish that book.

5 Russell's Propositional Attitudes

For contemporary philosophers and logicians, it is fairly clear that the introduction of the term of belief in logic was a risky move that, as already seen, Russell nevertheless made, leaning on Lotze's epistemology. As we are going to show in the lines below, eventually, it turned out to be the Trojan horse for the introduction of practical elements into his logic.

The problem with the understanding that we believe propositions—and not, for example, simply grasp them (as Frege maintained) or entertain them (as maintained by the influential Cambridge logician of the turn of the century William E. Johnson)—was that it was in palpable tension with Russell's extensional logic. More precisely, it was in contest with its Principle of Extensionality, which holds that

> the truth or falsehood of any statement about a proposition *p* depends only upon the truth or falsehood of *p* and that the truth or falsehood of any statement involving a propositional function depends only upon the extension of the function. (Russell 1959, p. 87)

Russell realised the problems in his new conception of proposition a few years later. In *The Analysis of Mind*, where he showed more interest in problems of psychology, he noted that belief "is an actual experienced *feeling*" (1921, p. 140; italics added) in the way in which asserting is not. Apparently, by introducing the concept of "belief" into his logic, Russell made major concessions to psychologism.

Before to carry out our analysis of the problems that the concept "believing propositions" posed into Russell's logic, it should be observed that while reflecting on that concept in "On Propositions", he introduced the term "propositional attitudes", maintaining that

> A form of words, unless artificially constructed, usually expresses not only the content of a proposition, but also what may be called a "propositional attitude"—memory, expectation, desire, etc.[226] (Russell 1919, p. 309)

The main kind of propositional attitude is belief, however.

In order to better understand Russell's concept of "propositional attitude", it should be observed that in 1913 and 1914, he worked hard on problems of epistemology. The results of these explorations were the books *Theory of Knowledge* (1913) and *Our Knowledge of the External World* (1914). In these years, Russell maintained that

---

[226] Russell already toyed with the idea of introducing the term "propositional attitudes" in his lectures "The Philosophy of Logical Atomism" where he concluded: "But I should not like that because it [the term 'attitudes'] is a psychological term" (1918a, p. 227).

"the distinguishing mark of what is mental, or at any rate what is cognitive, is not to be found in the particulars involved, but only in the nature of the *relations* between them" (1913, p. 45; italics added). In other words, the difference between believing, dreaming, remembering, and imagining is not a function of their objects or propositions but rather of the mental attitude to them. There is no difference in the mental objects *per se*. The objects in a dream, for example, are different from the objects that we perceive when we are awake only because the relation between the "I" and the object is different. Importantly enough, we have cognitive attitudes not only toward objects but also toward facts, events and, in logic, propositions.

Russell became aware of the deficiency of his theory of believing propositions only through Wittgenstein's critique of his *Theory of Knowledge* book-project (see n. 225). According to Russell's "puzzle about the nature of belief", as set out in "The Philosophy of Logical Atomism", in which Russell reassessed his philosophical ideas of the period before the Great War that he stopped exploring for more than three years,

> You cannot make what I should call a map-in-space of a belief. You can make a map of an atomic fact but not of a belief, for the simple reason that space-relations always are of the atomic sort or complications of the atomic sort. ... [The point is that] belief cannot strictly be logically one in all different cases but must be distinguished according to the nature of the propositions that you believe (Russell 1918a, pp. 224 ff.).

In other words, propositions of the form "Othello believes that 'Desdemona loves Cassio'" do not relate two terms, *a* and *b*. This is obvious when the judgment happens to be false. Russell's conclusion was that propositions with propositional attitudes as their constituents are "apparent propositions"—they violate the Principle of Extensionality.

In a sense, Russell was right—one cannot make a map of a belief. Still, his interpretation shows that he failed to grasp the full force of Wittgenstein's argument. It is not only beliefs of which we cannot make maps; we cannot make maps of any fact whatsoever. This is because maps are produced in space and can only represent spatial objects. They cannot depict facts because these are not spatial. We can only map complexes (Milkov 2013b; see § 7 below).

Gradually realizing that the concept of "believing propositions" is problematic, in his lectures "The Philosophy of Logical Atomism", Russell toyed with the idea of replacing it with "propositional verbs". In this context, he reminded his audience that from most general point of view, the universe can have attributes that are neither psychic nor material (1918a, p. 227). Hence, propositions are not necessarily to be embraced by minds. Of course, propositional verbs are very well exemplified by beliefs. But they can also be exemplified by non-psychological terms.

But Russell explicitly revolted against the concept of belief in propositions only in "On Propositions" (1919) and in *The Analysis of Mind* (1921); in them, he adopted William James' conception of neutral monism and also John B. Watson's behaviourism in interpreting beliefs. To be more explicit, now Russell ceased to claim that there is a place for propositional attitudes in logic since he, being now a neutral monist, stopped maintaining that there are subjects.

6 Analytic Revolt Against Russell's Propositional Attitudes

As can be expected, the two most talented followers of Russell of the time, Wittgenstein and Frank Ramsey, severely criticized the introduction of propositional attitudes into logic. They claimed, correctly, that this assumption contests the central principle of Russell's logic—the Principle of Extensionality:

i. In contrast to Russell, who eliminated the subject when he adopted the theory of neutral monism, Wittgenstein simply analysed "A believes that p" to "'p' says p" (5.542). In this way, the Principle of Extensionality was saved. Propositions occur in other propositions only as bases of truth-operations.
ii. Ramsey criticized Russell's beliefs from the other direction. He maintained that belief is an ambiguous term that can be interpreted in many different ways.

It is, for instance, possible to say that a chicken believes a certain sort of caterpillar to be poisonous, and mean by that merely that it abstains from eating such caterpillars on account of unpleasant experience connected with them. (Ramsey 1927, p. 46)

In fact, in "On Propositions", Russell himself suggested similar interpretation and attributed it to pragmatism. According to it, "there is no single occurrence which can be described as 'believing a proposition', but belief simply consists in causal efficiency" (Russell 1919, p. 310). Exactly this position gave Ramsey ground to state: "My pragmatism is derived from Mr Russell" (1927, p. 51).

A similar correction to Russell was made by another young and promising philosopher of the early 1930s in Cambridge—R. B. Braithwaite. In his paper "The Nature of Believing" (1932/1933), Braithwaite adopted a behaviourist account of believing. To be more specific, he joined the statement made by Alexander Bain that "belief has no meaning, except in reference to our action" (1859, p. 568). On the continent of Europe, Carnap was exactly as resolute against the Russellian propositional attitudes as his British colleagues were, defending the Principle of Extensionality: "*all propositions are extensional*" (1928, p. 63). This position was later argued for by Carnap's friend Quine (1960, pp. 191 ff.).

In Russell's defence, it can be said that his conception of propositional attitudes was his answer to Frege's claim that we state propositions with "affirmative *force*".

The problem with this conception was that it connected logic to a kind of logical voluntarism (Milkov 2015b), which explains why Russell decisively repudiated it.[227] Russell, in his indirect answer to Frege's position, maintained that "the vehicles of truth and falsehood" are our beliefs, not our will (1921, p. 139).

In conclusion, it should be observed that both Frege and Russell made concessions to the intensional understanding of logic at the cost of extensional logic. It deserves notice, however, that also Wittgenstein, who was thus critical of the Russellian propositional attitudes in the *Tractatus*, failed to shun the relatedness of his philosophy of language to pragmatism[228]—despite the fact that we cannot agree with A. J. Ayer's claim that the principle of verification that Wittgenstein adopted in the early 1930s "is indeed identical" with the "pragmatic maxim" (1968, p. 45).

7 James' Late Influence on Russell: Truth-Making

The mainstream scholars of pragmatism today maintain that while Russell showed some sympathy to pragmatism in and after 1919, he was still against "the pragmatist account of truth" (Misak 2019, p. 72). In this section, we are going to show, however, that in those years and in this respect, Russell was closer to James than it is usually believed. Furthermore, we shall see that this relatedness was supported by the fact, already discussed in § 4 above, that both philosophers, James and Russell, started their philosophical development based on some seminal ideas of Hermann Lotze.

In the late 1900^s, James' theory of truth or his "pragmatic maxim" was severely criticized by Moore (1908) and Russell (1908 and 1909). In particular, they decisively rejected the concept of truth-making. The truth is not *made*—it is not a process. Truth is valid.[229] It is something that pertains to logic and there are simply no processes in logic. Even more importantly, the truth is not made by men. It is objective.

Russell rejected James' theory of truth-making also in *The Problems of Philosophy* (1912a). Typically, however, he was already toying with the idea of using it. In particular, against James, as Russell understood him at this point in time, he argued that "what makes a belief true [if anything at all] is a *fact*", not a mind (Russell 1912a, p. 203). Despite the fact that Russell's use of the term "making-true" was only rhetorical here—in an effort to refute James—this was a step towards its adoption.

---

[227] In § 7 below, we shall review Russell's struggle between 1907 and 1909 against William James' alleged logical voluntarism.
[228] On the relatedness of pragmatism and Wittgenstein, see Boncompagni (2016).
[229] Incidentally, this was another idea of Lotze that G. E. Moore and Russell adopted—this time through their tutor James Ward.

Things changed after Russell read, or actually wrote down, Wittgenstein's "Notes on Logic" in September 1913. When Wittgenstein visited Frege in December 1912, the latter convinced him that propositions do not correspond to complexes but rather to facts, which are individuals.[230] The implication was the theory of truth-making that Wittgenstein now adopted (1979, pp. 95, 105).[231] This correction of the joint program of Russell and Wittgenstein of the second half of 1912 (Milkov 2013b) was important since, in contrast to complexes, which are simply there, facts are not unfolded in space (despite the fact that they are situated in space). They happen and are unities of necessity. Without any doubt, Frege adopted this idea from his professor in Göttingen, Lotze (Chapter 2, § 12). Wittgenstein transformed these remarks into the conception that facts of the real world, which are a kind of organic unity, *make* specific propositions that we construct true and others false (Milkov 2013b).

In order to better understand the sense in which Wittgenstein spoke about truth-"making" here, we must remind the reader of his thesis that "in the proposition we—so to speak—arrange things experimentally" with the aim to imitate reality (Wittgenstein 1979, p. 13). Practices such as using dolls for modelling a car accident function in this way. In a sense, the whole of language is a concatenation of such models or, as Wittgenstein would have it, a concatenation of pictures. The important point here is Wittgenstein's insistence that language is a product of our "*activity* to construct languages capable of expressing every sense" (1922, 4.002; italics added). This claim automatically assigns pragmatist qualities to reality—reality *determines* if these particular language products are true or false. In this sense, it *produces* their truth/falsity. In other words, the *act* of depicting entails a virtual *act* of truth-*making*.

Surprisingly enough, this understanding is not far from that of James. The problem, however, is that James' theory of truth is rather difficult to understand and interpret unambiguously. As Hilary Putnam pointed out, to state its real point is not easier than to set out the real point of Wittgenstein's philosophy (1994). One reason for this is that James deliberately wrote in a popular style and, for this purpose, he often overstated his position. This went together with the fact that his theory of truth was nothing but a summary of different themes that had accumulated in his thought over the years.

---

[230] As we have already seen in § 5 above, this assumption already contained in itself the indication that Russell's multiple relation theory of judgment is false.

[231] We can only speculate about Russell's role by coining the term of truth-making in Wittgenstein's "Notes on Logic". The point is that it was Russell who translated, in September 1913, Wittgenstein's "Notes" into English and also rearranged them, while the German original text of the "Notes" was not preserved. And, as just seen, Russell already spoke about "truth-making" in *The Problems of Philosophy*.

Be this as it may, it is clear that James' theory of truth is a correspondence theory (Putnam 1997, p. 170). He was convinced that what makes our beliefs true is the external world and nothing beyond it. In *Pragmatism*, in particular, James contended:

> Truth *happens* to an idea. It *becomes* true, is *made* true by events. Its verity is in fact an event, a process: the process namely of its verifying itself, its veri-*fication*. Its validity is the process of its vali-*dation*. (1907, p. 89)

It is the facts or the events that make propositions true.

But James also held, similarly to Wittgenstein, that truth-making is a fitting of two sides. Not only does the matter fit the ideas; the ideas are also to fit the matter. To be more explicit, James claimed that "when they [ideas] add themselves to being, they partly *predetermine* the existent, so that reality as a whole appears incompletely definable unless ideas also are kept account of" (James 1909, pp. 185–186). What distinguished James' position from that of Wittgenstein here was only his insistence that truth-making is a *process*.

8 Russell's Troubles with Truth-Making

Ironically enough, whereas Wittgenstein abandoned the theory of truth-making shortly afterwards while working on his *Notebooks 1914–1916*, so that it found no place in the *Tractatus*,[232] Russell embraced it without reservations in "The Philosophy of Logical Atomism", in "On Propositions", and in *The Analysis of Mind*. Apparently, he did not notice Wittgenstein's change in view on this point. Presumably, Russell's adoption of the phrase "making true" happened in the same way as his adoption of the phrase "belief in propositions" that we discussed in § 4.2 above. At first, Russell rejected it, but at the same time it entered his head. Eventually, after a long period of ruminations, he adopted it.

But Russell also failed to notice that the adoption of the concept of truth-making put him close to James' theory of truth. In fact, this cannot be a surprise since Russell misunderstood James' theory of truth from the very beginning, in particular, in his critical papers against it from 1908–1909. And he had a good excuse for this. The point is that to this conception of truth, James added the idea of usefulness. He, namely, claimed that when a fact "verifies" or makes an idea or a proposition true, the proposition (the idea) is "useful": "You can say of it either that 'it is useful because

---

[232] The reason for this was that in or about May 1915, Wittgenstein realized that language is not an autonomous entity but is only a way of arrangements of objects of reality in propositions (Milkov 2020c). The truth-making relation, however, requires the autonomy of language units (Simons 1992).

it is true' or that 'it is true because it is useful'" (James 1907, p. 90). It was exactly this notion of "usefulness" that the realists Russell and Moore fiercely opposed. It was in strong disparity with Moore's and Russell's "robust sense of reality". For our analysis, it is of special importance that James adopted this idea directly from Lotze—it followed the principle of primacy of the practical reason over the theoretical in Lotze's form (§ 4.1 above). As we already have seen (in Chapter 6, § 1), however, Russell was deeply critical of Lotze's anthropological stance.

It was only after 1940 that Russell, becoming increasingly critical of Wittgenstein, realised that the concept of truth-making he adopted is heavily pregnant with pragmatism. In consequence, in his lectures published as *The Impact of Science on Society*, he explicitly repudiated it (1951, p. 75). Instead of facts as truth-makers, he now spoke of "verifiers",[233] apparently failing to realize that this term too was introduced by William James, the pragmatist. Russell also continued to use the term "verifiers" in his later works—in *Human Knowledge: Its Scope and Limits* (1948, pp. 166 ff.) and in *My Philosophical Development* (1959, pp. 138 ff.).

9 Epilogue

Today, some authors insist that the dominance of analytic philosophy in North America after the 1930s was not exclusively connected with the influence of the logical empiricists who immigrated to the USA in the 1930s and 1940s. It was also prepared by the radical empiricism of the pragmatist movement. The smooth process of merging of the tradition of pragmatism with that of the logical empiricism is to be understood in this key. In Europe, however, that merger came to light already in the mid-1930s, when Charles Morris delivered his paper "The Concept of Meaning in Pragmatism and Logical Positivism" (1936) at the World Congress of Philosophy in Prague. It received loud acclaim from Carnap (Dahms 1992, pp. 240, 248).

Our concluding contention in this chapter is that this painless merger between logical empiricism and pragmatism was facilitated by the circumstance that Russell's conceptions of propositional attitudes and truth-makers made significant concessions to pragmatism. All three, however, have their roots in the philosophy of Hermann Lotze.

---

[233] This he did for the first time in *An Inquiry into Meaning and Truth* (Russell 1940, p. 227).

Part IV: **Lotze and the Philosophy of Logical Empiricism**

Chapter 9
Lotze, Heinrich Rickert, and Logical Empiricism

1 Opening

Over the past three decades, Alberto Coffa and Michael Friedman have brought to light traces of the Marburg Neo-Kantian Ernst Cassirer's impact on the early logical empiricists. Recently, however, some authors made it clear that Rudolf Carnap's *Aufbau* (1928), a paradigmatic text of early logical empiricism, was influenced not only by Cassirer but also by Heinrich Rickert. The present chapter shows that the latter's role extended beyond the early Carnap to early logical empiricism as a whole, most notably by way of Rickert's theory of concept formation. What is more, the cryptic connection of Rickert to the early logical empiricists was of more importance to it than that of Cassirer.

The logical empiricists had their own program, which had clearly closer contact than Rickert to the revolutionary changes in science and mathematics of the time. Be this as it may, they followed the pace of Rickert, specifically, in making the problem of conceptual construction in science a key philosophical subject, despite the fact that they did this in their own way. Rickert also facilitated the enthusiastic reception of Wittgenstein's early philosophy by the members of the Vienna Circle. Ultimately, we are going to show that Rickert's fruitful impact on the logical empiricists started from some ideas of Hermann Lotze.

2 The Philosophy of Logical Empiricism and the Southwest Neo-Kantians

According to the leading proponents of logical empiricism, the sudden disappearance of Neo-Kantianism from the philosophical scene after the First World War was an implication of new theories in science and mathematics. The logical empiricists maintained that the new ideas introduced in physics by Albert Einstein and in mathematics by David Hilbert completely discredited Kant's philosophy of nature and of mathematics.[234] In particular, the logical empiricists were convinced that Einstein and Hilbert demonstrated that there is no credible basis for invoking perceptual intuition in science and mathematics.

---

[234] This is especially true of the members of the Vienna Circle, in contrast to the members of the Berlin Group, who were not so quick to dismiss Kant (Milkov 2013a).

How problematic this position was is clear from the fact that Hilbert himself, especially after he adopted the "proof theory" in 1918, put great store in a kind of Neo-Kantian basis for his philosophy of mathematics. After displaying an initial enthusiasm for empiricism in the decade from 1915 to 1925, Einstein, in turn, was drawn toward Pierre Duhem's holism. These developments suggest that the principal concern of the logical empiricists of that period was not Kant exclusively and that the way forward was not seen to lie only in a turn to empiricism. As Michael Friedman has shown (2001), Kant's philosophy of science can be successfully transformed or relativized in order to meet the challenges of the new ideas in science and mathematics. The critical stance toward German philosophy that thrived in the English-speaking academy until around 1970 can be explained to a considerable extent by reference to the *Zeitgeist* of animosity. Division into antagonistic parties and blocs was the banner of the epoch: Germans against Britons and French, analytic against continental philosophy. The critical position of the logical empiricists toward Kant arose in this context of animosity and antagonistic political and sociocultural ideologies.

The objective of this chapter is to show, in ways that break with the received history, that early logical empiricism was at least in part a continuation and transformation of mainstream academic German philosophy from the second half of the 19th century and the first years of the 20th century.

This divergence from the standard accounts is not simply a result of chasing after idiosyncrasy but rather a reading of the evidence that is borne out, as we shall see, both philosophically and historically. It is consistent, moreover, with the new efforts of reassessment made by the 20th century exact philosophy, which has been on rise over the last three decades. On that score, studies by Alberto Coffa, Alan Richardson and Michael Friedman have revealed the considerable influence on early logical empiricists exerted by Ernst Cassirer, who through his middle years was a Marburg Neo-Kantian (Coffa 1993, Richardson 1998, and Friedman 1999). However, the task in these pages, by contrast, is to demonstrate that the Southwest Neo-Kantians played an even more important role in the development of logical empiricism.

First steps in this direction have already been made. Over a decade ago, Thomas Mormann declared that "the basic architectonic and agenda of [Rudolf Carnap's] *Aufbau* was marked by the Neo-Kantian school of Heidelberg (and Jena) school and not by that of Marburg" (2006, p. 26). More recently, Mikko Leinonen (2016) added that Heinrich Rickert exerted an influence on Carnap that is discernible in the younger man's work throughout his entire career. This, incidentally, is hardly surprising given that Carnap studied at Jena with both the Southwest

Neo-Kantian Bruno Bauch[235] and Gottlob Frege who, as we know today, was considerably under Lotze's influence (Introduction, § 3). In 1912, Carnap also attended lectures by Rickert in Freiburg and found them rather inspiring (Carnap 2022, pp. 94ff., 117f.). One detects Rickert's influence in particular, notes Leinonen, in Carnap's 1922 manuscript *Vom Chaos zur Wirklichkeit* (Kulyk 2019), and its traces persist in Carnap's later work, for example, in the paper "Empiricism, Semantic and Ontology" (1950). What is clear in these works is that both Rickert and Carnap took a constructivist view of reality according to which the concepts of science are to be drawn up before starting scientific exploration.

3 Rickert's Impact on the Logical Empiricists: A First Approximation

Heinrich Rickert was a doctoral student of Wilhelm Windelband at the University of Strasburg, and Windelband became "a major source of inspiration for Rickert's work" (Staiti 2013). Windelband, for his part, was a former doctoral student of Hermann Lotze. Rickert's *magnum opus, The Limits of Concept Formation in Natural Science (Die Grenzen der naturwissenschaftlichen Begriffsbildung)*, the first Part of which appeared in 1896, was instrumental in putting the subject of concept formation in science at the center of the philosophical discourse of the time. With the publication of the second edition (1902), to which Rickert added a second Part (Rickert 1896/1902), the book won a considerable readership among academic philosophers and scientists in Germany and beyond. It set the agenda for mainstream philosophical debate for years, influencing the thinking of distinguished scholars, such as Max Weber, whose theoretical interests extended beyond strictly philosophical concerns.[236]

It was during this period that the young Moritz Schlick published a paper on concept formation, a critical analysis occasioned precisely by Rickert's *Die Grenzen* (Schlick 1910/1911). This engagement with Rickert's thought proved to be—and this is a principal finding in the discussion that follows in the present chapter—a significant factor in the formative role that concept formation played in Schlick's philosophy of science. While Schlick could not be regarded as a champion of Rickert's theory of concept formation, he nonetheless appropriated Rickert's lead *subject* of concept formation in science, developing it in his own idiosyncratic way.

---

235 Bruno Bauch himself studied with Wilhelm Windelband and Heinrich Rickert.
236 Weber wrote in 1902 in a letter to his wife Mariane: "[Rickert] is very good. I partly find in him ideas that I myself entertained" (1950, p. 235).

What goes some way toward explaining this move on Schlick's part is that he was drawn to Rickert's subject—the epistemology of concept formation in science—because it suggested the radical aposteriority of scientific concepts. It assumed, namely, that the concepts required by scientific inquiry are not a priori but are rather *constructed* by scientists themselves. Crucially for Schlick, this position cohered with his deep-running predisposition to privilege empiricism.

After Schlick's pioneering works, the problem of concept formation became a core concern of the logical empiricists. In the forty years following the appearance of Schlick's paper on Rickert, the topic of concept formation emerged as a pivotal issue in book-length studies by such influential exponents of logical empiricism as Rudolf Carnap, Friedrich Waismann, Paul Oppenheim, and Carl Hempel (Carnap 1926, Oppenheim 1928, Waismann 1936, and Hempel 1952). And while Hans Reichenbach has left us no case treatment of the topic, concept formation was a defining component to his epistemology of science as well (1938, p. 91) (§ 7 below). Walter Dubislav, another leading figure of the Berlin Group of logical empiricism, also dealt at length with the problem of concept formation (Dubislav 1931, §§ 9 and 61; 1933, pp. 74–93).

It should be noted that between 1910 and 1960, the exponents of no other school of philosophical thought were as deeply engaged with the problematics of concept formation as were the logical empiricists. After the decline of logical empiricism in the 1960s, the problem of concept formation was scarcely discussed in philosophy for decades. This is attested, in a negative way, by the article on "concept formation" (*Begriffsbildung*) that appeared in the 1st volume of the twelve-volume *Historisches Wörterbuch der Philosophie* (1971/2007) (Foppa 1971), which restricted its treatment of concept formation only to psychology, ignoring its cardinal relevance to logic and philosophy of science. This omission reflects nothing so much as a widespread bias at the time of the *Wörterbuch*, Vol. I, toward the first of three discrete areas of philosophical inquiry that can address concept formation in principle: (i) the massively influential philosophical *psychologies* of Aristotle, Hume, Herbart and Mill, according to which concepts are nothing but abstractions from sense impressions; (ii) *logic*, where concepts are simply instrumental moments deployed to construct definitions; and, lastly, (iii) the *philosophy of science* originated by Lotze and Rickert that practically all of the early logical empiricists adopted and developed along their own lines.

4 History of the Notion of Concept Formation in Science

But how was it that Heinrich Rickert played a leading role by introducing the notion and thereby the very *topic* of concept formation in philosophy of science? To address this question calls, as a preliminary step, for a word about the historical development of this notion.

4.1 Kant and Fries

Kant was the first to set out, in the clear and forensically acute way that was typical of him, the role of logical concept formation in human knowledge. According to Kant, we construct the concepts only of mathematics but not those of the natural sciences (A713/B741). Concepts of science are simply "pure concepts" that unify sense-data spontaneously, in a transcendental-psychological way (McRobert 1994). They are not constructed by scientists themselves (Kant 1800, § 103).

Of special interest here is that Kant also introduced a logical dichotomy that sheds additional light on the problem of concept formation—the dichotomy between philosophy and mathematics. Philosophy operates with analytic concepts a priori while mathematics proceeds by way of synthetic concepts a priori. This makes the difference between these two disciplines a radical one. Whereas philosophy starts with complex elements of knowledge and analyzes them until it reaches clear and distinct ideas that underpin them, mathematics takes as its point of departure clear and distinct premises of intuition in order to construct complex concepts and theories. The method of philosophy is thus regressive and analytical, while that of mathematics is progressive and constructive.[237] The method of mathematics is dogmatic, while the method of philosophy is critical (analytical).

The first to turn full attention to this idea of Kant was Jakob Friedrich Fries. Fries found that Kant's position on mathematical method is also valid in what he had called "mathematical natural sciences"—i.e., in physics and chemistry. The task of physics and chemistry is to provide explanations. In contrast, the method that philosophy follows holds for the "descriptive natural sciences" (biology, geology, geography) and also in the humanities (Fries 1811, p. 303 f.). As this formulation suggests, the objective of these sciences is to advance descriptions. Furthermore, while the task of the mathematicized natural sciences is to achieve understanding (*Einsicht*), the task of descriptive sciences is to achieve cognition (*Kenntnis*) (p. 304).

Commenting on Kant's and Fries' theory of concepts, Walter Dubislav characterized their accounts as two alternative theories of conceptual construction (Dubislav 1931, pp. 7–17): (i) Mathematics and the mathematicized natural sciences are engaged in concept construction (in concept formation) and in explanation. (ii)

---

[237] This conception was repeated almost *mot-à-mot* by Bertrand Russell in (1907a).

Conceptual construction in philosophy, in humanities and in the descriptive natural sciences proceeds under the rubric of concept analysis, or exposition (*Aufweisung*). These disciplines are analytic in this sense (pp. 15 f.). Their objective, according to Dubislav, is to "discuss" (*erörtern*) concepts, so as to present them critically in order to foreground their defining moments.

4.2 Hermann Lotze

Hermann Lotze addressed the problem of concept formation along lines that track far beyond Kant and Fries on the topic. In his "greater" *Logic* (1874), especially in the section "Construction of Concept" ("*Die Bildung des Begriffs*") (pp. 36–56), Lotze criticized the position attributed to Plato that concepts are hyperuranian realities, David Hume's view that they ("ideas") are "intense impressions", and Mill's contention that concepts are the summary of the general characteristic of a class of particulars. On the other hand, Lotze also opposed Hegel's teaching that concepts shed light on the nature of the objects under review.

To Lotze, the concepts of science are not mirror images of "real" objects but are systematically constructed (made) from the manifolds of our perceptions by knowing subjects—the scientists. To be more explicit, he took concepts of science to be a product of our "logical work", or work of thinking, that exhibits four principal, progressively more developed epistemic stages, or forms of synthesis. The first is Kant's synthesis of apprehension. The second level is a synthesis of intuition (*Anschauung*). The third one engenders concepts that correspond to the "factual order of the multiplicity", while the fourth stage of synthesis is axiological, yielding concepts of the value of the objects of knowledge. A signal implication of Lotze's understanding is that the concepts of science are to be formulated by the scientists themselves (1874, § 27).

In his *Logik*, Christoph von Sigwart was the first prominent thinker to adopt Lotze's ideas of concept formation methodologically (Sigwart 1873/1878). Importantly enough, Sigwart took up the problem of concept formation only in Vol. II (pp. 176–222), which was published in 1878, i.e., four years after the appearance of Lotze's widely known "greater" *Logic* in 1874. This fact indicates that it was Sigwart who adopted his position from Lotze and not vice versa. Be this as it may, later influential philosophers who were drawn to the problematic of concept formation in the epistemology of science—Johannes Volkelt (1881), for example, and, more notably here, Heinrich Rickert[238]—referred to Sigwart's work much more frequently and in detail than to that of Lotze. That said, the problematic of concept formation was anything but an abiding preoccupation of mainstream logicians of the time in Germany. Important thinkers like Benno Erdmann and Wilhelm Wundt never so much as mentioned the topic of concept formation. The same is true of the Marburg Neo-Kantians Hermann Cohen and Paul Natorp. This seems especially unaccountable in the case of Cohen (1902), which totally ignored the theme of concept formation in science.

5 Heinrich Rickert on Concept Formations in Science

Although Sigwart and Volkelt had previously espoused Lotze's theory of concept formation, Heinrich Rickert was the first to develop it in detail. Like Kant and Fries, who saw concept formation in a logical way, as a kind of definition, Rickert's interest in this topic was first stimulated by his inquiry into definition. At the same time, however, he connected it with philosophy of science from the very beginning. In his PhD dissertation (1888), Rickert argued that the concepts of science are to be produced by definitions (p. 57). To this, however, Rickert made an important addendum. The experience presents us with a messy manifold of individuals and with what Kant called "pure concepts". The task of the scientist, before he starts to construct theories, is to define the concepts of his discipline precisely. This was a clear step beyond Kant, who maintained that when our mind is confronted with reality, the a priori ideas step in spontaneously in order to fuse with the data of experience.[239]

After Rickert defended his dissertation, the problem of concept formation in science became a leading topic in his works. We see this first in his 1894 paper "On the Theory of Concept Formation in Science". Two years later, Rickert pro-

---

238 Only in his late works did Rickert distance himself from Sigwart because of Sigwart's psychologism in logic.
239 Interestingly enough, the pressing nature of Rickert's problem of concept formation in science and mathematics was underscored in an elegant way by the leading (meta-) mathematician of the time, the already mentioned David Hilbert—an important point of reference of the logical empiricists. He saw as the main source of the paradoxes of classes, discovered by Bertrand Russell, the fact that Georg Cantor, the originator of the set theory, did not define the concept of "set" in a precise way before he started to develop his theory (Hilbert 1925, pp. 375 ff.). In order to correct this fault, Hilbert asked his student Ernst Zermelo to advance an axiomatic of set theory in which the concept of set is clearly defined at the very beginning. (Today, it is known as Zermelo–Fraenkel axiomatic system.) Hilbert was convinced that this approach eliminates the paradox of classes by itself.

duced the first volume of his monograph *The Limits of Concept Formation in Natural Science* (§ 2 above). The declared objective of both the paper and the book was to advance "a theory of concept formation that embraces all sciences" (Rickert 1896/1902, p. v)—it would elucidate the logic of both natural science and humanities (p. ix).[240]

True to his theory of concepts in science, Rickert claimed that reality is not rational, so it cannot, in itself, be an object of human knowledge. As Emil Lask, Rickert's doctoral student in Freiburg, put it (Lask 1902), there is a *hiatus irrationalis* (J. G. Fichte's term) between concepts and reality.[241] *Pace* Aristotle and Hume, concepts on this view are not merely products of abstraction. They are purely intellectual constructs that are the most important instruments of knowledge in the sense that without concepts we cannot achieve knowledge (Oakes 1986, p. xviii). Rickert further contended that concepts actually, in the words of Guy Oakes, "recast and transform reality in such a way that its complexity is reduced and simplified in the interest of systematic comprehensibility" (1986, p. xx). To be more explicit, "what is asserted by the propositions [of science] holds *validly* for reality" (Oakes 1986, p. xviii.)[242] and is not its direct representation. This account discredits both epistemological naïve realism and the correspondence theory of truth.

The brief analysis we conducted in this section shows that Rickert's contribution to the philosophy of science constitutes a genuine and historically significant advance that went ways beyond Fries. As we have seen (in § 3.1 above), Fries' theory of concepts gave birth to the view that there are two types of natural science: mathematical natural sciences and descriptive natural sciences. Rickert transformed this dichotomy into one between the natural and the cultural sciences, a distinction he introduced under the influence of Wilhelm Dilthey's life-philosophy. Breaking with Dilthey, however, Rickert identified Dilthey's "sciences of mind" (*Geisteswissenschaften*) as "cultural sciences" (*Kulturwissenschaften*). Rickert maintained that the defining characteristic of the humanities is that they refer to values, following here Lotze's doctoral student, and Rickert's doctoral supervisor, Wilhelm Windelband. To anticipate, no less a Marburg luminary than Ernst Cassirer chose to adopt Rickert's classificatory terminology over that of Dilthey

---

240 We turn to Rickert's logic of the humanities in § 9 below.
241 These are clear traces of J. G. Fichte's activism in Rickert's theory of concepts. On the influence of Fichte on Rickert, see Heinz (1995).
242 Gottlob Frege, who was ostensibly influenced by Lotze and the Southwest Neo-Kantians (Gabriel 2002), argued in the similar direction. Frege's propositions (thoughts) do not mirror facts; they enter the logic with their truth-value. On the relatedness between Frege's and Rickert's "problem of sense", see Bauch (1923, p. 119).

(Cassirer 1942). This brings us to the problem of comparing Rickert's and Cassirer's philosophy of science we are going to discuss in the next section.

6 Comparing Heinrich Rickert and Ernst Cassirer

Nearly a decade after the appearance of Rickert's *Die Grenzen*, the most distinguished younger representative of the Marburg school of Neo-Kantians, Ernst Cassirer, published *Substanzbegriff und Funktionsbegriff* (1910), the now classic systematic prolegomenon to the philosophy of science, which contains a detailed treatment of concept formation in science. Cassirer, the first philosopher in Marburg who took this problematic seriously, took issue, like Rickert before him, with the old Aristotelian logic, which maintains that the material objects are directly available for our knowledge and that science abstractively derives from them general characteristics, or concepts. Rather than following the Aristotelian genetic understanding of concepts, according to which concepts are generalizations of empirical data, Cassirer embraced a theory of scientific conceptualization keyed to the model of the mathematical notion of function.

Cassirer explicitly credited Hermann Lotze as the father of this new theory of concepts. What is of signal interest here, however, is that Cassirer evidently echoed Rickert in following Lotze on this point.[243] Indeed, it is a matter of record that already in his 1888 dissertation, Rickert defended "relation-concepts" against "thing-concepts" (1888, pp. 62f.) referring to Lotze in that context (pp. 66f.). In this key move, Rickert criticized the Aristotelian claim that concepts are general ideas (*Vorstellungen*). It is also clear that the new theory of concepts of Rickert–Cassirer was close to Frege's insistence that concept is rather a kind of function and not a kind of object.[244]

Especially instructive for understanding this development is Cassirer's penetratingly critical analysis of Rickert's theory of concept formation. Cassirer took issue, in particular, with Rickert's diremption of concepts from reality (1910, pp. 293ff.). According to Rickert, the system of concepts does not represent reality. That is why, on his view, the scientist's preliminary task is to posit a generally valid definition of every concept of his discipline to which the rigorously formal methods of scientific research and analysis are to be applied. Cassirer objected that this conception of Rickert's annihilates the individual character of the facts in the real

---

243 On pp. 299f. of his book, Cassirer explicitly admits that here he shakes hands with Rickert.
244 See Frege (1997). We are going to say more about the relatedness between Rickert and Frege in § 9 below.

world and implicitly supposes that science is not about the facts but is instead no more than a logical system that helps advance our understanding of the world. In other words, Cassirer faulted Rickert from the standpoint of *realism*. By contrast with Rickert, he contended that the concepts of science are not only "meanings of words" without any content; they also represent the world.[245] Cassirer held this to be the case because science, as he understood it, is connected with reality through the so-called "serial principle" as functionally related to the "serial members"—the scientist is to view scientific theory as referring to concrete, intuitively grasped reality. Hence, there is no radical split, to Cassirer's mind, between science and the world. In this way, Cassirer's theory of concepts at least partly reinstates the representing (mirroring) understanding of scientific knowledge (Kubalica 2012, p. 106). In contrast, Rickert consequently rejected the idea that science undertakes to represent reality. In this sense, Rickert's epistemology of science was resolutely *anti-realist*.

7 Comparing Marburg and Southwest Neo-Kantians

Having briefly reviewed how Cassirer differentiated his theory of concepts from that of Rickert, we are now better placed to understand the relation between the Marburg and the Southwest Neo-Kantians in general. The consensus in our time—particularly as exemplified by Michael Friedman and his followers—is that the Marburg Neo-Kantians were doctrinally closer to the logical empiricists than any other school of German thinkers of the period. This reading is *prima facie* plausible enough. To be sure, Hermann Cohen, Paul Natorp, and Ernst Cassirer published a whole range of penetrating and masterfully informed philosophical analyses of the latest findings of mathematics and science in order to bring to light the "relative a priori" in them. A signature example is Cohen's monograph *Das Prinzip der infinitesimal-Methode und seine Geschichte* (1883). Passing in review through the history of the idea of calculus down to his day, Cohen concluded that "contemporary (i. e., the post-Kantian) pure mathematics", in particular, the infinitesimal calculus and the exploration of the concepts of infinite, limit and continuity, has disclosed what "pure thinking" is (1902, p. 499). The only real objects of pure thinking are ordered series that can be seen either as functions, or as numbers.

---

[245] In contrast, according to Lotze, the scientist can learn something about the structure of the world, but science does not *represent* it (Chapter 2, § 9).

The received view has it that in a manner similar to the logical empiricists some thirty years later, the Marburg Neo-Kantians saw philosophy as logic of scientific knowledge. They maintained that the task of philosophy is to reveal the logical foundations of the exact sciences—philosophy investigates the logical structure of the existing body of science, of science as we have it in "printed books". The Southwest Neo-Kantians, by contrast, were preoccupied with problems relating to the "sciences of culture" (Luft 2015).[246]

But we find much more promising Emil Lask's differentiation of the two philosophical schools. The Marburg Neo-Kantians, he explained, were committed to a kind of "pan-logism" in that they tried to exclude the role previously accorded to perceptual intuition in scientific thinking. In addition, Lask noted, they sought to expand the place and function of logic in science—in particular, we should note, the role of formal logic, including the rising mathematical logic, and of pure mathematics in it (Cohen 1883). The Marburgers saw the data of experience, understood in the sense of the observations, made by the existing science, as organized in conceptual schemes that communicate their meaning. The task of philosophy of science is nothing but to explore these conceptual schemes from the point of view of logic understood in this sense.

The Southwest Neo-Kantians, in contrast, argued for a kind of logical "panarchy" (Lask 1923, p. 133),[247] in the sense of securing the unchallengeable supremacy of the logical necessity in science. They held that what is given in perception, the phenomena, could not in principle be articulated—it only appears, is shown. In order to become the subject of knowledge, phenomena, on this account, must be *translated* into the logic of concepts—logical necessity operates only on this level. As Andrea Staiti recently put it, "[t]o conceptualize, for Rickert, is to *recast* the materials delivered immediately by the senses into a conceptual form" (2013).[248] The task of science is not to represent reality.

To be more explicit, the core of the logic understood in this sense by the Southwest Neo-Kantians was the concept of value and the normativity of logical laws, exhibited in the course of their validation. Rickert and his colleagues sedulously worked out this approach (Gabriel 2007, p. 96) in a project that closely followed the logic of Hermann Lotze in ways that have been long and unwarrantably obscured in the historical record. Their logic also paralleled the work of Gottlob

---

246 In § 9 below, we are going to say in more detail why this claim is not correct.
247 Wilhelm Windelband, one of Lotze's many distinguished doctoral students, saw logic as "[the] quintessence of the whole theoretical philosophy" (1912, p. 2).
248 See how close this position of Rickert is to Wittgenstein's philosophy of science as developed in *Tractatus*, 6.34 ff.

Frege (another beneficiary of Lotze's thought) in that area, which he pursued at approximately the same period.[249]

The next section looks forward and explores the influence of Rickert's theory of concept construction on the founding fathers of logical empiricism in its Vienna and Berlin variants, Moritz Schlick and Hans Reichenbach.

8 Rickert and the Logical Empiricists before the Vienna Circle

Schlick too opposed Kant's idea that science employs concepts constructed in a spontaneous synthesis of manifolds. In conspicuous agreement with Fries, Lotze, Rickert, and Cassirer, he argued that concepts are to be formed, or constructed, by scientists themselves at the outset of their research programs.[250] Manifestly a constructivist program, this amounts to no less than "a new kind of empiricism, one that negotiates a careful path between a crudely reductive Machian and Humean positivism and the excesses of Kantian apriorism" (Howard 1994, p. 47). In contrast, following Ernst Mach, the members of the "first Vienna Circle" (1907–1912), such as Otto Neurath, Philipp Frank, and Hans Hahn, evinced negligible interest in the problematic of concept formation.

To be more explicit, Schlick claimed, in argument with Cassirer, that concept formation is produced in a process of coordinating (*Zuordnung*) the concepts to their objects. Against Cassirer, however, he insisted that such acts of coordination are arbitrary, or conventional. They do not involve grasping objects of reality. They are simply a mode of recognizing, for example, *a* as *b*. In his *Allgemeine Erkenntnislehre* (*General Theory of Knowledge*) (1918), Schlick maintained that transformative recent developments in mathematics and the revolutionary scientific discoveries radically changed the way we operate with concepts. More particularly, Schlick was convinced, they helped to successively purge concepts of evidential content sponsored by perceptual intuition (§ 1 above). Schlick singled out for his sharpest criticism "the school of the Neo-Kantians [who] believe that the world as such is found in scientific knowledge, whereas in fact it [scientific knowledge] is only a conceptual system of signs" (1918, p. 309). As it turns out, however, Schlick's critique could apply only to the Marburg Neo-Kantians, to Paul Natorp and Ernst Cassirer in particular—not to Heinrich Rickert. To be sure, as we have already mentioned (in § 4 above), Rickert rejected epistemological realism and the

---

[249] Among other things, the Frege connection explains the correlations of Rickert's philosophy of science with that of the Tractarian Wittgenstein (see § 9 below).
[250] Similarly, already in his dissertation, Rickert insisted that "the logical act of thinking must be already done, before to fix it in language form" (1888, p. 21).

correspondence theory of truth. He did not concur with the view that science explores the world itself, a position of Rickert's that, we have seen (in § 6 above), Cassirer tellingly criticized (Cassirer 1910, pp. 292ff.).

In contrast, Hans Reichenbach's program in philosophy of science was much closer to that of the Marburg Neo-Kantians. This should not be surprising, however. It will be remembered that in 1913–1914, Reichenbach was Ernst Cassirer's student in Berlin. With Cassirer's recommendation in his hands, in the summer of 1914, Reichenbach asked Paul Natorp to be his PhD supervisor in Marburg University and was unhappy when he received a negative answer. Cassirer and Reichenbach both strove to distil new relative principles a priori from the latest developments of science and mathematics. This objective informed Reichenbach's program for logical analysis of science first articulated in *Theory of Relativity and A Priori Knowledge* (1920). According to it, "Kant's notion of a priori has two different meanings. First, it means 'necessary true' or 'true at all times', and secondly, 'constituting the concept of object' of science". (1920, p. 49) By 1920, the young Reichenbach had abandoned the first concept of a priori although he still subscribed to the second one, in the form of principles of coordination. Like Schlick—and also like Rickert—Reichenbach was convinced that the principles of coordination are not realized spontaneously. Rather, he maintained, they must be first established in order to ensure the empirical material of scientific theory, which is to say, the "availability" of the objects of science. In other words, the principles of coordination constitute the concepts of scientific theories, and in this sense, they qualify as a priori. Of course, these a priori principles are not timelessly valid, as Kant believed they are, but instead change with every significant innovation of scientific theory. This justifies calling them, with Michael Friedman, "relativized a priori" (2001, pp. 71ff.). In *that* sense, the principles of coordination are empirical, or perhaps better, observable, at least so far as one distils them from scientific observations and experiments.

Understandingly, Moritz Schlick took Reichenbach to task, in 1920, for propounding a view that retains elements of what, to Schlick's mind, was discredited Kantian a priori doctrine. Consistent with an orientation linked to the cutting-edge mathematics and physical science of his day, Schlick insisted that rather than in terms of the Kantian a priori, we properly interpret the principles of coordination as "conventions" in Henri Poincaré's sense. Schlick's criticism led the young Reichenbach to rethink his entire approach, and from 1922 on, in place of "principles of coordination", he spoke of "definitions of coordination". Similar to the principles of coordination, Reichenbach's definitions of coordination feature relative a priori content in that the researcher is understood as positing them antecedently to the acquisition of scientific knowledge. In this respect, following Schlick, Reichenbach's epistemology of science became clearly *anti-realistic* and tracked closer to Rickert.

After 1924, however, Reichenbach returned to Cassirer's variant of philosophy of physics, declaring himself a philosophical realist (1925a, 1925b). The fact that he did not engage with the works of the Southwest Neo-Kantians in the past came to the surface. About the same time, Schlick, already experienced in discussions with Rickert, readily adopted the theoretical orientation of Wittgenstein's *Tractatus*.

9 Rickert and the Logical Empiricists of the Vienna Circle

It is a well-known fact that the Vienna Circle was founded under the decisive influence of Wittgenstein. After 1924, its members read and discussed his *Tractatus* sentence by sentence. This, however, is only the tip of a "logico-philosophical iceberg". Well-known is also Wittgenstein's avowal from the Preface to the *Tractatus* that he is "indebted to Frege's great works"—obviously, more indebted than to the works of "his friend" Russell. Moreover, as we know today (for example, from Frege's "17 Key Sentences on Logic", 1882) and as already mentioned in earlier pages of the book, Frege himself was heavily indebted to the great works of Hermann Lotze (n. 242). In order to bring the circle full, we remind the reader once again (§ 2 above) that Lotze was also the great inspiration of the Southwest Neo-Kantians, in particular of Heinrich Rickert.

Traditionally, scholars are divided by the evaluation of Schlick's philosophical development. Many students of his thought, including Anthony Quinton (1985) and Massimo Ferrari (2008), have identified a radical change in Schlick's philosophy after 1924. Other close readers of Schlick, however, such as Ludovico Geymonat (1985) and Rudolf Haller (1993), maintain that the influence that Wittgenstein's *Tractatus* exerted on Schlick was no sudden epiphany on Schlick's part, but was rather clearly in the cards given his earlier philosophical development. In fact, "Schlick developed himself, [although] in another form, a number of those ideas that attracted him to the *Tractatus before* he got acquainted with Wittgenstein's work or with its echo in Russell" (Haller 1993, p. 104). We join this interpretation here, simultaneously highlighting the genealogical connection between the ideas of Lotze, Rickert and Schlick, on the one hand, with those of Lotze, Frege and Wittgenstein, on the other.

One recalls in this context that already in 1910, in a period during which Schlick discussed Rickert's works intensively, Schlick adopted the view he preserved in his later years, namely, that knowledge is not an act of mirroring the world but rather of validating its facts. Correlatively, the Tractarian "pictures" are not mirror-images of facts (of states of affairs);[251] they are their models or, to be more exact, their *"tableaux vivant"* (4.0311). What counts in the Tractarian epistemology is the truth-value of propositions.

It remains to be said that, similarly, Carnap's contact with the thought of Rickert and Bruno Bauch contributed to his predisposition readily to assimilate the ideas of Wittgenstein's philosophy of language after he moved to Vienna in 1926 —and this to such an extent that in 1932, Wittgenstein openly charged Carnap with plagiarism.[252] This point partly explains why the core members of the Vienna Circle, Neurath, Hahn, and Frank (§ 7 above), were reluctant to adopt Wittgenstein's ideas in their full form. Unlike Schlick and Carnap, they had no contact, whether direct or indirect, either with Rickert's or Bruno Bauch's thought. The same also concerns the leading figures of the Berlin Group, Hans Reichenbach and Walter Dubislav.

10 Heinrich Rickert as a Philosopher of Science

Given Heinrich Rickert's implicit influence on the thinking of the logical empiricists, one might question why he came in for such severe criticism by those same philosophers and those who would qualify as their fellow travelers, such as Karl Popper and Carl Hempel. The answer appears to be mainly ideological (§ 1 above). Motivated by their world-view beliefs, the early logical empiricists committed themselves to establishing that there is but one science and that the humanities, so far as they constitute a coherent, epistemologically sound constellation of disciplines follow the method of the natural sciences. Precisely this position led the logical empiricists to oppose Rickert's philosophy of "cultural sciences" as an autonomous sub-discipline. Hence, they refrained even from discussing, let alone probing in any detail, Rickert's philosophy of science in general.

A closer look at Rickert's doctrine helps shed more light on the grounds of this resistance on the part of the logical empiricists. Rickert's critique of epistemological realism set the stage for his attack on the "methodological monism". Briefly stated, he argued that there are two types of individuals in science and, correspondingly, two types of concept formation. The natural sciences group their individuals into classes, putting their idiosyncratic properties in brackets. The principal instrument that natural science brings to bear in this process is the concept of

---

251 According to the *Tractatus*, *logic*, not science, is "a mirror-image of the world" (6.13). However, since the Tractarian logic is tautological, it does not produce knowledge (Milkov 2022b).
252 This is well-documented in Wittgenstein's letter to Carnap from August 20, 1932 (Nedo 2012, p. 300), in which he accuses Carnap of using in print his ideas without acknowledgement.

the "laws of nature". These laws hold validity for all members of a certain class of events while bracketing their specific spatio-temporal location. Clearly, natural laws of science do not represent the perceptual manifold of reality.

But the humanities also strive to formulate concepts that are sufficiently precise and objective to be implemented in scientific studies. Unlike the natural sciences, however, they preserve the idiosyncrasy of their individuals as marked by specific, yet objective values. Thus, when one engages with them in axiological terms, the humanities can achieve epistemic precision and exactness no less than the natural sciences. Developing the philosophical implications of this position, Rickert termed natural science a "science of concepts" (*Begriffswissenschaft*) and the humanities a "science of the actual" (*Wirklichkeitswissenschaft*). It was by these means that Rickert categorically distinguished between the natural sciences and the "cultural sciences". It thus turns out that Rickert was an anti-realist as a philosopher of natural science but a realist as a philosopher of the human sciences.

One of the sources of Rickert's conception of two types of science, cultural and natural, was the specific theory of concepts, previously touched upon (in § 3.1 above), found in the thought of Kant and Fries. On that view, there are *explanatory* and *descriptive* natural sciences. Another prime source for Rickert, as noted previously (in § 4 above), was Dilthey's doctrine that discriminates between natural sciences and sciences of mind (*Gesiteswissenschaften*). Crucial to the historical record is the often-overlooked fact that it was Lotze's concept of value that prompted Rickert to emend what he learned from Dilthey by drawing a distinction between sciences of nature and sciences of culture—the first explores events and phenomena, while the second explores values. Rickert's dissatisfaction with Dilthey concerned the fact that the latter's concept of "mind" is tainted by psychologism and for that reason cannot serve, Rickert was convinced, as a theoretical ground of thought and modes of inquiry in the humanities—alongside Frege and Husserl, Rickert was a dedicated anti-psychologist. A significant historical fact, one far too downplayed or altogether missing in the literature, is that the anti-psychologism that characterizes the thought of all three philosophers is due to the seminal influence of Hermann Lotze (Introduction, § 4.2).

It should be clear by now that Rickert richly repays serious reconsideration in our time as, in the words of Guy Oakes, "an advocate of 'scientific' philosophy as a legitimate academic discipline with valid standards and objective methods" (1986, p. xxix). His ambition was nothing less than "to develop a comprehensive system of *philosophy of science* and to demonstrate in it the logical structure of theology, the system of law, political economy and of all other, so called, sciences of culture" (Rickert 1921, p. ix; italics added). Perhaps the most innovative and historically significant element of Rickert's project was the prominent role he accorded to what we already have called (in Introduction, § 4.3) philosophical logic (as opposed to formal, including mathematical logic) in the philosophy of science. This move, one that was seen as counter to the formalist trends in the philosophy of the period, enabled Rickert to distill the principal concept of orientation of various humanistic disciplines—the concept of value.

Importantly enough, the foregoing analysis makes it difficult to see a profound difference between Rickert's doctrine and the philosophy of science propounded by his sharpest critics, Karl Popper and Carl Hempel. For like Rickert, Popper and Hempel saw a divide between the natural sciences and the cultural sciences; and this notwithstanding the fact that unlike Rickert, Popper and Hempel conceived the difference as a matter merely of the generality associated with the natural sciences and the particularity characteristic of the cultural sciences. Further, the categorical diversity that Rickert saw between natural sciences and sciences of culture, something that Popper and Hempel were so quick to fault in his system, was predicated upon something that Popper and Hempel could not have opposed since they never adequately accounted for it, namely, the clear difference that Fries originally introduced between explanatory and descriptive natural science. Taking inspiration from Fries—through Lotze—Rickert taught that the descriptive natural sciences treat empirical generic terms (*Gattungsbegriffe*), such as those of biological taxonomies. Explanations, according to Rickert's account, are only a function of the mathematical natural sciences, where we typically locate an object or event under a formal concept, and then explain it as an instance or exemplification of a law of nature that is generally valid (1986, p. 81). "Something is explained", declares Rickert, "inasmuch as it can be put under a *law*" (1986, p. 82). The more general and more comprehensive an explanation the more it recommends itself over alternative accounts. Ironically enough, half a century later this very conception pioneered by Rickert was restated virtually *mot-à-mot* by the logical empiricists Carl Hempel and Paul Oppenheim (1948), and this without so much as a word in recognition of its origination with Rickert.

11 Epilogue

We have undertaken in this chapter a concise review of the progress in philosophy of science from the standpoint of some of its most prominent German exponents: Kant, Fries, Lotze, Rickert, Schlick, Reichenbach and Carnap. *Pace* Michael Friedman and the historians of philosophy who follow him, we have found that following ideas of Hermann Lotze, Heinrich Rickert and the Southwest Neo-Kantians substantially assisted the emergence and development of logical empiricism. Our principal finding is that Rickert played the role of pace-maker by setting the course for the logical empiricists by causing concept formation to become a focal concern of the philosophy of science of the time. In addition, there was another genealogical connection between Rickert and the Vienna logical empiricists that helped them to embrace the ideas of Wittgenstein's *Tractatus* enthusiastically.

References

Abbagnano, Nicola (2006): "Verso il pensiero contemporaneo: dallo spiritualismo all'esistenzialismo". In: *Storia della filosofia*. Vol. 5. Bergamo: Gruppo Editoriale l'Espresso.
Adair-Toteff, Christopher (1994): "The Neo-Kantian *Raum* Controversy". In: *British Journal for the History of Philosophy* 2, pp. 131–148.
Anscombe, Elisabeth (1990): "Wittgenstein: Whose Philosopher?". In: *Royal Institute of Philosophy Supplement* 28, pp. 1–10.
Armstrong, David M. (1978): *Universals and Scientific Realism*. 2 Volumes. Cambridge: Cambridge University Press.
Arnold, Mathew (1873): *Literature & Dogma: An Essay Towards a Better Apprehension of the Bible*. London: Smith & Elder.
Ayer, Alfred (1936): *Language, Truth, and Logic*. London: Gollancz.
Ayer, Alfred (1968): *The Origins of Pragmatism*. London: Macmillan.
Bain, Alexander (1859): *The Emotions and the Will*. London: Parker.
Baldwin, Thomas (1991): "Identity Theory of Truth". In: *Mind* 100, pp. 35–52.
Bauch, Bruno (1918): "Lotzes Logik und ihre Bedeutung im deutschen Idealismus". In: *Beiträge zur Philosophie des Deutschen Idealismus* 1, pp. 45–58.
Bauch, Bruno (1923): *Wahrheit, Wert und Wirklichkeit*. Leipzig: Felix Meiner.
Baumann, Julius (1869): *Die Lehren von Raum, Zeit und Mathematik in der neueren Philosophie nach ihrem ganzen Einfluß dargestellt und beurteilt*. Berlin: Reimer.
Baumann, Julius (1909): "Persönliche Erinnerungen an Hermann Lotze". In: *Annalen der Naturphilosophie* 8, pp. 175–182.
Becher, Erich (1917): "Hermann Lotze und seine Psychologie". In: *Die Naturwissenschaften* 5. No. 20, pp. 325–334.
Becher, Erich (1929): *Deutsche Philosophen*. München und Leipzig: Duncker & Humblot.
Beiser, Frederick (2008): *German Idealism: The Struggle against Subjectivism, 1781–1801*. Cambridge: Harvard University Press.
Beiser, Frederick (2013): *Late German Idealism: Trendelenburg and Lotze*. Oxford: Oxford University Press.
Beiser, Frederick (2014): *The Genesis of Neo-Kantianism, 1796–1880*. Oxford: Oxford University Press.
Beiser, Frederick (2016): "Lotze's *Mikrokosmus*". In: Schliesser, Eric (Ed.): *Ten Neglected Classics of Philosophy*. Oxford: Oxford University Press, pp. 84–119.
Bell, David (1999): "The Revolution of Moore and Russell: A Very British Coup?". In: O'Hear, Anthony (Ed.): *German Philosophy since Kant*. Cambridge: Cambridge University Press, pp. 137–166.
Blackwell, Kenneth (2015): "Russell's Personal Shorthand". In: *Russell* 35, pp. 66–70.
Boccaccini, Federico (Ed.) (2015): *Lotze et son héritage: Son influence et son impact sur la philosophie du XXe siècle*. Bruxelles: Peter Lang.
Bolzano, Bernard (1984): *Philosophische Texte*. Neemann, Ursula (Ed.) Stuttgart: Reclam.
Bonacchi, Silvia and Boudewijnse, Geert-Jan (Eds.) (2011): *Carl Stumpf—From Philosophical Reflection to Interdisciplinary Scientific Investigation*. Vienna: Krammer.
Boncompagni, Anna (2016): *Wittgenstein and Pragmatism: On Certainty in the Light of Peirce and James*. London: Palgrave.
Bradley, Francis Herbert (1893): *Appearance and Reality*. London: Swan Sonnenschein.
Braithwaite, Richard Bevan (1932/1933): "The Nature of Believing". In: *Proceedings of the Aristotelian Society* 33, pp. 129–146.

Brentano, Franz (1862): *Von der mannigfachen Bedeutung des Seienden nach Aristoteles*. Freiburg: Herder.
Brentano, Franz (1874, 1924a): *Psychologie vom empirischen Standpunkt*. Vol. I. 2nd ed. Oskar Kraus (Ed.) Leipzig: Felix Meiner.
Brentano, Franz (1895): *Die vier Phasen der Philosophie und ihr augenblicklicher Stand*. Stuttgart: Cotta.
Brentano, Franz (1921): *Die Lehre Jesu und ihre bleibende Bedeutung*. Alfred Kastil (Ed.) Leipzig: Felix Meiner.
Brentano, Franz (1924b): *Psychologie vom empirischen Standpunkt*. Vol. II. 2nd ed. Oskar Kraus (Ed.) Leipzig: Felix Meiner.
Brentano, Franz (1925): *Versuch über die Erkenntnis*. Alfred Kastil (Ed.) Leipzig: Felix Meiner.
Brentano, Franz (1933): *Kategorienlehre*. Alfred Kastil (Ed.) Leipzig: Felix Meiner.
Brentano, Franz (1988): *Grundzüge der Ästhetik*. Franziska Mayer-Hillebrand (Ed.) Hamburg: Felix Meiner.
Brentano, Franz (1989): *Briefe an Carl Stumpf*. Gerhard Oberkofler (Ed.) Graz: Akademische Druck- und Verlagsanstalt.
Carnap, Rudolf (1922): *Vom Chaos zur Wirklichkeit*. ULS Digital Collections. University of Pittsburgh. https://digital.library.pitt.edu/islandora/object/pitt%3A31735061814202/manuscript/pages (last accessed on December 3, 2022).
Carnap, Rudolf (1926): *Physikalische Begriffsbildung*. Karlsruhe: Braun.
Carnap, Rudolf (1928): *Der logische Aufbau der Welt*. Berlin: Weltkreis Verlag.
Carnap, Rudolf (1950): "Empiricism, Semantic and Ontology". In: *Revue Internationale de Philosophie* 4, pp. 20–40.
Carnap, Rudolf (2022): *Tagebücher, 1908–1919*. Vol I. Christian Damböck (Ed.) Hamburg: Felix Meiner.
Cassirer, Ernst (1910): *Substanzbegriff und Funktionsbegriff*. Berlin: Bruno Cassirer.
Cassirer, Ernst (1942): *Zur Logik der Kulturwissenschaften*. Götteborg: Elanders Bovetryckerie aktiebolag.
Centi, Beatrice (2011): "Stumpf and Lotze on Space, Reality, Relation". In: Bonacchi, Silvia and Boudewijnse, Geert-Jan (Eds.): *Carl Stumpf—From Philosophical Reflection to Interdisciplinary Scientific Investigation*. Vienna: Krammer, pp. 69–81.
Chrudzimski, Arkadiusz (2004): *Die Ontologie Franz Brentanos*. Berlin: Springer.
Coffa, Alberto (1981): "Russell and Kant". In: *Synthese* 46, pp. 247–263.
Coffa, Alberto (1993): *The Semantic Tradition from Kant to Carnap: To the Vienna Station*. Cambridge: Cambridge University Press.
Cohen, Hermann (1883): *Das Prinzip der infinitesimal-Methode und seine Geschichte*. Berlin: Dümmler.
Cohen, Hermann (1902): *Logik der reinen Erkenntnis*. Berlin: Bruno Cassirer.
Collingwood, Robin (1944): *An Autobiography*. Harmondsworth: Penguin [1st ed. 1939].
Collingwood, Robin (1946): *The Idea of History*. Oxford: Oxford University Press.
Cuming, Agnes (1917): "Lotze, Bradley, and Bosanquet". In: *Mind* 26, pp. 162–170.
Dahms, Hans-Joachim (1992): "Positivismus und Pragmatismus". In: Bell, David Bell and Vossenkuhl, Wilhelm (Eds.): *Wissenschaft und Subjektivität. Der Wiener Kreis und die Philosophie des 20. Jahrhunderts*. Berlin: Akademie Verlag, pp. 239–257.
Darwin, Charles (1859): *On the Origin of Species*. London: John Murray.
Dedekind, Richard (1888): *Was sind und was sollen die Zahlen?* Braunschweig: Vieweg.
De Santis, Daniele (Ed.) (2018): *Lotze's Back!*. In: *Philosophical Readings* 10. No. 2, https://philosophicalreadings.org/ (last accessed on December 3, 2022).

Dilthey, Wilhelm (1894): "Ideas Concerning Descriptive and Analytic Psychology". In: Dilthey, Wilhelm (2012): *Descriptive Psychology and Historical Understanding*. Richard Zaner and Kenneth Heiges (Trans.). The Hague: Martinus Nijhoff, pp. 21–120.

Dilthey, Wilhelm (1933): *Der junge Dilthey. Ein Lebensbild in Briefen und Tagebüchern 1852–1870*. Clara Misch (Ed.) Leipzig: Teubner.

Dubislav, Walter (1931): *Die Definition*. Leipzig: Felix Meiner.

Dubislav, Walter (1933): *Naturphilosophie*. Berlin: Junker & Dünnhaupt.

Dummett, Michael (1956): "Nominalism". In: Dummett, Michael (1978): *Truth and Other Enigmas*. London: Duckworth, pp. 38–49.

Dummett, Michael (1973): *Frege: Philosophy of Language*. London: Duckworth.

Dummett, Michael (1993): *Origins of Analytical Philosophy*. London: Duckworth.

Ewen, Wolfgang (2008): *Carl Stumpf und Gottlob Frege*. Würzburg: Königshausen & Neumann.

Fechner, Gustav Theodor (1860): *Elemente der Psychophysik*. 2 Volumes. Leipzig: Breitkopf und Hartel.

Ferenczi, Sandor (1913): "Aus der Psychologie von Lotze". In: *Imago. Zeitschrift für Anwendungen der Psychoanalyse auf die Geisteswissenschaften* 2, pp. 238–241.

Fernándes-Armesto, Felipe (2001): *Civilizations: Culture, Ambition, and the Transformation of Nature*. New York: The Free Press.

Ferrari, Massimo (2008): "Moritz Schlick in Wien: Die Wende der Philosophie". In: Engler, Fynn O. and Iven, Mathias (Eds.): *Moritz Schlick: Leben, Werk und Wirkung*. Berlin: Parerga, pp. 91–113.

Ferreirós, José (2004): "The Motives Behind Cantor's Set Theory". In: *Science in Context* 17. No. 1, pp. 49–83.

Fisette, Denis (2011): "Love and Hate: Brentano and Stumpf on Emotions and Sense Feelings". In: Bonacchi, Silvia and Boudewijnse, Geert-Jan (Eds.): *Carl Stumpf—From Philosophical Reflection to Interdisciplinary Scientific Investigation*. Vienna: Krammer, pp. 37–49.

Flanagan, Owen (1991): *The Science of the Mind*. Boston: MIT Press.

Føllesdal, Dagfinn (2001): "Bolzano, Frege, and Husserl on Reference and Object". In: Floyd, Juliet and Shieh, Sanford (Eds.): *Future Pasts: The Analytic Tradition in Twentieth Century Philosophy*. Oxford: Oxford University Press.

Foppa, Klaus (1971): "Begriffsbildung". In: Ritter, Joachim, Gründer, Karlfried, and Gottfried, Gabriel (Eds.): *Historisches Wörterbuch der Philosophie*. 12 Volumes. Basel: Schwabe (1971/2007). Vol I. Columns 787 f.

Frege, Gottlob (1879): *Begriffscshrift*. Halle: Nebert.

Frege, Gottlob (1882): "17 Key Sentences on Logic". In: Frege, Gottlob (1979): *Posthumous Writings*. Brian McGuinness (Ed.). Oxford: Blackwell, pp. 174–175.

Frege, Gottlob (1884): *Grundlagen der Arithmetik*. Breslau: Koebner.

Frege, Gottlob (1891): *Funktion und Begriff*. Jena: Pohle.

Frege, Gottlob (1892): "Über Sinn und Bedeutung". In: *Zeitschrift für Philosophie und philosophische Kritik* NF 100, pp. 25–50.

Frege, Gottlob (1893/1903): *Die Grundgesätze der Arithmetik*. 2 Volumes. Jena: Pohle.

Frege, Gottlob (1918/1919): "Der Gedanke. Eine logische Untersuchung". In: *Beiträge zur Philosophie des Deutschen Idealismus* 1, pp. 58–77.

Frege, Gottlob (1997): "On Function and Concept". In: Beaney, Michael (Ed.): *The Frege Reader*. Oxford: Blackwell, pp. 130–148.

Friedman, Michael (1999): *Reconsidering Logical Positivism*. Cambridge: Cambridge University Press.

Friedman, Michael (2001): *Dynamics of Reason*. Stanford: CSLI Publications.

Fries, Jacob Friedrich (1811): *Logik*. Heidelberg: Winter 1837.

Gabriel, Gottfried (1984): "Fregean Connection: *Bedeutung*, Value and Truth-Value". In: Wright, Crispin (Ed.): *Frege: Tradition & Influence*. Oxford: Blackwell, pp. 186–194.

Gabriel, Gottfried (1986): "Frege als Neukantianer". In: *Kant-Studien* 77, pp. 84–101.

Gabriel, Gottfried (1989a): "Einleitung des Herausgebers: Lotze und die Entstehung der modernen Logik bei Frege". In: Lotze, Hermann: *Logik, Erstes Buch. Vom Denken (Reine Logik)*. Hamburg: Meiner, pp. xi–xxxv.

Gabriel, Gottfried (1989b): "Einleitung des Herausgebers: Objektivität, Logik und Erkenntnistheorie bei Lotze und Frege". In: Lotze, Hermann: *Logik, Drittes Buch. Vom Erkennen (Methodologie)*. Hamburg: Meiner, pp. xi–xxvii.

Gabriel, Gottfried (2002): "Frege, Lotze, and the Continental Roots of Early Analytic Philosophy". In: Reck, Erich (Ed.): *From Frege to Wittgenstein: Perspectives on Early Analytic Philosophy*. Oxford: Oxford University Press, pp. 39–51.

Gabriel, Gottfried (2007): "Windelband und die Diskussion um die Kantischen Urteilsformen". In: Heinz, Marion and Krijnen, Christian (Eds.): *Kant im Neukantianismus. Fortschritt oder Rückschritt*. Würzburg: Königshausen & Neumann, pp. 91–108.

Gabriel, Gottfried, and Schlotter, Sven (2017): *Frege und die kontinentalen Ursprünge der analytischen Philosophie*. Paderborn: Mentis.

Geach, Peter Thomas (1976): "Saying and Showing in Frege and Wittgenstein". In: *Acta Philosophical Fennica* 28, pp. 54–71.

Geymonat, Ludovico (1985): "Entwicklung und Kontinuität im Denken Schlicks", In: McGuinness, Brian (Ed.): *Zurück zu Schlick*. Vienna: Hölder–Pichler–Tempsky, pp. 24–31.

Griffin, Nicholas (1991): *Russell's Idealistic Apprenticeship*. Oxford: Clarendon Press.

Griffin, Nicholas (1996): "F. H. Bradley's Contribution to the Development of Logic". In: Bradley, James (Ed.): *Philosophy after F. H. Bradley*. Bristol: Thoemmes Press, pp. 195–230.

Griffin, Nicholas and Lewis, Albert C. (1990): "[Comments to] 'An Analysis of Mathematical Reasoning'". In: Russell, Bertrand: *The Collected Papers of Bertrand Russell*. Vol. II. Griffin, Nicholas and Lewis, Albert (Eds.). London: Routledge, pp. 155–161.

Habermas, Jürgen (1992): "Staatsbürgerschaft und nationale Identität". In: Habermas, Jürgen: *Faktizität und Geltung*. Frankfurt am Main: Suhrkamp, pp. 632–660.

Hacker, Peter (1975): "Frege and Wittgenstein on Elucidations". In: *Mind* 84, pp. 601–609.

Hager, Paul (1994): *Continuity and Change in the Development of Russell's Philosophy*. Dordrecht: Kluwer.

Hahn, Hans, Neurath, Otto, and Carnap, Rudolf (1929): *Wissenschaftliche Weltauffassung der Wiener Kreis*. Vienna: Wolf.

Hall, Stanley (1912): *Founders of Modern Psychology*. New York: Appleton.

Haller, Rudolf (1993): *Neopositivismus*. Darmstadt: Wissenschaftliche Buchgesellschaft.

Hamacher-Hermes, Adelheit (1994): *Inhalts- oder Umfangslogik? Die Kontroverse zwischen E. Husserl und A. H. Voigt*. Freiburg: Alber.

Hannequin, Arthur (1895): *Essai critique sur l'hypothese des atomes dans la science contemporaine*. Paris: Alcan.

Hartmann, Eduard von (1888): *Lotze's Philosophie*. Leipzig: Friedrich.

Hawking, Stephen (2004): *Das Universum in der Nussschale*. Hainer Kober (Ed.) München: dtv.

Hegel, Georg Wilhelm Friedrich (1806, 2006): *Phänomenologie des Geistes*. Hamburg: Meiner.

Hegel, Georg Wilhelm Friedrich (1830, 1986): *Enzyklopädie der philosophischen Wissenschaften im Grundrisse 1830*. 3 Volumes. Frankfurt am Main: Suhrkamp.

Heidegger, Martin (1978): "Neuere Forschungen über Logik". In: Heidegger, Martin: *Frühe Schriften. Gesamtausgabe.* Vol. I. Frankfurt am Main: Klostermann, pp. 16–43.
Heinz, Marion (1995): "Die Fichte-Rezeption in der Südwestdeutschen Schule des Neukantianismus". In: *Fichte-Studien* 13, pp. 109–129.
Helmholtz, Hermann von (1867): *Handbuch der physiologischen Optik.* Hamburg and Leipzig: Voss.
Hempel, Carl (1942): "The Function of General Laws in History". In: *The Journal of Philosophy* 39, pp. 35–48.
Hempel, Carl (1952): *Fundamentals of Concept Formation.* Chicago: University of Chicago Press.
Hempel, Carl and Oppenheim, Paul (1948): "Studies in the Logic of Explanation". In: *Philosophy of Science* 15, pp. 135–175.
Herder, Johann Gottfried (1784/1791, 1966): *Ideen zur Philosophie der Geschichte der Menschheit.* 4 Volumes. Gerhart Schmidt (Ed.). Darmstadt: Melzer.
Hilbert, David (1925, 1967): "On the Infinite". In: van Heijenoort, Jean (Ed.): *From Frege to Gödel: A Source Book in Mathematical Logic, 1879–1931.* Boston: Harvard University Press, pp. 367–392.
Hill, Claire Ortiz (1998): "Introduction to Paul Linke's 'Gottlob Frege as Philosopher'". In: Poli, Roberto (Ed.): *The Brentano Puzzle.* Aldershot: Ashgate, pp. 45–47.
Høffding, Harald (1896): *Geschichte der neueren Philosophie.* 2 Volumes. Leipzig: Reisland.
Honneth, Axel (1992): *Kampf um Anerkennung: zur moralischen Grammatik sozialer Konflikte.* Frankfurt am Main: Suhrkamp.
Howard, Don (1994): "Einstein, Kant, and the Origins of Logical Empiricism". In: Salmon, Wesley and Wolters, Gereon (Eds.): *Logic, Language, and the Structure of Scientific Theories.* Pittsburgh and Konstanz: University of Pittsburgh Press and Universitätsverlag Konstanz, pp. 45–105.
Humboldt, Alexander von (1845/1862): *Kosmos.* 5 Volumes. Stuttgart: Cotta.
Husserl, Edmund (1887): *Über den Begriff der Zahl: psychologische Analysen.* Halle: Heinemann.
Husserl, Edmund (1900): *Prolegomena zur reinen Logik.* Hamburg: Meiner.
Husserl, Edmund (1900/1901): *Logische Untersuchungen.* 2 Volumes. Hamburg: Meiner.
Husserl, Edmund (1939a): "Entwurf einer 'Vorrede' zu den 'Logischen Untersuchungen' (1913)". In: *Tijdschrift voor Philosophie* 1. No. 1, pp. 106–133.
Husserl, Edmund (1939b): "Entwurf einer 'Vorrede' zu den 'Logischen Untersuchungen' (1913)". In: *Tijdschrift voor Philosophie* 1. No. 2, pp. 319–339.
Imaguire, Guido (2001): *Russells Frühphilosophie: Propositionen, Realismus und die sprachontologische Wende.* Hildesheim: Olms.
Jaeger, Werner (1945): *Paideia: The Ideals of Greek Culture.* 3 Volumes. Gilbert Highet (Trans.). Oxford: Oxford University Press.
James, William (1890, 1950): *The Principles of Psychology.* 2 Volumes. New York: Dover Publications.
James, William (1892): *Psychology: Brief Course. The Works of William James*, 19 Volumes, Vol. XIV. Cambridge: Harvard University Press.
James, William (1902): *The Varieties of Religious Experience.* New York: Longmans.
James, William (1907): *Pragmatism.* New York: Longmans.
James, William (1909): *The Meaning of Truth.* New York: Mackay.
James, William (1995): *The Correspondence of William James.* 7 Volumes. Vol. V. Skrupskelis, Ignas and Berkeley, Elizabeth (Eds.): Charlottesville: University Press of Virginia.
Kaiser-el-Safti, Margaret (Ed.) (2014): *Franz Brentano—Carl Stumpf: Briefwechsel 1867–1917.* Frankfurt am Main: Peter Lang.
Kant, Immanuel (1781): *Kritik der reinen Vernunft.* Riga: Hartknoch.

Kant, Immanuel (1800): *Logik*. Gottlob Benjamin Jäsche (Ed.). Königsberg: Nicolovius. In: Kant, Immanuel (1968): *Werke. Akademie Textausgabe*. Vol. 9. Berlin and New York: De Gruyter, pp. 1–150.

Karinskij, Michail Iwanowitsch (1873): *Critical Outline of the Latest Period of German Philosophy* (in Russian). Saint Petersburg: Department udelov.

Kastil, Alfred (1912): "Jakob Friedrich Fries' Lehre von der unmittelbaren Erkenntnis". In: *Abhandlungen der Fries'schen Schule* Neue Folge 4. No. 1, pp. 5–336.

Kenneally, Christine (2018): "The Cultural Origins of Language: What makes language distinctly human". In: *Scientific American*. https://www.scientificamerican.com/article/the-cultural-origins-of-language/ (last accessed on December 3, 2022).

Kneale, William and Kneale, Martha (1962): *The Development of Logic*. Oxford: Clarendon Press.

Koffka, Kurt, Köhler, Wolfgang, Wertheimer, Max, Goldstein, Kurt, and Gruhle, Hans (1923): *Festschrift für Carl Stumpf*. In: *Psychologische Forschung. Zeitschrift für Psychologie und ihre Grenzwissenschaften* 2.

Köhnke, Klaus (1986): *Entstehung und Aufstieg des Neukantianismus*. Frankfurt: Suhrkamp.

Kölliker, Albert (1850): *Mikroskopische Anatomie, oder Gewebelehre des Menschen*. Leipzig: Engelmann.

Kraus, Oskar (1925): *Offene Briefe an Albert Einstein und Max von Laue über die gedanklichen Grundlagen der speziellen und allgemeinen Relativitätstheorie*. Vienna: Braumüller.

Kraus, Oskar (1974): "Einleitung des Herausgebers". In: Brentano, Franz: *Wahrheit und Evidenz*. Hamburg: Meiner, pp. xi–xxiii.

Kraushaar, Otto (1936): "Lotze's Influence on the Psychology of William James". In: *Psychological Review* 43, pp. 235–257.

Kraushaar, Otto (1940): "Lotze's Influence on James' Pragmatism". In: *Journal of the History of Ideas* 1, pp. 439–458.

Kriegel, Uriah (2017): "Brentano's Concept of Mind: Underlying Nature, Reference-Fixing, and the Mark of the Mental". In: Lapointe, Sandra and Pincock, Christopher (Eds.): *Innovations in the History of Analytic Philosophy*. London: Palgrave Macmillan.

Kronenberg, Moritz (1899): *Moderne Philosophen. Porträts und Charakteristiken*. München: Beck.

Kubalica, Tomasz (2012): "Die Abbildtheorie bei Rickert and Cassirer". In: Krijnen, Christian and Noras, Andrzej (Eds.): *Marburg versus Südwestdeutschland: Philosophische Differenzen zwischen den beiden Hauptschulen des Neukantianismus*. Würzburg: Königshausen & Neumann, pp. 97–114.

Kulyk, Oleksandr (2019). "Khaos u Flosofi Henrikha Rykkerta [Chaos in Heinrich Rickert's Philosophy]". *Grani*, 22. No. 8, pp. 37–46.

Kuntz, Paul Grimley (1971): "Rudolf Hermann Lotze, Philosopher and Critic". In: Santayana, George (1889): *Lotze's System of Philosophy*. Bloomington and London: Indiana University Press, pp. 3–94.

Kusch, Martin (1995): *Psychologism. A Case Study in the Sociology of Philosophical Knowledge*. London: Routledge.

Landini, Gregory (2019): "Russell's Logic as the *Essence* of Philosophy". In: Wahl, Russell (Ed.): *Bloomsbury Companion to Bertrand Russell*. London: Bloomsbury, pp. 205–236.

Lapointe, Sandra (2019): "Introduction". In: Lapointe, Sandra (Ed.): *Logic from Kant to Russell: Laying the Foundations for Analytic Philosophy*. London: Routledge, pp. 1–27.

Lask, Emil (1902): *Fichtes Idealismus und die Geschichte*. Tübingen: Mohr.

Lask, Emil (1923): *Die Logik der Philosophie und die Kategorienlehre*. Tübingen: Mohr.

Lehmann, Gerhardt (1943): *Die deutsche Philosophie der Gegenwart*. Stuttgart: Kröner.

Leibniz, Gottfried Wilhelm (1714, 1998): *Monadologie* (in French and German). Hartmut Hecht (Ed.). Stuttgart: Reclam.
Leibniz, Gottfried Wilhelm (1923/Present): *Akademie Ausgabe*. Berlin and New York: De Gruyter.
Leinonen, Mikko (2016): "Assessing Rickert's Influence on Carnap". In: *Vienna Circle Institute Yearbook* 18, pp. 213–230.
Levy, Donald (1967): "Macrocosm and Microcosm". In: Edwards, Paul (Ed.): *The Encyclopedia of Philosophy*. 8 Volumes. Vol. V. London and New York: Macmillan and The Free Press, pp. 121–125.
Libardi, Massimo (1996): "Franz Brentano (1838–1917)". In: Arbertazzi, Liliana (Ed.): *The School of Franz Brentano*. Dordrecht: Kluwer, pp. 25–79.
Liebmann, Otto (1865): *Kant und die Epigonen*. Stuttgart: Schober.
Linke, Paul (1961): *Niedergangs-Erscheinungen in der Philosophie der Gegenwart*. München: Ernst Reinhardt Verlag.
Lorhard, Jacob (1606): *Ogdoas scholastic*. St. Gallen.
Lotze, Hermann (1838): *De futurae biologiae principiis philosophicis*. Leipzig: Typis Breitkopfio-Haertelianis. In: Lotze, Hermann (1885/1891): *Kleine Schriften*. 4 Volumes. Vol. I. David Peipers (Ed.). Leipzig: Hirzel, pp. 1–25.
Lotze, Hermann (1840): *Gedichte*. Leipzig: Weidmann.
Lotze, Hermann (1841): *Metaphysik*. Leipzig: Weidmann.
Lotze, Hermann (1842): *Allgemeine Pathologie und Therapie als mechanische Naturwissenschaft*. Leipzig: Weidmann.
Lotze, Hermann (1843a): *Logik*. Leipzig: Weidmann.
Lotze, Hermann (1843b): "Leben, Lebenskraft". In: Lotze, Hermann (1885/1891): *Kleine Schriften*. 4 Volumes. Vol. I. David Peipers (Ed.). Leipzig: Hirzel, pp. 257–267.
Lotze, Hermann (1844): "Instinct". Lotze, Hermann (1885/1891): *Kleine Schriften*. 4 Volumes. Vol. I. David Peipers (Ed.). Leipzig: Hirzel, pp. 221–250.
Lotze, Hermann (1845): "Über den Begriff der Schönheit". In: Lotze, Hermann (1885/1891): *Kleine Schriften*. 4 Volumes. Vol. I. David Peipers (Ed.). Leipzig: Hirzel, pp. 291–341.
Lotze, Hermann (1846): "Seele und Seelenleben". In: Lotze, Hermann (1885/1891): *Kleine Schriften*. 4 Volumes. Vol. II. David Peipers (Ed.). Leipzig: Hirzel, pp. 1–204.
Lotze, Hermann (1847): "Über die Bedeutung der Kunstschönheit". In: Lotze, Hermann (1885/1891): *Kleine Schriften*. 4 Volumes. Vol. II. David Peipers (Ed.). Leipzig: Hirzel, pp. 205–272.
Lotze, Hermann (1850): "Recension von Ottomar Domrich, *Die psychischen Zustände*". Lotze, Hermann (1885/1891): *Kleine Schriften*. 4 Volumes. Vol. II. David Peipers (Ed.). Leipzig: Hirzel, pp. 444–470.
Lotze, Hermann (1851): *Allgemeine Physiologie des körperlichen Lebens*. Leipzig: Hirzel.
Lotze, Hermann (1852a): *Medicinische Psychologie oder Physiologie der Seele*. Leipzig: Weidmann.
Lotze, Hermann (1852b): "Quaestiones Lucretianae". In: Lotze, Hermann (1885/1891): *Kleine Schriften*. 4 Volumes. Vol. III. Part I. David Peipers (Ed.). Leipzig: Hirzel, pp. 100–144.
Lotze, Hermann (1856a): *Mikrokosmus: Ideen zur Naturgeschichte und Geschichte der Menschheit, Versuch einer Anthropologie*. Vol. I. Leipzig: Hirzel.
Lotze, Hermann (1856b): "Selbstanzeige des ersten Bandes des *Mikrokosmus*". In: Lotze, Hermann (1885/1891): *Kleine Schriften*. 4 Volumes. Vol. III. Part I. David Peipers (Ed.). Leipzig: Hirzel, pp. 303–314.
Lotze, Hermann (1857): *Streitschriften*. Part I. Leipzig: Hirzel.
Lotze, Hermann (1858): *Mikrokosmus*. Vol. II, Leipzig: Hirzel.

Lotze, Hermann (1864): *Mikrokosmus*. Vol. III, Leipzig: Hirzel.
Lotze, Hermann (1874): *Logik*. Leipzig: Hirzel.
Lotze, Hermann (1878): *Mikrokosmus*. 3rd ed. Leipzig: Hirzel.
Lotze, Hermann (1879): *Metaphysik*. Leipzig: Hirzel.
Lotze, Hermann (1882): *Geschichte der deutschen Philosophie seit Kant*. Leipzig: Hirzel.
Lotze, Hermann (1885): *Microcosmus: An Essay Concerning Man and his Relation to the World*. 2 Volumes. Elizabeth Hamilton and Constance Jones (Trans.). Edinburgh: T&T Clark.
Lotze, Hermann (1885/1891): *Kleine Schriften*. David Peipers (Ed.) 4 Volumes. Leipzig: Hirzel.
Lotze, Hermann (1887a): *Logic*. Bernard Bosanquet et al. (Trans.) 2nd ed. Oxford: Clarendon Press [1st ed. 1884].
Lotze, Hermann (1887b): *Metaphysic*. Bernard Bosanquet et al. (Trans.) 2nd ed. Oxford: Clarendon Press [1st ed. 1885].
Lotze, Hermann (1912) *Logik*. 2th ed. Georg Misch (Ed.). Leipzig: Felix Meiner.
Lotze, Hermann (1913): *Der Zusammenhang der Dinge*. Berlin: Deutsche Bibliothek.
Lotze, Hermann (1923): *Mikrokosmos*. 3 Volumes. 6th ed. Raymund Schmidt (Ed.). Leipzig: Meiner.
Lotze, Hermann (1989): *Logik*, Erstes Buch. *Vom Denken* (1874). Gottfried Gabriel (Ed.) Hamburg: Felix Meiner.
Lotze, Hermann (2003): *Briefe und Dokumente*. Reinhardt Pester (Ed.). Würzburg: Königshausen & Neumann.
Lotze, Hermann (2017): *Mikrokosmos*. 3 Volumes. 7th ed. Nikolay Milkov (Ed.). Hamburg: Felix Meiner.
Lotze, Hermann (2021a): *Medicinische Psychologie oder die Physiologie der Seele*. Nikolay Milkov (Ed.) Berlin: Springer [1st ed. 1852].
Lotze, Hermann (2021b): "Selbstanzeige". In: Lotze, Hermann (2021a): *Medicinische Psychologie oder die Physiologie der Seele*. Nikolay Milkov (Ed.) Berlin: Springer Spektrum, pp. 669–679.
Luft, Sebastian (2015): *The Space of Culture: Towards a Neo-Kantian Philosophy of Culture (Cohen, Natorp, and Cassirer)*. Oxford: Oxford University Press.
Manser, Anthony (1983): *Bradley's Logic*. Oxford: Blackwell.
Martinelli, Riccardo (2006): "Descriptive Empiricism: Stumpf on Sensation and Presentation". In: *Brentano Studien* 10, pp. 81–100.
Marx, Karl (1867): *Das Kapital*. Hamburg: Otto Meissner.
Marx, Karl and Engels, Friedrich (1845/1846, 1932): *Die deutsche Ideologie*. Berlin.
Mayer, Emil Walter (1892): "Christliche Moral in ihrem Verhältnis zum (staatlichen) Recht". In: *Jahres-Bericht über das Königliche Friedrich-Wilhelms-Gymnasium zu Berlin*, pp. 3–31.
McGuinness, Brian (Ed.) (1985): *Zurück zu Schlick*. Vienna: Hölder–Pichler–Tempsky.
McGuinness, Brian (2002): *Approaches to Wittgenstein: Collected Papers*. London: Routledge.
McRobert, Jennifer (1994): *Concept Construction in Kant's "Metaphysical Foundations of Natural Science"*. PhD Dissertation. London (Ontario): The University of Western Ontario.
McTaggart, John Ellis (1896): *Studies in Hegelian Dialectic*. Cambridge: Cambridge University Press.
Milkov, Nikolay (1992): *Kaleidoscopic Mind: An Essay in Post-Wittgensteinian Philosophy*. Amsterdam: Rodopi.
Milkov, Nikolay (1997): *The Varieties of Understanding: English Philosophy Since 1898*. 2 Volumes. Frankfurt am Main: Peter Lang.
Milkov, Nikolay (2000): "Lotze and the Early Cambridge Analytic Philosophy". In: *Prima philosophia* 13, pp. 133–153.
Milkov, Nikolay (2001): "The History of Russell's Terms 'Sense-data' and 'Knowledge by Acquaintance'". In: *Archiv für Begriffsgeschichte* 42, pp. 221–231.

Milkov, Nikolay (2002a): "Lotze's Concept of 'States of Affairs' and its Critics". In: *Prima philosophia* 15, pp. 437–450.
Milkov, Nikolay (2002b): "Logical Forms of Biological Objects". In: *Analecta Husserliana* 77, pp. 13–28.
Milkov, Nikolay (2003): *A Hundred Years of English Philosophy*. Dordrecht: Kluwer.
Milkov, Nikolay (2004): "Leo Tolstois Darlegung des Evangelium und seine theologisch-philosophische Ethik". In: *Perspektiven der Philosophie. Neues Jahrbuch* 30, pp. 311–333.
Milkov, Nikolay (2005a): "The Formal Theory of Everything: Explorations of Husserl's Theory of Manifolds (Mannigfaltigkeitslehre)". In: *Analecta Husserliana* 88, pp. 119–135.
Milkov, Nikolay (2005b): "Bertrand Russell Early Philosophy of Time (1899–1913)". In: Stadler, Friedrich and Stoelzner, Michael (Eds.). *Time and History. Contributions of the Austrian Ludwig Wittgenstein Society* 13, pp. 188–190.
Milkov, Nikolay (2006a): "A New Interpretation of Leibniz's Concept of characteristica universalis". In: Poser, Hans (Ed.): *Einheit in der Vielheit. Proceedings of the 8th International Leibniz-Congress*. Hannover, pp. 606–614.
Milkov, Nikolay (2006b): "Hermann Lotze's *Microcosm*". In: Tymieniecka, Anna-Teresa (Ed.): *Islamic Philosophy and Occidental Phenomenology on the Perennial Issue of Microcosm and Macrocosm*. Vol 2. Berlin: Springer, pp. 41–65.
Milkov, Nikolay (2006c): "Mesocosmological Descriptions: An Essay in the Extensional Ontology of History". In: *Essays in Philosophy* 7. No. 2, pp. 170–186. https://www.pdcnet.org/collection/fshow?id=eip_2006_0007_0002_0170_0186&pdfname=eip_2006_0007_0002_0015_0031.pdf&file_type=pdf (last accessed on December 3, 2022).
Milkov, Nikolay (2008a): "Russell's Debt to Lotze". In: *Studies in History and Philosophy of Science, Part A*, 39, pp. 186–193.
Milkov, Nikolay (2008b): "Die Berliner Gruppe und der Wiener Kreis: Gemeinsamkeiten und Unterschiede". In: Fürst, Martina, Gombocz, Wolfgang, and Hiebaum, Christian (Eds.): *Analysen, Argumente, Ansätze*. Frankfurt am Main: Ontos, pp. 55–63.
Milkov, Nikolay (2010): "Rudolf Hermann Lotze". *Internet Encyclopedia of Philosophy*. http://www.iep.utm.edu/lotze/ (last accessed on December 3, 2022).
Milkov, Nikolay (2011a): "Einleitung: Hans Reichenbachs wissenschaftliche Philosophie". In: Reichenbach, Hans: *Ziele und Wege der heutigen Naturphilosophie*. Nikolay Milkov (Ed.). Hamburg: Felix Meiner, pp. vii–xliv.
Milkov, Nikolay (2011b): "Towards a Reistic Social-Historical Philosophy". In: Petrov, Vesselin (Ed.): *Ontological Landscapes: Recent Thought on Conceptual Interfaces between Science and Philosophy*. Frankfurt am Main: Ontos, pp. 245–262.
Milkov, Nikolay (2012): "The Construction of the Logical World: Frege and Wittgenstein on Fixing Boundaries of Human Thought". In: Nemeth, Elisabeth, Dunshirn, Alfred, and Unterthurner, Gerhard (Eds): *Crossing Borders: Thinking (Across) Boundaries. Proceedings of the 9th Congress of Austrian Philosophical Society*. Vienna: University of Vienna, pp. 151–161.
Milkov, Nikolay (2013a): "The Berlin Group and the Vienna Circle: Affinities and Divergences". In: Milkov, Nikolay and Peckhaus, Volker (Eds.) (2013): *The Berlin Group and the Philosophy of Logical Empiricism*. Dordrecht: Springer, pp. 3–32.
Milkov, Nikolay (2013b): "The Joint Philosophical Program of Russell and Wittgenstein and Its Demise". In: *Nordic Wittgenstein Review* 2, pp. 81–105.
Milkov, Nikolay (2013c): "Kant's Transcendental Turn as a Second Step in the Logicalization of Philosophy". In: Bacin, Stefano, Ferrarin, Alfredo, La Rocca, Claudio, and Ruffing, Margit (Eds.):

Kant and Philosophy in a Cosmopolitan Sense. Proceedings of the XI. International Kant Congress. Vol. I. Berlin and New York: De Gruyter, pp. 655–667.

Milkov, Nikolay (2015a): "Carl Stumpf's Debt to Hermann Lotze". In: Fisette, Denis and Martinelli, Riccardo (Eds.): *Philosophy from an Empirical Standpoint. Essays on Carl Stumpf*. Leiden: Brill, pp. 101–122.

Milkov, Nikolay (2015b): "Frege and the German philosophical Idealism". In: Schott, Dieter (Ed.): *Frege: Freund(e) und Feind(e)*. Berlin: Logos, pp. 88–104.

Milkov, Nikolay (2015c): "Einleitung: Die Berliner Gruppe des logischen Empirismus". In: Milkov, Nikolay (Ed.): *Die Berliner Gruppe: Texte zum Logischen Empirismus. Eine Anthologie*. Hamburg: Felix Meiner, pp. ix–lxi.

Milkov, Nikolay (2016a): "Hermann Lotze: Innovative philosopher in the context of his time: William R. Woodward: Hermann Lotze: An intellectual biography". In: *Metascience* 25. No. 2, pp. 221–224.

Milkov, Nikolay (2016b): "The 1900-Turn in Bertrand Russell's Logic, the Emergence of His Paradox, and the Way Out". In: *Siegener Beiträge Zur Geschichte und Philosophie der Mathematik* 7, pp. 29–50.

Milkov, Nikolay (2017a): "Lotze und Brentano". In: Vollbrecht, Jürgen (Ed.): *Denken im Zwiespalt. Zum 200. Geburtstag des Philosophen Rudolph Hermann Lotze*. Bautzen: Museum, pp. 24–29.

Milkov, Nikolay (2017b): "Hermann Lotzes philosophische Synthese". In: Lotze, Hermann (2017): *Mikrokosmos*. 3 Volumes. 7th ed. Nikolay Milkov (Ed.). Hamburg: Felix Meiner, pp. xi–lxxv.

Milkov, Nikolay (2017c): "The Method of Wittgenstein's *Tractatus*: Toward a New Interpretation". In: *Southwest Philosophy Review* 33. No. 2, pp. 197–212.

Milkov, Nikolay (2018): "Hermann Lotze and Franz Brentano". In: *Philosophical Readings* 10. No. 2, pp. 115–122. https://philosophicalreadings.org/ (last accessed on December 3, 2022).

Milkov, Nikolay (2019): "Russell Wahl (ed.), The Bloomsbury Companion to Bertrand Russell". In: *Notre Dame Philosophical Reviews* 2019.12.02. https://ndpr.nd.edu/news/the-bloomsbury-companion-to-bertrand-russell/ (last accessed on December 3, 2022).

Milkov, Nikolay (2020a): "Stumpf, Carl (1848–1936)". In: *Bloomsbury Encyclopedia of Philosophers*. London: Bloomsbury. https://doi.org/10.5040/9781350994997.0009 (last accessed on December 3, 2022).

Milkov, Nikolay (2020b): *Early Analytic Philosophy and the German Philosophical Tradition*. London: Bloomsbury Academic.

Milkov, Nikolay (2020c): "The Composition of Wittgenstein's *Tractatus*: Interpretative Study". In: Lozev, Kamen and Bakalova, Marina (Eds.): *130 Years Ludwig Wittgenstein*. Blagoevgrad: Bon, pp. 67–87.

Milkov, Nikolay (2020d): "Wittgenstein's Ways". In: Wuppuluri, Shyam and da Costa, Newton (Eds.): *Wittgensteinian (adj.): Looking at sciences from the viewpoint of Wittgenstein's philosophy*. Berlin: Springer, pp. 7–20.

Milkov, Nikolay (2020e): "Introduction: Bertrand Russell's 'Notes on McTaggart's Lectures on Lotze'". In: *Russell* 40, pp. 53–56.

Milkov, Nikolay (2021a): "Kurt Grelling and the Idiosyncrasy of the Berlin Logical Empiricism". In: Lutz, Sebastian and Tuboly, Ádám (Eds.): *Logical Empiricism and the Physical Sciences: From Philosophy of Nature to Philosophy of Physics*. London: Routledge, pp. 64–83.

Milkov, Nikolay (2021b): "The Berlin Group and the Society for Scientific Philosophy". In: Uebel, Thomas and Limbeck-Lilienau, Christoph (Eds.): *The Handbook of Logical Empiricism*. London: Routledge, pp. 118–126.

Milkov, Nikolay (2021c): "Einleitung: Hermann Lotzes Philosophie der Psychologie". In: Lotze, Hermann (2021a): *Medicinische Psychologie oder die Physiologie der Seele*. Nikolay Milkov (Ed.) Berlin: Springer, pp. 1–25.

Milkov, Nikolay (2022a): "Bertrand Russell's Philosophical Logic and Its Logical Forms". Paper presented at the Workshop "Philosophical Roots of Mathematical Logic", *Programma Rita Levi Moltancini*, University of Turin, Italy, April 4, 2022.

Milkov, Nikolay (2022b): "Mauro Luiz Engelmann: *Reading Wittgenstein's Tractatus*. Cambridge: Cambridge University Press, 2021". In: *Nordic Wittgenstein Review* 11. https://doi.org/10.15845/nwr.v11.3640 (last accessed on December 3, 2022).

Milkov, Nikolay and Peckhaus, Volker (Eds.) (2013): *The Berlin Group and the Philosophy of Logical Empiricism*. Dordrecht: Springer.

Misak, Cheryl (2019): "Russell and the Pragmatists". In: Wahl, Russell (Ed.): *Bloomsbury Companion to Bertrand Russell*. London: Bloomsbury, pp. 59–74.

Misch, Georg (1912): "Einleitung". In: Lotze, Hermann: *Logik*. Leipzig: Felix Meiner, pp. ix–cxxii.

Monk, Ray (1996): *Bertrand Russell*. Vol. I. New York: Free Press.

Moog, Willy (1922): *Die deutsche Philosophie des 20. Jahrhunderts*. Stuttgart: Enke.

Moore, George Edward (1908): "William James's 'Pragmatism'". In: Moore, George Edward (1922): *Philosophical Studies*. London: Routledge & Kegan Paul, pp. 97–146.

Moore, George Edward (1942): "An Autobiography". In: Schilpp, Paul Arthur (Ed.): *The Philosophy of G. E. Moore*. Evanston: Northwestern University Press, pp. 1–39.

Mormann, Thomas (2006): "Between Heidelberg and Marburg: The *Aufbau*'s Neo-Kantian Origins and the AP/CP-Divide". In: *Sapere aude* 1, pp. 22–50.

Morris, Charles (1936): "The Concept of Meaning in Pragmatism and Logical Positivism". In: *Actes du Huitième Congrès International de Philosophie, Prague, Czechoslovakia, 2–7 September*, Prague, pp. 130–138.

Mulligan, Kevin (1985): "'Wie die Sachen sich zueinander verhalten'. Inside and Outside the Tractatus". In: *Teoria* 2, pp. 145–174.

Mulligan, Kevin (2013): "Acceptance, Acknowledgment, Affirmation, Agreement, Assertion, Belief, Certainty, Conviction, Denial, Judgment, Refusal and Rejection". In: Textor, Mark (Ed.): *Judgement and Truth in Early Analytic Philosophy and Phenomenology*. Basingstoke: Palgrave Macmillan, pp. 97–136.

Münch, Dieter (2006): "Erkenntnistheorie und Psychologie: Die wissenschaftliche Weltauffassung Carl Stumpfs". In: *Brentano Studien* 10, pp. 11–64.

Murphey, Murray G. (1968): "Kant's Children: The Cambridge Pragmatists". In: *Transactions of the Charles S. Peirce Society* 4, pp. 3–33.

Natorp, Paul (1902): *Platons Ideenlehre*. Leipzig: Dürr.

Nedo, Michael (2012): *Ludwig Wittgenstein. Ein biographisches Album*. München: Beck.

Nelson, Leonard (2015): *Vom Selbstvertrauen der Vernunft. Schriften zur kritischen Philosophie und ihrer Ethik*. Hamburg: Felix Meiner.

Neugebauer, Matthias (2002): *Lotze und Ritschl: Reich-Gottes-Theologie zwischen nachidealistischer Philosophie und neuzeitlichem Positivismus*. Frankfurt am Main: Peter Lang.

Nicholson, Peter (1990): *The Political Philosophy of the British Idealists*. Cambridge: Cambridge University Press.

O'Shaughnessy, Brian (2000): *Consciousness and the World*. Oxford: Clarendon Press.

Oakes, Guy (1986): "Rickert's Theory of Historical Knowledge". In: Rickert, Heinrich (1986): *The Limits of Concept Formation in Natural Science*. Guy Oakes (Ed. and Trans.). Cambridge: Cambridge University Press, pp. vii–xxx.
Oppenheim, Paul (1928): *Die Denkfläche. Statische und dynamische Grundgesetzte der wissenschaftlichen Begriffsbildung*. Berlin: Kurt Metzner.
Orth, Ernst Wolfgang (1983): "Der Anthropologiebegriff Rudolf Hermann Lotzes und seine Bedeutung für Philosophie und Wissenschaft der Gegenwart". In: Frey, Gerhard and Zelger, Josef (Eds.): *Der Mensch und die Wissenschaften vom Mensch*. 2 Volumes. Vol. I. Innsbruck: Solaris, pp. 371–382.
Orth, Ernst Wolfgang (1984a): "Dilthey und Lotze. Zur Wandlung des Philosophiebegriffs im 19. Jahrhundert". In: *Dilthey-Jahrbuch* 2, pp. 140–158.
Orth, Ernst Wolfgang (1984b): "Einleitung". In: Orth, Ernst Wolfgang (Ed.): *Dilthey und der Wandlung des Philosophiebegriffs im 19. Jahrhundert*. Freiburg: Alber, pp. 7–23.
Orth, Ernst Wolfgang (1986): "R. H. Lotze: Das Ganze unseres Welt- und Selbstverständnisses". In: Speck, Josef (Ed.): *Grundprobleme der großen Philosophen. Philosophie der Neuzeit*. 6 Volumes. Vol. IV. Göttingen: Vandenhoeck & Ruprecht, pp. 9–51.
Orth, Ernst Wolfgang (1995/1996): "Brentanos und Diltheys Konzeption einer beschreibenden Psychologie in ihrer Beziehung zu Lotze". In: *Brentano Studien* 6, pp. 13–29.
Orth, Ernst Wolfgang (1997): "Metaphysische Implikationen der Intentionalität, Trendelenburg, Lotze, Brentano". In: *Brentano Studien* 7, pp. 13–30.
Orth, Ernst Wolfgang (2018): "Rezension zu: Rudolf Hermann Lotze: *Mikrokosmos. Ideen zur Naturgeschichte und Geschichte der Menschheit. Versuch einer Anthropologie*. 3 Volumes. (Neu hrsg. v. Nikolay Milkov, Hamburg 2017)". In: *Kant-Studien* 109, pp. 504–509.
Padovani, Flavia (2013): "Genidentity and Topology of Time: Kurt Lewin and Hans Reichenbach". In: Milkov, Nikolay and Peckhaus, Volker (Eds.) (2013): *The Berlin Group and the Philosophy of Logical Empiricism*. Dordrecht: Springer, pp. 97–122.
Passmore, John (1966): *A Hundred Years of Philosophy*. 2nd ed. Harmondsword: Penguin.
Passmore, John (1995): "Editing Russell's Papers: A Fragment of Institutional History". In: *Grazer Philosophische Studien* 49, pp. 189–205.
Perry, Ralf Barton (1935): *The Thought and Character of William James*. 2 Volumes. Boston: Little, Brown, and Co.
Pester, Reinhardt (1997): *Hermann Lotze. Wege seines Denkens und Forschens*. Würzburg: Königshausen & Neumann.
Poggi, Stefano and Vagnetti, Michele (2015): "James lecteur de Lotze". In: Boccaccini, Federico (Ed.): *Lotze et son héritage: Son influence et son impact sur la philosophie du XXe siècle*. Bruxelles: Peter Lang, pp. 161–169.
Poli, Roberto (Ed.) (1998): *The Brentano Puzzle*. Aldershot: Ashgate.
Priest, Graham (2014): *One: Being an Investigation into the Unity and Its Parts*. Oxford: Oxford University Press.
Puglisi, Mario (1913): "Prefazione". In: Brentano, Franz: *La classificazione delle attività psichiche*. Lanciano: Rocco Carabba.
Putnam, Hilary (1994): *Pragmatism*. Oxford: Blackwell.
Putnam, Hilary (1997): "James's Theory of Truth". In: Putnam, Ruth Anna (Ed.): *The Cambridge Companion to William James*. Cambridge: Cambridge University Press, pp. 166–185.
Quine, Willard van Orman (1960): *Word and Object*. Cambridge: MIT Press.

Quinton, Anthony (1985): "Vor Wittgenstein: Der Frühere Schlick". In: McGuinness, Brian (Ed.): *Zurück zu Schlick*. Vienna: Hölder-Pichler-Tempsky, pp. 114–133.
Ramsey, Frank (1927, 1978): "Facts and Propositions". In: Ramsey, Frank: *Foundations: Essays in Philosophy, Logic, Mathematics and Economics*. David Hugh Mellor (Ed.). London: Routledge & Kegan Paul, pp. 40–57.
Reichenbach, Hans (1920): *Relativitätstheorie und Erkenntnis A Priori*. Berlin: Springer.
Reichenbach, Hans (1925a): "Die Kausalstruktur der Welt und der Unterschied von Vergangenheit und Zukunft". In: *Sitzungsberichte, Bayerische Akademie der Wissenschaften, mathematisch-naturwissenschaftliche Abteilung*, München, pp. 133–175.
Reichenbach, Hans (1925b): "Metaphysics and Natural Science". In: *Symposion* 1. No. 2, pp. 158–176.
Reichenbach, Hans (1928): *Philosophie der Raum-Zeit Lehre*. Berlin and New York: De Gruyter.
Reichenbach, Hans (1938): *Experience and Prediction*. Chicago: University of Chicago Press.
Reichenbach, Hans (1956): *The Direction of Time*. Los Angeles: University of California Press.
Rescher, Nicholas (2011): *Productive Evolution: On Reconciling Evolution with Intelligent Design*. Frankfurt am Main: Ontos.
Ribot, Théodule (1879, 1892): *La psychologie Allemande contemporaine: école expérimentale*. 4th ed. Paris: Félix Alcan.
Richardson, Alan (1998): *Carnap's Reconstruction of the World*. Cambridge: Cambridge University Press.
Rickert, Heinrich (1888): *Zur Lehre von der Definition*. Tübingen: Siebeck.
Rickert, Heinrich (1894): "Zur Theorie der wissenschaftlichen Begriffsbildung". In: *Vierteljahrsschrift für wissenschaftliche Philosophie* 18, pp. 277–319.
Rickert, Heinrich (1896): *Die Grenzen der naturwissenschaftlichen Begriffsbildung*. 2nd ed. Tübingen: Mohr, 1902.
Rickert, Heinrich (1921): *Die Grenzen der naturwissenschaftlichen Begriffsbildung*. 3rd ed. Tübingen: Mohr.
Rickert, Heinrich (1986): *The Limits of Concept Formation in Natural Science*. Guy Oakes (Ed. and Trans.). Cambridge: Cambridge University Press.
Rödl, Sebastian (2018): *Selbstbewusstsein und Objektivität. Eine Einführung in den deutschen Idealismus*. Berlin: Suhrkamp.
Rollinger, Robin (2001): "Lotze on the Sensory Representation of Space". In: Albertazzi, Liliana (Ed.): *The Dawn of Cognitive Science: Early European Contributors*. Dordrecht: Kluwer, pp. 103–122.
Roth, John K. (Ed.) (1982): *The Philosophy of Josiah Royce*. Indianapolis: Hackett.
Royce, Josiah (1970): *The Letters of Josiah Royce*. John Clendenning (Ed.). Chicago: University of Chicago Press.
Russell, Bertrand (1895): "Review of Hannequin". In: Russell, Bertrand (1990): *The Collected Papers of Bertrand Russell*. Vol. II. Nicholas Griffin and Albert Lewis (Eds.). London: Routledge, pp. 35–43.
Russell, Bertrand (1896): "On Some Difficulties of Continuous Quantity". In: Russell, Bertrand (1990): *The Collected Papers of Bertrand Russell*. Vol. II. Nicholas Griffin and Albert Lewis (Eds.). London: Routledge, pp. 44–58 [textual notes pp. 563–566].
Russell, Bertrand (1897a): *An Essay on the Foundations of Geometry*. Cambridge: Cambridge University Press.
Russell, Bertrand (1897b): "Why Do We Regard Time, But Not Space, as Necessarily a Plenum?". In: Russell, Bertrand (1990): *The Collected Papers of Bertrand Russell*. Vol. II. Nicholas Griffin and Albert Lewis (Eds.). London: Routledge, pp. 91–97.

Russell, Bertrand (1897c): "Can We Make a Dialectical Transition from Punctual Matter to the Plenum?". In: Russell, Bertrand (1990): *The Collected Papers of Bertrand Russell*. Vol. II. Nicholas Griffin and Albert Lewis (Eds.). London: Routledge, pp. 22–23.

Russell, Bertrand (1898): "An Analysis of Mathematical Reasoning". In: Russell, Bertrand (1990): *The Collected Papers of Bertrand Russell*. Vol. II. Nicholas Griffin and Albert Lewis (Eds.). London: Routledge, pp. 163–222.

Russell, Bertrand (1899): "The Classification of Relations". In: Russell, Bertrand (1990): *The Collected Papers of Bertrand Russell*. Vol. II. Nicholas Griffin and Albert Lewis (Eds.). London: Routledge, 136–146.

Russell, Bertrand (1900a): *A Critical Exposition of the Philosophy of Leibniz*. Cambridge: Cambridge University Press.

Russell, Bertrand (1900b): "Is Position in Time Absolute or Relative?" In: Russell, Bertrand (1993): *The Collected Papers of Bertrand Russell*. Vol. III. Gregory Moore (Ed.): London: Routledge, pp. 219–233.

Russell, Bertrand (1901a): "The Notion of Order and Absolute Position in Space and Time". In: Russell, Bertrand (1993): *The Collected Papers of Bertrand Russell*. Vol. III. Gregory Moore (Ed.): London: Routledge, pp. 241–258.

Russell, Bertrand (1901b): "Is Position in Time and Space Absolute or Relative?" In: Russell, Bertrand (1993): *The Collected Papers of Bertrand Russell*. Vol. III. Gregory Moore (Ed.): London: Routledge, pp. 259–282.

Russell, Bertrand (1901c): "Idée d'ordre et la position absolue dans l'espace et le temps". In: *Bibliothèque du Congrès International de Philosophie* 3, pp. 241–277.

Russell, Bertrand (1903): *The Principles of Mathematics*. London: Allen & Unwin.

Russell, Bertrand (1905a): "On Denoting". In: Russell, Bertrand (1956): *Logic and Knowledge*. Robert Charles Marsh (Ed.). London: Kegan Paul, pp. 39–56.

Russell, Bertrand (1905b): "The Nature of Truth". In: Russell, Bertrand (1992): *The Collected Papers of Bertrand Russell*. Vol. VI. John Greer Slater (Ed.). London: Routledge, pp. 492–506.

Russell, Bertrand (1907a): "The Regressive Method of Discovering the Premises of Mathematics". In: Russell, Bertrand (1973): *Essays in Analysis*. Douglas Lackey (Ed.). London: George Allan & Unwin, pp. 272–283.

Russell, Bertrand (1907b): "On the Nature of Truth". In: *Proceedings of the Aristotelian Society* 7, pp. 28–49.

Russell, Bertrand (1908): "William James's Conception of Truth". In: Russell, Bertrand (1910, 1966): *Philosophical Essays*. 2nd ed. London: George Allen & Unwin, pp. 112–130.

Russell, Bertrand (1909): "Pragmatism". In: Russell, Bertrand (1910, 1966): *Philosophical Essays*. 2nd ed. London: George Allen & Unwin, pp. 79–111.

Russell, Bertrand (1910, 1966): *Philosophical Essays*. 2nd ed. London: George Allen & Unwin.

Russell, Bertrand (1911a): "On the Relations of Universals and Particulars". In: Russell, Bertrand (1956): *Logic and Knowledge*. Robert Charles Marsh (Ed.). London: Kegan Paul, pp. 103–124.

Russell, Bertrand (1911b): "Knowledge by Acquaintance and Knowledge by Description". In: Russell, Bertrand (1992): *The Collected Papers of Bertrand Russell*. Vol. VI. John Greer Slater (Ed.). London: Routledge, pp. 147–161.

Russell, Bertrand (1912a, 1932): *The Problems of Philosophy*. 2nd ed. London: Butterworth.

Russell, Bertrand (1912b): "On Matter". In: Russell, Bertrand (1992): *The Collected Papers of Bertrand Russell*. Vol. VI. John Greer Slater (Ed.). London: Routledge, pp. 77–95.

Russell, Bertrand (1913, 1984): *Theory of Knowledge: The 1913 Manuscript*. London: Allen & Unwin.

Russell, Bertrand (1914, 1926): *Our Knowledge of the External World*. 2nd ed. London: Allen & Unwin.
Russell, Bertrand (1918a): "The Philosophy of Logical Atomism". In: Russell, Bertrand (1956): *Logic and Knowledge*. Robert Charles Marsh (Ed.). London: Kegan Paul, pp. 175–281.
Russell, Bertrand (1918b, 1963): *Mysticism and Logic*. 3rd ed. Totowa: Barnes & Noble.
Russell, Bertrand (1919): "On Propositions: What they are and how they mean". In: Russell, Bertrand (1956): *Logic and Knowledge*. Robert Charles Marsh (Ed.). London: Kegan Paul, pp. 285–320.
Russell, Bertrand (1921): *The Analysis of Mind*. London: Allen & Unwin.
Russell, Bertrand (1940): *Inquiry into Meaning and Truth*. London: Allen & Unwin.
Russell, Bertrand (1948): *Human Knowledge: Its Scope and Limits*. London: Allen & Unwin.
Russell, Bertrand (1951): *The Impact of Science on Society*. London: Allen & Unwin.
Russell, Bertrand (1956): *Logic and Knowledge*. Robert Charles Marsh (Ed.). London: Kegan Paul.
Russell, Bertrand (1959): *My Philosophical Development*. London: Allen & Unwin.
Russell, Bertrand (1967): *The Autobiography of Bertrand Russell*. 3 Volumes. Vol. I. London: Allen & Unwin.
Russell, Bertrand (1990): *The Collected Papers of Bertrand Russell*. Vol. II. Nicholas Griffin and Albert Lewis (Eds.). London: Routledge.
Russell, Bertrand (1992): *The Collected Papers of Bertrand Russell*. Vol. VI. John Greer Slater (Ed.). London: Routledge.
Russell, Bertrand (1993): *The Collected Papers of Bertrand Russell*. Vol. III. Gregory Moore (Ed.): London: Routledge.
Ryle, Gilbert (1949): *The Concept of Mind*. London: Hutchinson.
Santayana, George (1889, 1971): *Lotze's System of Philosophy*. Paul Grimley Kuntz (Ed.). Bloomington: Indiana University Press.
Schafer, Matthew and Schiller, Daniela (2020): "In Search of the Brain's Social Road Maps". In: *Scientific American*, February 1, 2020.
Schatzki, Theodore (2002): *The Site of the Social: A Philosophical Account of the Constitution of Social Life and Change*. University Park: Penn State University Press.
Scheler, Max (1997): *Gesammelte Werke*. 16 Volumes. Vol. XV. Manfred Frings (Ed.). Bonn: Bouvier.
Schlick, Moritz (1910/1911): "Die Grenze der naturwissenschaftlichen und philosophischen Begriffsbildung". In: *Vierteljahrsschrift für wissenschaftliche Philosophie und Soziologie* 34–35, pp. 121–142.
Schlick, Moritz (1918): *Allgemeine Erkenntnislehre*. Berlin: Springer.
Schmidt, Raymund (1923): "Vorwort des Herausgebers". In: Lotze, Hermann: *Mikrokosmos*. 3 Volumes. 6th ed. Leipzig: Meiner, pp. vii–xxv.
Schnädelbach, Herbert (1983): *Philosophie in Deutschland 1831–1933*. Frankfurt am Main: Suhrkamp.
Schuhmann, Karl (2000/2001): "Stumpfs Vorstellungsbegriff in seiner Hallenser Zeit". In: *Brentano Studien* 9, pp. 63–88.
Sen, Amartya (1970): "The Impossibility of a Paretian Liberal". In: *Journal of Political Economy* 78. No. 1, pp. 152–157.
Seron, Denis (2015): "Lotze et la psychologie physiologique". In: Boccaccini, Federico (Ed.): *Lotze et son héritage: Son influence et son impact sur la philosophie du XXe siècle*. Bruxelles: Peter Lang, pp. 21–43.
Sigwart, Christoph von (1873/1878): *Logik*. 2 Volumes. Tübingen: Laupp.
Simons, Peter (1992): "Logical Atomism and Its Ontological Refinement: A Defence". In: Mulligan, Kevin (Ed.): *Language, Truth and Ontology*. Dordrecht: Kluwer, pp. 157–179.
Sluga, Hans (1980): *Frege*. London: Routledge.

Smith, Barry (1992): "Sachverhalt". In: *Historisches Wörterbuch der Philosophie*. Vol. VIII. K. 1102–1013. Basel: Schwabe.
Smith, Barry (1994): *Austrian Philosophy: The Legacy of Franz Brentano*. Chicago and La Salle: Open Court.
Smith, Barry (1998): "Ontologie des Mesocosmos. Soziale Objekte und Umwelten". In: *Zeitschrift für philosophische Forschung* 52, pp. 522–541.
Smolensky, Paul (1988): "On the proper treatment of connectionism". In: *Behavioral and Brain Sciences* 11. No. 1, pp. 1–23.
Staiti, Andrea (2013): "Heinrich Rickert". In: Zalta, Edward (Ed.): *Stanford Encyclopedia of Philosophy*. http://plato.stanford.edu/entries/heinrich-rickert/ (last accessed on December 3, 2022).
Stebbing, Susan (1914): *Pragmatism and French Voluntarism*. Cambridge: Cambridge University Press.
Steinvorth, Ulrich (2007): "Descartes. Willensfreiheit als Verneinungsfreiheit". In: an der Heiden, Uwe and Schneider, Helmut (Eds.), *Hat der Mensch Freien Willen?* Stuttgart: Reclam, pp. 128–141.
Stevens, Graham (2005): *The Russellian Origin of Analytic Philosophy*. London: Routledge.
Stone, Peter (2019): "Russell's Literary Approach to History". In: Wahl, Russell (Ed.): *Bloomsbury Companion to Bertrand Russell*. London: Bloomsbury, pp. 361–386.
Stout, George (1886): *Analytic Psychology*. London: Allen & Unwin.
Stumpf, Carl (1870): *Über die Grundsätze der Mathematik*. Wolfgang Ewen (Ed.). Würzburg: Königshausen & Neumann, 2008.
Stumpf, Carl (1873): *Über den psychologischen Ursprung der Raumvorstellung*. Leipzig: Hirzel.
Stumpf, Carl (1883): *Tonpsychologie*. Vol I. Leipzig: Hirzel.
Stumpf, Carl (1888): *Logik*. Karl Schuhmann (transcription of the lithographed text Q13). Cologne: Husserl Archive.
Stumpf, Carl (1890): *Tonpsychologie*. Vol. II. Leipzig: Hirzel.
Stumpf, Carl (1891): "Psychologie und Erkenntnistheorie". In: *Abhandlungen der bayerischen Akademie der Wissenschaften, Philosophisch-Philologische und Historische Klasse* 19, pp. 465–516.
Stumpf, Carl (1899): "Über den Begriff der Gemütsbewegung". In: Stumpf, Carl (1928): *Gefühl und Gefühlsempfindung*. Leipzig: Barth, pp. 1–53.
Stumpf, Carl (1906): "Zur Einteilung der Wissenschaften". In: *Abhandlungen der Königlich-Preußischen Akademie der Wissenschaften, Philosophisch-historische Klasse*. Berlin: Verlag der Königliche Akademie der Wissenschaften, pp. 1–94.
Stumpf, Carl (1907): "Die Wiedergeburt der Philosophie". In: Stumpf, Carl (1910): *Philosophische Reden und Vorträge*. Leipzig: Barth, pp. 161–196.
Stumpf, Carl (1908): "Vom ethischen Skeptizismus". In: Stumpf, Carl (1910): *Philosophische Reden und Vorträge*. Leipzig: Barth, pp. 197–224.
Stumpf, Carl (1910): *Philosophische Reden und Vorträge*. Leipzig: Barth.
Stumpf, Carl (1917): "Zum Gedächtnis Lotzes". In: *Kant-Studien* 22, pp. 1–26.
Stumpf, Carl (1919): "Erinnerungen an Franz Brentano". In: Kraus, Oskar (Ed.): *Franz Brentano. Zur Kenntnis seines Lebens und seiner Lehre*. München: Beck, pp. 87–149.
Stumpf, Carl (1924): "Selbstdarstellung". In: Schmidt, Raymund (Ed.): *Die Philosophie der Gegenwart in Selbstdarstellungen*. Vol. V. Leipzig: Felix Meiner, pp. 205–265.
Stumpf, Carl (1928): *William James nach seinen Briefen*. Berlin: Pan.
Stumpf, Carl (1939/1940): *Erkenntnislehre*. 2 Volumes. Leipzig: Barth.
Sullivan, David (2018): "Hermann Lotze". In: Zalta, Edward (Ed.): *The Stanford Encyclopedia of Philosophy* (Winter 2018 Edition). https://plato.stanford.edu/entries/hermann-lotze/ (last accessed on December 3, 2022).

Sweet, William (1995): "Was Bosanquet a Hegelian?" In: *Bulletin of the Hegel Society of Great Britain* 31: 39–60.
Textor, Mark (2017): *Brentano's Mind*, Oxford: Oxford University Press.
Thiel, Christian (1993): "Carnap und die wissenschaftliche Philosophie auf der Erlanger Tagung 1923". In: Haller, Rudolf Stadler, Friedrich (Eds.): *Wien–Berlin–Prag: Der Aufstieg der wissenschaftlichen Philosophie*. Vienna: Hölder–Pichler–Tempsky, pp. 175–188.
Thomas, Emily (2012): "John McTaggart Ellis McTaggart (1866–1925)". In: *Internet Encyclopedia of Philosophy*. https://iep.utm.edu/mctaggar/ (last accessed on December 3, 2022).
Thomas, Geoffrey (1987): *The Moral Philosophy of T. H. Green*. Oxford: Clarendon Press.
Thompson, D'Arcy Wentworth (1917): *On Growth and Form*. Cambridge: Cambridge University Press.
Trendelenburg, Adolf (1840, 1870): *Logische Untersuchungen*. 2 Volumes. 2nd ed. Leipzig: Hirzel.
Vagnetti, Michele (2020a): "Rudolph Hermann Lotze: *Mikrokosmos: Ideen zur Naturgeschichte und Geschichte der Menschheit. Versuch einer Anthropologie*". In: *Balkan Journal of Philosophy*. 12. No. 2, pp. 143–146.
Vagnetti, Michele (2020b): *Hermann Lotze on the mind-body problem and the 19th century philosophy and psychology: with special attention to William James*. Dissertation. Paderborn: Universität Paderborn.
Vallicella, William (2000): "Three Conceptions of States of Affairs". In: *Noûs* 34, pp. 237–259.
van der Schaar, Maria (2013): *G. F. Stout*. London: Palgrave.
van Heijenoort, Jean (1967): "Logic as a Calculus and Logic as Language". In: *Synthese* 17: pp. 324–330.
Varga, Peter Andras (2013): "The Missing Chapter from the *Logical Investigations:* Husserl on Lotze's Formal and Real Significance of Logical Laws". In: *Husserl Studies* 29, pp. 181–209.
Voegelin, Eric (1956/1987): *Order and History*. 5 Volumes. Baton Rouge: University of Louisiana Press.
Volkelt, Johannes (1881): "Über die logischen Schwierigkeiten in der einfachsten Form der Begriffsbildung". In: *Philosophische Monatshefte* 17, pp. 129–150.
Volkmann, Alfred (1836): *Neue Beiträge zur Physiologie des Gesichtssinnes*. Leipzig: Breitkopf und Härtel.
Vorländer, Karl (1927): *Geschichte der Philosophie*. 3 Volumes. Leipzig: Felix Meiner.
Wahl, Russell (Ed.) (2019): *Bloomsbury Companion to Bertrand Russell*. London: Bloomsbury.
Waismann, Friedrich (1936): *Einführung in das mathematische Denken: die Konzeptbildung in der modernen Mathematik*. Vienna: Gerold.
Weber, Marianne (1950): *Max Weber. Ein Lebensbild*. Heidelberg: Schneider.
Weber, Max (1904/1905): *The Protestant Ethic and the Spirit of Capitalism*. Baehr, Peter and Wells, Gordon (Eds.). New York: Penguin, 2002.
Weiße, Christian Hermann (1865): "Rezension von Mikrokosmus by H. Lotze". In: *Zeitschrift für Philosophie und philosophische Kritik* 47, pp. 272–315.
Whitehead, Alfred North (1898): *A Treatise of Universal Algebra*. Vol. I. Cambridge: Cambridge University Press.
Windelband, Wilhelm (1882): "Was ist Philosophie?" In: Windelband, Wilhelm (1922): *Präludien*. 9th ed. Vol. II. Tübingen: Mohr, pp. 1–54.
Windelband, Wilhelm (1884): "Beiträge zur Lehre vom negativen Urteil". In: Zeller, Eduard: *Strassburger Abhandlungen zur Philosophie. Eduard Zeller zu seinem siebzigsten Geburtstage*. Freiburg und Tübingen: Mohr, pp. 165–195.
Windelband, Wilhelm (1912): "Die Prinzipien der Logik". In: Ruge, Arnold (Ed.): *Enzyklopädie der philosophischen Wissenschaften*. Vol. I. *Logik*. Tübingen: Mohr, pp. 1–201.

Wittgenstein, Ludwig (1922): *Tractatus Logico-Philosophicus*. Charles Ogden and Frank Ramsey (Trans.). London: Allen & Unwin.
Wittgenstein, Ludwig (1953): *Philosophische Untersuchungen*. Elizabeth Anscombe (Ed.). Oxford: Blackwell.
Wittgenstein, Ludwig (1979): *Notebooks 1914–1916*. 2nd ed. Elizabeth Anscombe (Ed.). Oxford: Blackwell.
Wittgenstein, Ludwig (1984): *Bemerkungen über der Philosophie der Psychologie*. Elisabeth Anscombe and Georg Henrik von Wright (Eds). Frankfurt am Main: Suhrkamp.
Woodward, William Ray (2015): *Hermann Lotze: An Intellectual Biography*. Cambridge: Cambridge University Press.
Wundt, Wilhelm (1877): "Philosophy in Germany". In: *Mind* o.s. 2, pp. 493–513.

Index

Abbagnano, Nicola   41
absolute
– contents   98–99, 102
– motion   133
aggregate   37, 50, 113
Agrippa of Nettesheim   59
analysis, analyze
– concept   27, 164
– logical   171
– regressive   18–19, 38–39, 57, 61
analytic, analytical   1, 25, 127, 151, 163–164
– method   98
– philosophy   ix–xi, 1, 3–4, 11, 42, 81, 83, 93, 95, 99, 109, 145, 155, 160
– psychology   33, 96, 98–99
anthropology   11, 18, 20–21, 56–58, 60–61
– Lotze's philosophical   xi, xiii, 56, 61
– theoretical   21, 58
– transcendental   39
anti-psychologism   2, 8–9, 54, 111, 141, 174
anti-realist, anti-realism   168, 172, 174
anti-semitic   64
Apelt, Ernst Friedrich   17, 30, 141
Aquinas, Thomas   84
Aristotle   6, 10, 40, 45, 50, 54, 70, 79, 84, 86, 87, 141, 162
atom(s)   31, 48, 113–114, 122, 134, 136
– extensionless   31
– Lotze's   31, 48, 114
– philosophical   37
– metaphysical   49
atomism   17, 22, 31, 54, 91, 99, 114, 121–122, 149–150, 154
Austin, John Langshaw   9, 88
axiom(atic)   9, 50, 71, 88, 165
Ayer, Alfred Jules   152

Bain, Alexander   77, 151
Baldwin, Thomas   109, 148
Balfour, Arthur   95
Bauch, Bruno   10, 161, 166, 173
Baumann, Julius   79, 102
Becher, Erich   8, 33

Beiser, Frederick   ix, 1, 9, 38, 41–43, 48, 65, 84, 178
belief(s)   20, 23, 72, 139, 146, 148–152, 154, 173
– Lotze on   8, 42, 94, 138
– in proposition   147, 154
– religious   18
– Russell on   109, 144, 151
Bennett, Jonanthan   46
Blackwell, Kenneth   124–125
Bloch, Marc   68
Boccaccini, Federico   1
body, bodies   45–47, 51, 57, 59–60, 135
– mind-   17, 27, 33, 34, 36–39, 41–44, 54, 57, 61, 71, 98
– physiology of   34
– functions of   47
– human   52, 60, 140
– movement of   52
– and soul   136, *see also* soul
Böhme, Jakob   20, 31, 59
Bolzano, Bernard   2–3, 111
Bonitz, Hermann   87
Boole, George   87
Bosanquet, Bernard   1, 4, 5, 10, 95, 112
Bradley, Andrew Cecil   5
Bradley, Francis Herbert   1, 4, 5, 10, 110–112, 112, 125, 129
brain   36, 39, 50–51, 66, 136
Braithwaite, Richard Bevan   151
Brentano, Franz   x–xi, xiii, 2, 5, 9, 29, 33, 47–48, 55, 69, 77–94, 96–104, 120, 146
Broad, Charlie Dunbar   5
Büchner, Ludwig Friedrich   18, 36
Burckhardt, Jacob   70

Cantor, Georg   94, 109, 111, 142, 165
Carlyle, Thomas   140
Carnap, Rudolf   10, 101, 104, 144, 151, 155, 159–162, 173, 175
Cassirer, Ernst   1, 25, 141, 159–160, 166–168, 170–172
categorical imperative   23
cause, causal   48, 51, 67, 126–130, 133–135, 142

Centi, Beatrice   103
Chomsky, Noam   42
Christ, Jesus   139, Christianity   72–73
Coffa, Alberto   117, 159–160
cognitio rei/cognitio circa rem   40
Cohen, Hermann   165, 168–169
Collingwood, Robin Geroge   4, 69
color(s), coloring   9, 20, 26, 63, 67, 99, 119
- colorless   63
common sense   127–129, 133
compositionality   24
Comte, Auguste   77
concept(s), conceptual
- analytic, analysis   163–164
- construction   xi, 159, 163–164, 170
- formation   161–167, 170, 173, 175
- of home   20, *see also* Heimat
- of humanity, *see* humanities
- of idealities   7, 71, *see also* ideality
- of judgment, *see* judgment
- logical/logic of   121, 169, *see also* logic
- of movement, *see* movement
- and names   x
- notion   102
- philosophical   8, 83
- pure   163, 165
- of relation, *see* relation
- of science, *see* science
- science of   174
- of social order   62
- of space, *see* space
- of substance   41–42
- synthetic   163
- system of   167, 170
- theory of   25, 163, 166–168, 174
- of value(s)   9, 23, 87, 169, 174–175
conceptualization   81, 167, 169
conciousness   3, 49, 51, 55, 63, 71, 130, 136, 138
- contents of   96
- relation of   82, 85, 133
- self-   33, 131
- stream of   28, 55, 86
- unity of   135
connectionism   26–27, 81, 110
construction   41, 44, 86, 104, 119, 164
- concept   163, 170
consume, consumption   20, 57, 66, 69

context principle   8–10, 29, 55, 82, 122, 141–142
Copernicus, Nikolaus   134
cosmology   10, 24, 29–30, 48, 50, 59, 116, 121, 124–125, 127, 131, 141
Couturat, Louis   117
culture   19, 39–40, 57–58, 66, 169
- history of   19, 39
- human   7, 19, 38, 40, 61–62, 64, 66
- philosophy of   58
- science of   169, 174–175
Czolbe, Heinrich   18

Darwin, Charles   65
Daubert, Johannes   3
de Santis, Daniele   1
Dedekind, Richard   109, 111, 116–117, 142
definition(s)   28, 117, 162, 165, 167, 171
Descartes, René   29
description(s), describe   xi, 4, 27–28, 40–41, 45–46, 85–86, 88–89, 144–145, 148, 151
- vs. explanation   86
desire(s)   7, 20, 45, 66–68, 70, 100, 139, 149
determinism   130, 132
dialectic(al)   11, 21, 28, 39, 51, 54, 109, 114, 122, 127, 134
Diels, Hermann   95
dignity   64, 73
Dilthey, Wilhelm   1, 6, 16, 20–21, 81, 86, 166, 174
dimension(s)   29, 38–40, 47–50, 54, 132
Diogenes of Sinope   67
division(s)   1, 23, 31, 70, 125, 160
- of work   67
dogma(s), dogmatic   9, 40, 72–73, 100–101, 139, 143, 163
Driesch, Hans   83
Drobisch, Moritz Wilhelm   17
Droysen, Johann Gustav   68
Dubislav, Walter   104, 162–164, 173
Duhem, Pierre   160
Dummett, Micheal   xi, 55, 77
dynamic, dynamically   30, 45–46, 51

Eckhart, Meister   20
economy, economic(al)   25, 57, 62, 70, 174
effort(s)   15, 20–21, 32, 58, 66, 86, 133, 160

Einstein, Albert   97, 159–160
elucidation(s)   25, 44, 52, 60, 166, *see also* explanation(s)
emotion(s)   52, 67–68, 81, 85, 87, 91, 100
empirical(ly)   xiv, 23, 30, 33–36, 44, 48, 53, 69, 77, 80, 84, 87–88, 96–97, 101, 105, 126, 140, 167, 171, 175
empiricism, empiricist(s)   47, 78, 96–97, 144, 155, 160–162, 170
– British   ix, 81, 123
– introspective   88, 97
– logical   x, xi, xiii, 104, 106, 155, 159–162, 165, 168–170, 172–173, 175–176
encyclopedia   x, xiii, 18, 60, 109
epistemology   2, 7, 17, 27, 47, 83–84, 86, 93, 96, 144–145, 149, 162, 164, 168, 172–173
Erdmann, Benno   111, 165
Erdmann, Johann Eduard   56, 94
existence, existent(s)   37, 43, 47, 84, 116, 122, 135, 137, 139, 141, 143, 154
– forms of   67
– human   59
– independent   51
– non-   127, 137
– self-   137
experience(s)   19–20, 32, 34–35, 84–85, 88–89, 105, 126–127, 165
– data of   165, 169
– of life   33
– psychological   53
explanation   22, 52, 58, 86, 96, 127, 144, 163, 175
– vs. elucidation   52
extension, extensional   26, 30–32, 39, 41, 48–49, 102, 113–114, 136, 149–152; extensionality   149–151

Fechner, Gustav Theodor   17, 33, 36–39, 43, 52, 54, 77, 95, 97–98, 104–105, 142
feeling(s)   20, 27, 47, 52, 65, 70–71, 84, 100, 131, 139, 149
– of life   71
– religious   139
– of pleasure   19, 57, 87
– theory of   52
feminism, feminist   64, 143
Ferenczi, Sandor   87

Fernandez-Armes, Felipe   63
Ferrari, Massimo   172
Fichte, Johann Gottlieb   8, 49, 52, 66, 98, 137, 166
Fick, Franz   18
Fischer, Kuno   4
Fodor, Jerry   42
force(s)   28, 37, 39–40, 50, 70, 82, 133–135, 139, 150–151
– life   37, 45, 52
– vital   135–136
form(s)
– axiomatic   50
– conceptual   169
– of existence, *see* existence
– of externality   112–113, 116, 118
– of language, *see* language
– of knowledge   40
– of life, *see* life
– logical   23, 61, 65, 99, 145
– of perceptions, *see* perception(s)
– of pleasure   140
– propositional   23, 25
– of psychology, *see* psychology
– of space, *see* space
– of synthesis   164
– theory of   6, 96
– of values   7, 27
– world of   23
Frank, Philipp   170, 173
freedom   135, 139
– of the will   20, 40, 46, 130, 139
Frege, Gottlob   ix, xi, 1–3, 8, 10, 20, 28–30, 32, 42, 52, 54, 77, 82, 85, 87–89, 94–95, 99–102, 111, 141, 143, 148–149, 151–153, 161, 166–167, 170, 172, 174
Freud, Sigmund   22, 87
Friedman, Michael   105, 159–160, 168, 171, 175
Fries, Jakob Friedrich   28, 78, 163

Gabriel, Gottfried   ix, 3, 15, 29, 42, 77, 85, 111, 121, 166, 169
gender   58, 62
Geymonat, Ludovico   172
given, the   2, 22, 30, 54, 82–83, 86
God   18, 43, 71–73, 92, 109, 130, 132, 135, 137–140, 142

– Almighty   125, 133, 136–140, 143
Green, Thomas   4–5, 10, 110, 135
Griffin, Nicholas   4–5, 111, 114, 116, 118–121, 123
Großmann, Hermann   50

Habermas, Jürgen   70
Hager, Paul   113
Hahn, Hans   144, 170, 173
Haldane, Richard   16
Haller, Rudolf   172
Hamilton, Elizabeth   5, 56
Hamilton, William   91
Hannequin, Arthur   114
harmony   38, 43, 45–46, 59, 66, 69, 127, 137
heart   19–20, 22, 27, 58, 62–64, 67
hedonism   20, 23, 140
Hegel, Georg Wilhelm Friedrich   ix, xi, 1–11, 15, 17, 21, 28, 35, 39, 49, 52–54, 61, 63, 65, 68–69, 91, 104, 109–111, 114, 117, 119, 122–124, 127–130, 132–134, 141, 164
Heidegger, Martin   10
Heimat   20, 62
Heisenberg, Werner   122
Hempel, Carl Gustav   36, 104, 162, 173, 175
Herbart, Johann Friedrich   ix, 6, 16–17, 22–23, 29–30, 33, 43, 52–53, 55, 59, 80, 82, 95, 111, 128–129, 133–134, 139, 142, 162
Hering, Ewald   47, 94, 96
Hilbert, David   159–160, 165
Hirzel, Samuel   60–61
history   ix, x, xiii, 3, 10, 19, 39, 56–57, 60–61, 67–69, 89, 111, 160, 162, 168
– human   57, 62–63, 67
– natural   60, 65
– of philosophy, *see* philosophy
– social   68
Hobbes, Thomas   70
Høffding, Harald   27, 121
humanities   71, 88, 105, 163–164, 166, 173–174
Hume, David   29, 32, 55, 81, 142, 162, 164, 166, 170
Husserl, Edmund   xi, 1–3, 8–9, 29, 33, 49–50, 59, 86, 90–91, 94, 98–99, 101, 104, 111, 141, 174

ideality, idealities   2, 7, 19, 23–24, 38, 48, 71, 84, 117–118
identity   vi, 36–38, 128–130, 142, 148
– of indiscernibles   118–119
– self-   121
– theory   37
imagination   4, 55, 62–63, 65, 67, 69–70, 72, 91
impression(s)   47, 51, 78, 98, 102, 104, 131, 136, 164
– sensory   38
– sense-   99, 162
indefinable   40, 112
intelligibility, intelligible   15, 19, 24, 71–72, 112, 131, 141
intention(ality)   2, 81, 84–85, 89

James, William   xi, xiii, 1, 5, 9, 37, 40, 47, 52, 55, 83, 86, 93–94, 101, 144–146, 151–155
Johnson, William Ernest   149
Jones, Emily Elizabeth Constance   5, 56
judgement   9–10, 23, 26, 29, 55, 66, 72, 81–83, 87, 91, 99, 116, 126, 139–140, 146–148, 150
– concept(s) of   81, 103, 148
– hypothetical   71
– nature of   120
– principle of   53
– theory of   98, 116–117, 119–120, 148, 153

Kant, Immanuel   ix, 4, 6, 8, 15, 17, 19, 21, 23, 30, 38, 48, 52, 54, 64, 72, 86–87, 90–91, 96, 98, 102, 109, 105, 111–114, 131–133, 136–137, 139–140, 146, 159–160, 163–165, 170–171, 174–175
Karinski, Michail Iwanowitsch   49
Kastil, Alfred   78
Klein, Felix   94
Kneale, William and Martha   10
knowledge
– of acquaintance   145
– discursive   40
– empirical   84
– form(s) of, *see* form(s)
– historic   68
– metaphysical   35
– subject and object of   9, 164, 169
– theory of   83, 88, 93, 142, 148–150, 170
– scientific   168–171

Koffka, Kurt   92, 94
Köhler, Wolfgang   92, 94, 98, 101, 104
Kraus, Oskar   82, 83, 97, 101, 103
Kraushaar, Otto   9, 40, 146
Kriegel, Uriah   84
Kuntz, Paul Grimley   5, 16, 21, 27, 31, 64

Landini, Gregory   117
language   ix, xiv, 3, 18, 32, 44–45, 50, 57, 66, 99, 153–154, 170
– form(s) of   32, 82, 170
– of the macrocosm   32
– philosophy of   32, 101, 124, 152, 173
– symbolic   118
Lask, Emil   166, 169
law(s)
– international   70
– of juxtaposition   118
– mathematical   45, 93–94
– mechanical   135, 137
– natural/of nature   70, 72, 174
– philosophy of   101
– of reality   53
– of science   35, 88, 96, 174
– of structure   96, 99
– of thoughts   137
Leibniz, Gottfried Wilhelm   129–131, 137–139
Leinonen, Mikko   160–161
Lewin, Kurt   92, 94, 101, 104
liberalism, liberal(s)   vi, 64, 70, 72, 77, 101, 143
Liebmann, Otto   95
life
– cosmic   22, 54
– force   37, 45, 52
– form(s) of   26, 57, 61, 65–67, 69
– human   18–20, 38, 62–63, 68–69, 71
– material   45
– mental   35, 43, 48, 122
– philosophy of   21, 166
– physiological   44
– political   70
– sensual   19
– solitary   16
– spiritual   34
– wild   62
Linke, Paul   85

local-sign(s)   26, 32, 46, 47, 51, 55, 91, 98, 136, 142
Locke, John   86
logic(al)
– of concepts   169
– empiricism   x, xi, 104, 106, 155, 159–162, 165, 168–170, 173, 175–176, *see also* empiricists
– form(s)   61, 65, 99, 145
– formal   17, 169
– mathematical   10, 123–124, 169, 175
– necessity   169
– philosophical   9–10, 58, 82, 96, 99, 118, 121, 174
– philosophy of   52
– positivists, positivism   88, 104, 155
– symbolic   77
– transcendental   6
– turn   3, 6, 8, 145
Lotze, Ferdinande Hoffmann   16
Lotze, Rudolf Hermann (*passim*)
– *Logic* (1843)   17, 32, 103, 111
– *Logic* (1874)   ix, 2–3, 5, 10, 18, 30, 57, 95, 146, 164
– *Metaphysic* (1841)   17, 23, 57, 111, 113
– *Metaphysic* (1879)   ix, 5, 18, 57, 95, 146
– *Medicinische Psychologie*   x, xiii, 1, 17, 33–34, 53, 60, 146
– *Mikrokosmus*   x, 1, 5, 11, 15, 17–18, 20, 24, 42, 56–63, 65, 66, 68, 79–80, 87, 118, 124, 143, 146
Luther, Martin   72

Mach, Ernst   37, 94, 170
magnitude(s)   19, 98, 117, 119
Malthus, Thomas   70
manifolds   50, 164, 170
– theory of   50, 117
Manser, Anthony   10, 121–122
Martinelli, Ricardo   xiii, 97
Marty, Anton   78, 89, 94, 101, 103
Marx, Karl   11, 18, 67
matter
– characteristic of   31
– element of   134
– indeterminate   128
– inorganic   135
– laws of   127

– properties of 30
– and spirit 15
material, materialism xiii, 19–20, 39, 44–45, 48, 51, 70, 128, 150, 167, 171
– contents 6
– reality 19, 84
– world 30–31
maxim(s) 23, 50, 86, 144, 152
Mayer, Emil Walter 136, 142–143
McGinn, Colin 42
McTaggart, John Ellis x, xiii, 4, 109, 115, 116, 123–127, 129–132, 135–139
measurement 38, 119
medicine, medical 15–17, 34–35, 41, 45, 60, 105
– philosophical 34
– psychology 35
Meinong, Alexius 89
Melanchton, Philipp 72
metaphysic(s) ix, xi, 19–21, 23–24, 35–40, 45–46, 48–49, 111, 113–114, 117–118, 121–125, 127, 135–136, 141–142, 146–147
– Lotze's 5, 7, 24, 33, 42, 114, 123–124
microcosm xiii, 15, 18, 32, 57, 59–61, 70, 136
Mill, John Stuart 77, 81, 94, 162, 164
mirror 49, 59, 164, 166, 168, 172–173
Misch, Georg 7, 23, 28, 41, 81, 116
Moleschott, Jacob 18, 36
Montesquieu, Charles 63
Moore, George Edward ix, 4–5, 9, 42, 83, 109, 119–121, 123, 141, 144–145, 148, 152, 155
Mormann, Thomas 160
Morris, Charles 155
movement ix, 15, 44–45, 47, 51, 68, 87, 95, 105, 131, 155
– of the body 52
– concept(s) of 15
– in God 139
– sense of 46
Müller, Johannes Peter 47
Münch, Dieter 97, 100, 103
music 50, 125, 140
Musil, Robert 94
mysticism 20, 59, 145

Nagel, Thomas 42
nativism, nativist(s) 47–48, 91, 96–97

Natorp, Paul 1, 3, 165, 168, 170–171
nature
– biological 40
– God's 139
– human 68
– law of 70, 72, 174–175
– mechanics of 27
– philosophy of 24, 30, 37, 141, 160
– physical 34
– spiritual 131
necessity 44, 72, 116, 133, 139, 153
– mathematical 45
– logical 129, 169
Nelson, Leonard 141
Neo-Brentanist(s) 78, 92, 103, 168
Neo-Kantian(ism) ix, xi, 1, 6, 95, 138, 159–160, 165–172, 175
nerve(s) 45–47, 49–50, 136
Nettleship, Richard Lewis 4, 6
Neurath, Otto 144, 170, 173
Newton, Isaac 48, 142
Nicholas of Cusa 59
Nicholson, Peter 4
number(s) 48–49, 51, 53, 101–102, 116–117, 119, 130–131, 134

O'Shaughnessy, Brian 51
Oakes, Guy 166, 174
objectivism 23, 29, 113
ontology
– connectionist 103
– Lotze's 15, 24, 26, 42, 121, 124, 141–142
– spatial 19, 47, 62
– Stumpf's 102
ontological(ly)
– conception 111, 116
– dependent 99, 102
– structure 62
– theory 65
Oppenheim, Paul 104, 162, 175
order
– formal 27
– higher 32
– regressive 39
– serial 119
– social 62
– spatial 19, 47, 110, 113

– theory of   15, 27, 117, 124
– in the world   31, 66
Orient   64, 72
orientation   7, 38, 53, 60, 99, 118, 171–172, 175
Orth, Ernst Wolfgang   21, 32, 41, 56, 64, 79, 84, 86

panpsychism   31, 48
Pappus of Alexandria   19
Paracelsus   59
Passmore, John   ix, 4, 8, 89–90
patriotism   70
perception(s)
– aesthetic   117
– content of   30, 81–83, 86, 103
– data of   146
– form of   60
– sense   32, 100, 110, 137, 140
– space   46–47, 49, spatial   43, 51
theory of   83, 91
– of time   132
perspective(s)
– aesthetic   17
– logical   8, 147
– metaphysical   147
– theoretical   42
perspectivism   22, 54, 121, 142, 147
phenomenology   xi, xiii, 1, 2, 3, 33, 86, 88, 95, 96
philosophy
– (early) analytic   ix–xi, 1, 3–4, 8, 81, 83, 95, 99, 109, 155, 160
– British   4
– continental   93, 160
– of culture, see culture
– German   ix, xi, 1, 4, 6, 10, 24, 59, 77–78, 81, 95, 124, 146
– Greek   59, 78
– history of   1, 4, 54, 69, 80, 89
– of history   57
– of language   32, 124
– of law, see law(s)
– of life   21, 166
– of mind   17, 20, 24, 124
– of nature/natural   24, 30, 52, 121, 124
– of physiology   34
– political   64, 70
– of psychology, see psychology
– of religion/religious   3, 5, 18, 71
– of science   114, 160–162, 165–167, 169–171, 173–176
– social   62–63
– of space   49–50, 102
– system of   5, 18, 58, 174
– theoretical   ix, 21–22, 58, 64, 110, 124–125, 169
– western   ix, xi, 1, 6, 10–11, 89, 124, 144
phrenology   50
physic(s), physical   23, 34, 47, 50–51, 66–67, 84, 134–135
– -psychological   18, 41–42, 44, 46, 62, 142
– science   171
physiology   15, 17, 34–36, 38–41, 46, 52, 54
piano   49–51
piecemeal (approach)   8–9, 81, 90, 101
Plato(nism), Platonic   2–3, 6, 10, 23, 28, 40, 45, 54, 59, 69–70, 84, 92–93, 115, 117, 119, 143, 164
pleasure   19, 23, 57, 63, 84, 87, 100, 117, 138–140
Poincare, Henri   117, 171
Popper, Karl   36, 173, 175
Prichard, Harold Arthur   9
principle(s)
– context   8–10, 29, 55, 82, 122, 141–142
– of extensionality   149–151
– Lotze's   18, 49, 91, 112, 141
– of mathematics   110, 124
– methodological   20, 43
– moral   23
– of psychology   145–146
– of reflection   47, 49
– serial   168
Prior, Arthur   ix
process
– dynamic   51
– mechanistic/mechanical   19, 44–45
– natural   20, 71
– physiological   43, 52
– psychological   34
progress   10, 45, 57, 66–69, 72, 105, 163–164, 175
propositions, propositional
– attitudes   xi, xiii

– ethical   140
– geometrical   126
– theory of   115, 117, 120
protestant(ism)   67, 73, 97
psychology
– analytic   33, 96, 98–99
– descriptive   81, 83–86, 88, 96, 98–99, 141
– empirical   35, 48, 88, 96
– experimental   55, 91, 97
– form(s) of   85–86
– genetic   85–86, 96
– mathematical   33, 43
– medical   35
– philosophical   33, 36, 48, 77, 86, 88
– philosophy of   xi, 33–34, 41, 57
– physiological   34, 36, 43–44, 47, 52, 54–55
– rational   51
– speculative   35
Putnam, Hilary   153–154

quantum mechanics   122
Quine, Willard   55, 151
Quinton, Anthony   172

Ramsey, Frank   151
reality
– description of   54
– dimensions of   38–40, 54
– law of   53
– levels of   49
– material   19
– objects of   3, 154, 170
– psychology of   127
– teleological   40, 45
realism, realist   3, 9, 20, 22, 49, 66, 68, 120, 130, 143, 166, 168, 170, 172–174
– anti-   168, 174
– logical   9, 145
– platonic   2, 115, 117, 119
reciprocally, reciprocal   24–25, 31, 48, 63, 70, 82, 134, 148, see also relations
reflection   18, 39, 47, 49, 52, 138
– scientific   33
– critical   47, 52
Rehmke, Johannes   83, 95
Reichenbach, Hans   x, 104–106, 162, 170–173, 175

Reinach, Adolf   3, 148
relationism   26, 110
relation(s)
– asymmetric   119
– between body and mind   17, 39, 54, 57, see also body
– concept of   15, 167
– between men and woman   64
– between microcosm and macrocosm   32
– reciproca tantum   25, reciprocal   82
– system of   26
– theory of   96, 124
– transitive   119
religion   3, 5, 19–20, 57, 71–72, 134, 136–138, 143
Rescher, Nicholas   x, 75
revelation   71, 73, 120
Ribot, Theodule   33, 35
Richardson, Alan   160
Rickert, Heinrich   xi, xiii, 1, 159–162, 165–176
Riemann, Bernard   50
Ritschl, Albrecht   72, 143
Rousseau, Jean-Jacques   67
Royce, Josiah   1, 5, 83
Russell, Bertrand   ix–xi, xiii, 1, 4–5, 8–9, 19, 22, 25, 30, 37, 42, 69, 83, 90, 93, 99, 101–102, 105, 109–125, 141–155, 163, 165, 172

Santayana, George   6, 21–22, 31, 54
Scheler, Max   56, 59
Schelling, Friedrich Wilhelm Joseph   8, 17, 61, 130
Schleiermacher, Friedrich   6, 17, 87
Schlick, Moritz   161–162, 170–173, 175
Schmidt, Raymund   1, 56
Schopenhauer, Arthur   58
Schwegler, Albert   87
science
– Cartesian   86, 96
– cultural/of culture   166, 169, 173–175
– concept of   48, 52, 161, 163–166, 168
– descriptive   86, 163–164, 166, and explanatory   86, 174–175
– empirical   36
– human   174
– law(s) of   35, 174
– medicinal   60

- of mind 174
- moral 123
- natural/of nature 36 – 38, 40, 43, 57, 59, 61, 88 – 89, 96 – 97, 105, 163 – 164, 166, 173 – 175
- object(s) of 171
- philosophical/philosophy of x, 34, 114, 160 – 162, 165 – 167, 169, 171, 173 – 176
- physical 134, 171, see also physic(s)
- pseudo- 60
- system of 30
- theory in 159
- truths of 32
sense
- common-sense spatiality 46
- of conscience 71
- -data 3, 9, 30, 83, 110, 144 – 146, 163
- of freedom 139
- -impression 99, 162
- of movement 46
- non-temporal 28
- -perception 32, 37, 100, 110, 137
- of place 47
- of propositions 85
- of truth 28
series 5, 16, 27, 58, 62, 78, 82, 86, 93, 100, 103, 116, 118 – 119, 130, 133 – 134, 168
Sidgwick, Henry 5, 124
Sluga, Hans 3, 77, 110
Smith, Barry 25, 62 – 63, 86, 103, 134
social 50, 57, 60, 62 – 63, 66 – 68, 70, 73, 105
- history 68
- ontology 62
- philosophy 62 – 63
- progress 66
- traditions 66
society 57, 62 – 63, 65 – 66, 68, 73, 93 – 94, 98, 104 – 105, 140, 155
Socrates 28
soul 20, 35 – 36, 38, 42, 46, 49 – 51, 62, 135 – 139, 142
- location of 50
- substantiality of 135
- world 59
space
- and/or time 3, 50, 96, 98, 112 – 116, 136, 147
- concept(s) of 38, 50, 102, 112 – 113, 115
- empty 113 – 114, 131 – 132

- forms of 132
- knowledge of 114
- nature of 126
- non-Euclidean 132, 142
- perception of 46 – 47, 49, 132
- philosophy of 49 – 50, 102
- theory of 49, 110, 113, 131
- view of 136
speculative theists 66
Spencer, Herbert 77
Spieß, Gustav Adolph 47
Spinoza 29, 37, 45, 138
spirit(ual), spiritualistic 15, 20, 32, 38 – 40, 52, 54, 63, 128, 134
- life 34
- nature 131
- needs 72
- organism 66
- world 26, 39, 68
spiritualism 36, 38 – 39, 41, 121
Staiti, Andrea 161, 169
Stebbing, Susan 144
Stout, George Frederick 5, 99, 120, 124
strive, -ing 20, 45, 48, 51, 91, 174
Stumpf, Carl x, xi, xiii, 1 – 2, 29, 33, 47 – 48, 55, 78 – 80, 82, 89 – 106, 111, 141 – 142, 146
subject(s) 9, 22, 38, 82, 102 – 103, 135, 151, 161
- knowing/of knowledge 49, 164, 169
- unity of 135
subjectivism 23, 95, 102, 114
substance(s) 19, 24 – 26, 29, 31, 37, 42, 48, 51, 85 – 86, 110, 114, 129 – 130, 140, 142
- conception of 85
- elements of 24 – 25
- ideal-real 37
- unity of 135
suffer(ing) 16, 31, 62, 85, 138
Sweet, William 4
symbol(s), symbolism 77, 118 125, 139, 148

theory
- of concept(s) 25, 159 – 160, 163, 165 – 168, 170, 174
- of causality 130
- cultural 39
- of forms 96
- of ideas 2

- of judgment 98, 116–117, 119–120, 148
- of knowledge 88 142, 145, 149–150, and perception 83
- of local-signs 32, 46–47, 55, 91, 98, 100
- of manifolds 50, 117
- ontological 65
- of order 27, 117, 124
- philosophical 7
- of relations 96, 116
- scientific 168, 171
- space 49, 110, 113, 131, and time 113, 116
- of truth 2, 144, 148, 152–154, 166, 171
- of the world 96

thing(s)
- connection of 24, 42, 53
- finite 131
- knowledge of 35
- living 59
- material 19
- nature of 128–129
- objective 26
- unity of 127, 141

Thomas, Geoffrey 4
Thompson, D'Arcy Wentworth 65
Tolstoy, Leo 73
thought(s) 27–28, 109, 112, 114, 117, 130, 132, 134–138, 173–174
- definition of 28
- formal 130
- -determinations 78
- human 27
- law of 137
- logical-metaphysical 17
- philosophical xi, 90, 162
- pure 130, 136
- secondary 28, 87

Trendelenburg, Friedrich Adolf 79–80, 84, 87, 95, 111, 113
Trevelyan, George 69
Treviranus, Gottfried Reinhold 37
truth 20, 28–29, 57–58, 67, 88, 120, 126, 138–139, 148–149, 152–154
- historical 77
- -making xi, 146, 152–155
- nature of 53, 147–148
- objective 127
- -operations 151

- realm of 88
- religious 71, 137
- sense of 28
- theory of 144, 148, 153–154, 166, 171
- -value 9, 30, 166, 173
Twardowski, Kazimierz 89
Tymieniecka, Anna-Teresa x, xiii

Ueberweg, Friedrich ix
unity 31, 37–38, 43, 53, 59–60, 131, 134–138, 140–141
- aestehic 31, 130
- dialectic 134
- minimal composite 24–25, 29, 42
- of God and humanity 18
- organic 24, 50, 99, 142, 153
- substantial/of substance 130, 135

vital(ism) 36, 40–41, 72, 135–136, 142
Voegelin, Eric 62
Vogt, Carl 18, 36
Volkelt, Johannes 95, 164–165
Volkmann, Alfred Wilhelm 34
von Autenrieth, Jakob Friedrich 37
von Hartmann, Eduard 21
von Helmholtz, Hermann 46, 77, 111
von Humboldt, Alexander 63
von Ranke, Leopold 68
von Savigny, Friedrich 70
von Sigwart, Christoph ix, 164–165

Wallace, William 4
Ward, James 5, 9, 124, 152
Watson, John Broadus 151
Weber, Ernst Heinrich 33, 36, 38–39, 43, 49
Weber, Max 71, 161
Weierstrass, Karl 109
Weiße, Christian 17, 31–32, 66
Wertheimer, Max 92
Whitehead, Alfred North 116–117, 123
Wilson, John Cook 5, 9
Windelband, Wilhelm 1, 28, 30, 95, 161, 166, 169
Wittgenstein, Ludwig 9, 11, 22, 25–26, 29, 32–33, 36, 42, 45, 52, 64, 66–67, 119, 123, 148, 150–153, 155, 159, 169–170, 172–173, 176

Wolff, Johannes   78
Woodward, William   x, 1, 36, 41, 56, 111, 143
world(s)
– of art   26
– examination of   20
– external   23, 46, 84, 147, 154
– finite   132
– of forms   23
– of ideas   23
– inner   46
– lesser   59–60
– life-   69
– material   30–31
– meaning of   40
– mental   32, 50
– order in   31
– -philosophies   58
– physical   47, 51, 67
– possible   24, 44, 141
– relations in   26
– real   24, 118, 141, 147, 153, 167
– sensual   32
– spiritual/of the spirit   26, 39, 68
– -soul   59
– theory of   96
worldview   10, 43, 144, 173
Wundt, Wilhelm   4, 97, 165

Zermelo, Ernst   165

www.ingramcontent.com/pod-product-compliance
Lightning Source LLC
Chambersburg PA
CBHW020231170426
43201CB00007B/384